Reza Banakar is Professor and Director of Research in the Sociology of Law Department at Lund University. He has previously held the positions of Professor of Socio-Legal Studies at the Department of Advanced Legal Studies, University of Westminster and Research Fellow at the Centre for Socio-Legal Studies, University of Oxford. His recent publications include *Normativity in Legal Sociology* (2015), *Law and Social Theory* (2013) and *Rights in Context* (2010).

'In this original and exciting book Reza Banakar and his collaborators use an investigation into driving practices in Iran – with its very high rate of road accidents – to cast light on a variety of crucial questions that surround that country's legal culture. They draw on fascinating interviews with taxi drivers, doctors, psychologists, insurance agents, and others. The result is an account particularly sensitive to male/female differences, to the way different groups in society relate to the state and to law, and the role religious ideology plays in maintaining order. A must read.'

David Nelken, Professor of Comparative & Transnational Law
in Context, and Head of Research, The Dickson Poon School
of Law, King's College London

'This is a fascinating study, which looks at Iranian legal culture (and Iranian culture in general) through the prism of driving habits and customs in the urban areas of this important country. It is a real contribution to our understanding of the interplay between law and society in a setting where traditional values and the values of the modern automotive and technological society collide.'

Professor Lawrence Friedman, Marion Rice Kirkwood
Professor of Law, Stanford University

'This brilliant and insightful investigation guides us through the current Iranian society. Although Iran is a country of mass automobility, there have been few efforts to reflect on the significance of (auto)mobility in the urban Iran. By disclosing how Iranians experience the traffic problem in everyday life this well-argued book helps us to reach a better understanding of the centrality of gender and class in the complex driving culture in Iran.'

Shahram Khosravi, Stockholm University

DRIVING CULTURE IN IRAN

Law and Society on the Roads of the Islamic Republic

REZA BANAKAR

with

SHAHRAD NASROLAHI FARD, BEHNOOSH PAYVAR
and ZARA SAEIDZADEH

I.B. TAURIS

LONDON · NEW YORK

Published in 2016 by
I.B.Tauris & Co. Ltd
London • New York
www.ibtauris.com

International Library of Iranian Studies 58

ISBN: 978 1 78453 448 6
eISBN: 978 0 85772 873 9

A full CIP record for this book is available from the British Library
A full CIP record is available from the Library of Congress

Library of Congress Catalog Card Number: available

Typeset in Garamond Three by OKS Prepress Services, Chennai, India
Printed and bound by CPI Group (UK) Ltd, Croydon, CR0 4YY

This book is dedicated to women taxi drivers in Iran.

CONTENTS

LIST OF ILLUSTRATIONS

ACKNOWLEDGEMENTS

I am grateful to the Economic and Social Research Foundation (ESRC) in the UK for funding this project, and to the School of Law at the University of Westminster, London, for providing a home for it. The background research for this book was conducted in two consecutive stages in collaboration with Dr Shahrad Nasrolahi Fard: during 2010, when a pilot study was carried out in Shiraz and Tehran, and in 2012, when the larger project funded by the ESRC was conducted in Tehran. Besides myself and Dr Nasrolahi Fard, Dr Behnoosh Payvar and Ms Zara Saeidzadeh have been involved in this project.

This project would not have come to fruition and this book would not have been possible without the kind and generous support of a number of people. Professor Andy Boon, the former Dean of the Law School at the University of Westminster, supported the project within the university at a crucial moment and allowed it to run. Dr Amir Hossein Abadi, Attorney in Law, facilitated the initial stage of our research, Mr Hamid Nasrolahi Fard assisted us in organizing the project in Tehran and Dr Shokouh Hossein Abadi provided us with invaluable legal advice and support at different stages of the project. Mr Keyvan Ziaee has kindly shared his experience of working as a researcher in Iran, and provided text and material which I have employed in Chapter Two, where 'conducting research in Iran' is discussed. Ms Zara Saeidzadeh provided invaluable intellectual support during the time I was writing up the first nine chapters of this book. Many of the insights regarding Iranian culture that appear in this book were developed through critical discussions with Zara. Finally, I am endebted to Ms Ann Williams, who kindly helped me with preparing the first draft of the manuscript and to Mr Ian McDonald who judiciously edited the final draft.

I also acknowledge the kind permission of Mr Sirus Banakar, Mr Gustaf Öhrnell, Mr Hamid Shojaee and Mr Jeppe Schilder to reproduce their images of traffic in Iran.

Reza Banakar

CHAPTER 1

INTRODUCTION: WHAT HAVE DRIVING HABITS GOT TO DO WITH LAW, GENDER AND CLASS CONFLICTS?

Reza Banakar

When I think about driving, law and traffic rules in Iran, I can't help but wonder if the social problems they jointly pose are not an integral part of a much larger societal problem. The causes should be searched for in the totality of our society, as it is at that level that we have serious shortcomings. The failure to obey the law is endemic [...], although it is very pronounced in our disrespect for traffic rules. But the roots of the problem should be sought in the totality of our society. [...] What people say and do are two different things, and in my opinion the gap between these two are very large in Iran, and this in itself causes a problem when we try to reform people's behaviour.

(A medical doctor interviewed as part of this study)[1]

There is an unusually large discrepancy between Iranians' actual driving behaviour, which displays a widespread disregard for traffic laws, and their expectations of how one should behave in traffic. This normative hiatus translates itself empirically into high levels of road traffic accidents (RTAs), generating thousands of fatalities and serious traffic-

Figure 1.1   Tehran Traffic. © Jeppe Schilder.

related injuries annually.[2] However, the driving habits of Iranians, their disregard for traffic laws and their attitude to the rights of other drivers are themselves indicators of how their social identities and relations are forged, how their social institutions are maintained and, ultimately, how Iranian society is organized. By focusing on the driving habits of Iranians and exploring their attitudes to traffic laws and authorities, on the one hand, their perception of traffic safety and the rights of others, on the other, this book will offer a snapshot of Iranian legal culture and political order. These, in turn, will provide us with vantage points from which to view and analyse Iranian society as a place where modernity merges with tradition to produce cultural dualities, contradictions and paradoxes.[3] The picture that will emerge from this study reveals Iranian society as a social space where contrasting ideologies, religious beliefs, loyalties, forms of political authority and personal and collective aspirations clash on a daily basis in order to uphold a form of social order. It will be argued, finally, that this social order is maintained partly by perpetuating class and gender conflicts.

The study presented in this book is based on over 70 hours of qualitative interviews with various groups of Iranians regarding their experiences of the traffic, road accidents and driving in Tehran and

Shiraz. Our interviews with male and female taxi drivers, lawyers, insurance managers and medical doctors, who study road traffic injuries, soon guide us towards the foundational problems of Iranian culture, society and politics. Although our interviewees start by describing how they have experienced the traffic problem, their reflections on the causes of the problem inadvertently lead them to talking about other topics, such as the lack of a driving culture, the role of education, and Iranians' excessive sense of individualism and their disrespect for the rights of strangers, law enforcement and authorities whom they distrust. Our interviews with women taxi drivers open up a different perspective on Iranian society by showing that no aspect of social order may be adequately analysed without considering the roles of gender and social class. This study shows that class and gender conflicts cut across all walks of life in Iranian society, thereby moulding relationships between individuals and groups of people and thus influencing how social institutions, from family to the legal system and higher education, are formed. We shall argue in the following pages that the two categories of class and gender are employed by the authorities and policy makers to fuel social conflicts and to pit social groups up against each other. This tendency to control sociopolitical developments through dissent can, arguably, be related to Shi'i culture's urge to protest and revolt (see Dabashi 2011). However, there are also more tangible reasons that compel the Iranian regime to incite class war and gender conflicts. More than three decades on, the spirit of the 1979 revolution has largely abated, and, as Khosravi (2008) has shown, a generation of middle-class youth, constituting a large portion of the country's population, has come of age, who no longer share the revolutionary aspirations of the previous generation to establish an Islamic order.[4] Under the onslaught of globalization, the lifestyle of these middle-class youths is gradually drifting away from the ideals of the founders of the Islamic Republic, and is being replaced by an apolitical sense of defiance towards the authorities and the dominant Islamic order, as well as towards their parents' generation. In order to maintain revolutionary zeal among its supporters and to mobilize the masses, the Islamic regime taps into Shi'i mythology to perpetuate the conflict between *mostazafin* (the oppressed) and *mostakberin* (the oppressors).[5] A concrete manifestation of this policy is found in the *Basij-e Mostazafin* (the Mobilisation of the Deprived), which initially consisted of bands of volunteers recruited to support the war against Iraq but was gradually turned into a paramilitary organization charged with policing 'cultural crimes' and imposing Islamic moral codes, such as the wearing of the *hijab* (headscarf) in public places, upon the populace (Golkar 2011).

Thus, to maintain its form of social order, the Islamic state needs to revolutionize Iranian society *internally* over and again, on a daily basis. The regime also revolutionizes the country *externally* through its uncompromising opposition to the policies of neocolonial powers in the Middle East. The Iranian nuclear project exemplifies how the country's government can mobilize public opinion by driving an international conflict with superpowers. This book will demonstrate that this social order, which is preserved by inflaming class and gender conflicts, is mirrored not only in Iranians' driving habits but also in how they experience and describe the traffic situation in their cities.

This introductory chapter consists of three parts. Part One will describe the rate of RTAs and fatalities in Iran, placing them in relation to other recent social developments in the country. This section will also provide an overview of the previous research on RTAs in Iran, most of which were conducted by groups of medical doctors using quantitative methods. These studies often conceptualize RTAs as a public health issue rather than a multifaceted problem with cultural and legal dimensions. Part Two will present a preliminary discussion on the interplay between law and culture, in an attempt to devise a concept of 'legal culture' appropriate for examining the sociolegal dimensions of RTAs in Iran. Finally, Part Three presents the layout of the book and explains how the discussions in various chapters are related to each other.

Road Traffic Accidents in Iran

The rate of road accidents in Iran is twenty times more than the world's average. Globally, road traffic accidents kill 1.2 million people every year and leave 20–50 million people injured and disabled. In Iran, among all unintentional fatal injuries inflicted on children under five, traffic-related fatalities are the leading cause of death. Each year, road traffic crashes kill nearly 28,000 people in Iran, and injure or disable 300,000 more. Every

19 minutes one person dies on Iran's roads, and every two minutes people will hear that one of their family members has survived a crash but with serious injury and perhaps lifelong disability.

(UNICEF 2014)

Iranian society has undergone a number of important changes during the last few decades. For example, the rate of literacy among women has improved considerably over the last 30 years and is now over 98 per cent among female youth under 24 (World Bank 2014).[6] In addition, 60 per cent of applicants who passed the university entry exam in Iran in 2,000 were women, and women constituted 62 per cent of the country's university graduates.[7] During the same period, general health has significantly improved and the infant mortality rate (IMR) has decreased by 59 per cent, while life expectancy has increased by 23.2 per cent (Amani and Kazemnejad 2010). This general improvement in health, combined with a decrease in IMR and a relatively high birth rate, has generated a young age structure for the population, which has increased the demand for education, health care and other public services as well as for employment, while at the same time it has accelerated the 'changing mortality pattern' particularly in regard to RTAs (Abbasi-Shavazi 2004: 2).[8] Although such developments suggest that Iran is capable of social change, despite attempts made by the authorities to address the growing problem of RTAs by introducing severe penalties for traffic offences, the reckless and dangerous driving habits of Iranians remain largely unchanged as they continue to disregard traffic laws in what appears to be an unconscious collective behaviour.[9]

In November 2013, an official Iranian agency, the Majles Research Center (MRC), published the first report on Iran's RTA death toll, according to which '117,256 [serious] accidents, leading to 20,068 deaths and 297,257 injuries' had occurred during the previous year (Al-Monitor website 2013). The 2012 official statistics on fatalities, however, are somewhat lower than those from previous years, as collected by UNICEF. The lower official numbers might indicate a reduction in death toll, but they might equally reflect the different methodology employed by the MRC to collect and process its data, as well as the need to demonstrate that the authorities' measures have had a positive impact on the rate of RTAs. By contrast, the data collected by UNICEF show a steadily rising number of accidents and fatalities. For example, according to UNICEF (2007), 'in 2006, nearly 28,000 people died in traffic accidents in Iran, compared with roughly 17,000 in 2000,' RTAs thus constituting the second most frequent single cause of mortality in the country.[10] Admittedly, RTAs are a major public health problem globally, and according to the World Health Organization they account for 25 per cent of all deaths from injury (Peden et al. 2002). However, while RTAs constitute the second highest cause of death in Iran, they are the ninth leading causes of death worldwide (Mohammadi 2013). According to Bahadori Monfard et al. (2013), RTAs per 100,000 people amount to 747 in Iran, 28 in the Azerbaijan Republic, 94 in Kazakhstan, 28 in Turkmenistan, 94 in Turkey and 370 in the UK. Behind the differences between the rates of the RTAs in these countries lie not only the culture of driving and attitudes to safety, but also the percentage of car ownership per 100,000 people, the frequency of car usage and a host of other factors.

RTAs in Iran have multiple and complex causes, including the culture of driving, which in turn comprises widespread disregard for traffic rules and indifference to others' rights, but also drivers' attitudes to 'risky driving', including 'speeding, passing violations, tailgating, lane-usage violations, right-of-way violations, illegal turns, and control signal violations' (Habibi et al. 2014). In addition to drivers' attitudes to their own and other people's safety, other factors – such as driver stress and fatigue, drunk-driving and driving under the influence of drugs – play an important part. Finally, the standards and the design of the roads, the safety standards of the automobiles, especially unsafe vehicles manufactured in Iran, and the age structure of the population play a significant role in the rate of RTAs. In 2010, the population of Iran was about 74 million, the majority (65 per cent) of which lived in urban areas. According to the Statistical Center of Iran, more than 50 per cent of the population is under the age of 25 years, which means that the country has one of the youngest – and thus, car accident-prone – populations in the world (see Abbasi-Shavazi 2004: 2; Ghajarieh 2010: 34).

It is estimated that as many as 70 per cent of Iranian RTAs may be due to reckless and dangerous driving, with illegal overtaking and high-speed driving being the main causes (see *Iran Car Accidents* 2010). According to a recent study by Rezaei et al. (2014), traffic fatalities cost Iran $7.2 billion, which amounted to 2.19 per cent of the country's gross domestic product (GDP) in 2009–10 (UNICEF's estimate, however, is 5 per cent of Iran's GDP). During a similar period, the cost of RTAs in Egypt was 1 per cent, and in Vietnam 0.45 per cent of the country's GDP. Rezaei et al. (2014) conclude that RTAs not only cause great grief and suffering for many Iranians, but they also constitute a significant drain on the country's public resources. Understandably, the Iranian Government has been concerned about the exceptionally high rate of the RTAs for some time, and has taken several measures to improve road safety records, including the introduction of a seat-belt law in 2005, a motorcycle helmet law and increased general traffic law enforcement. They have also created the National Information Traffic Management Centre and installed more traffic cameras, in order to enhance the enforcement of traffic laws. A new law, entitled 'Traffic Penalty', was approved by Parliament (*Majlis*) in 2011, and introduced severe fines for dangerous and reckless driving. This study shows, however, that it is doubtful whether tougher penalties have had the desired impact on the Iranians' driving behaviour. As we shall see, many of those we have interviewed either state that the new laws have had very little effect or argue that they only penalize the economically disadvantaged sections of society.

Traffic researchers recognize the importance of law in regulating traffic and driving behaviour, but they also point out that laws designed specifically to change driving habits are ultimately dependent on the legal culture both of those responsible for enforcing the law and of those who are expected to obey it accordingly (see McCartt and Geary 2004; Mashaw and Harfst 1990). The cultural dimension of driving, and the fact that it is mediated through the technology of the automobile, which in itself affects behaviour in particular ways, turns it into a highly complex activity. As a result of its sociocultural complexity, driving does not lend itself easily to formal methods of regulation. Referring to our interviews again, we find widespread awareness of the cultural dimension of driving behaviour among Iranians and the fact that driving must be tackled as a cultural problem. Despite the fact that most Iranians experience reckless driving and the dangerous traffic situation existing in their cities as a cultural problem, very few (if any) of the hundreds of studies conducted in Iran that explore the traffic problem and RTAs engage with the cultural aspects of driving or with the limits of enforcing traffic laws.

Iranian Research on RTAs

There is a growing body of Iranian research, conducted almost exclusively by various groups of medical doctors based at university hospitals, which describes and analyses the rising levels of RTAs as a new social problem 'caused by the rapid modernisation of society' (Salamati et al. 2009: 6). These studies often highlight burgeoning car ownership (or the rapid increase in output of Iran's car manufacturing industry), the constitution of the population in Iran (as mentioned above, Iran has a youthful populace) and the changed lifestyles of Iranians as the main causes of RTAs.[11] Moreover, they discuss RTAs in terms of morbidity, pathology, epidemiology, injury and trauma, and – unwittingly, as the case might be – they 'medicalise' them. What is otherwise a societal problem requiring public policy debate is thus presented from a medical or epidemiological angle – a 'neglected epidemic', as Muntazeri (2004: 110) calls it.[12] With very few exceptions,[13] these studies are based on hard data collected by hospitals and traffic authorities, and they conceptualize driving primarily as a set of skills or a form of performance, thus, as a result, disregarding the possible significance of perceptions, attitudes, culture, law, history or forms of regulation for driving habits.[14] In addition, they disregard the body of social-science research that examines the complex relationship between the automobile, which is a form of technology mediated socioculturally, and driving, as a sociocultural behaviour mediated through said technology.[15] One objective of this study is to bring some balance to the debate on RTAs in Iran by highlighting driving habits as a complex behaviour informed by cultural as well as legal and technological processes. By exploring how the interplay between law and culture has evolved in Iran, this study will also pay attention to the historical context of Iranian legal culture.

The neglect of the social, cultural and legal aspects of driving behaviour and the traffic situation in Iran is an important and complex topic in itself. We shall return to this problem in the course of our various discussions, but we can already identify two main factors that have drawn the attention of Iranian researchers away from the study of the cultural and sociolegal aspects of RTAs. Many of these studies are conducted by researchers who employ a positivist methodology and subscribe to quantitative methods, which they consider 'scientific'. This group stays clear of cultural studies, which require qualitative and interpretive methods of analysis and which in their particular academic circles – and many of them are trained in medicine – are regarded as 'unscientific'. It is also possible that the sociolegal aspects of the problem are neglected because, first, there is no tradition of sociolegal research in Iran and, second, because potentially it requires critical political analysis. Law is politics by other means, and exploring law enforcement in Iran amounts to engaging in political debates and questioning the role of the authorities. Looking at this problem from a different standpoint, we could argue that sociolegal research has not developed in Iran partly because it requires the freedom to study official institutions and question the actions taken by various authorities, which might lead subsequently to discussing politically sensitive issues (for a discussion, see Banakar 2011). We shall return to this topic in Chapter Two, where we briefly discuss the state of social research in Iran.

Road safety in different countries is often analysed using a combination of factors such as the quality of infrastructure, driving conditions, the culture of driving or the efficacy of traffic rule enforcement (McAndrews 2010). Since this study is concerned with driving behaviour in urban areas, it will focus on the cultural aspects of RTAs and the enforcement of traffic rules. Moreover, it will conceptualize driving habits as a social activity, with legal and cultural dimensions reflective of how groups of people interact with each other and with society at large to create a form of social order. It is further argued that the driving habits of Iranians need to be placed in a historical context that reflects the inherent tension between Iranians' cultural identity, sense of individuality and community, on the one hand, and Iranians' perception of law and order, on the other.

Law, Culture and Legal Culture

'Legal culture' is a subcategory of the concept of culture and is used in the following pages to refer to 'relatively stable patterns of legally-oriented social behaviour and attitudes' (Nelken 2004: 1).[16] 'Culture', having been invoked by all of our interviewees, constitutes the central concept of this study. There are many ways of defining the notion of culture, and all of them testify to the difficulties associated with conceptualising cultural phenomena.[17] In the following pages, we shall regard culture as a 'form of life', or a way of going about the world – seeing, making sense of and experiencing social life. We shall initially frame our definition in line with Clifford Geertz's understanding of culture as 'socially constructed and historically transmitted patterns of meaning', which are embodied in symbols, values, attitudes, perceptions, worldviews, conventions and customary practices (Geertz 1973: 89).

'Law' is understood somewhat broadly to encompass not only legislation and the rules of the legal system but also certain categories of social norms, which are used to regulate behaviour and social activities.[18] In the context of this study, *urf* (meaning custom) exemplifies this broader notion of law, which is embedded in Iranian culture and, where it is compatible with the principles of Shari'a, is employed as a secondary source of law. *Urf* helps us to focus on customary practices that people employ instinctively, unprompted by the threat of formal sanctions, to organize their everyday activities, exchanges and relationships. This book will therefore argue that the study of the intersection of law and culture is significant in understanding how Iranian society has developed historically and been organized politically. Certain laws, such as criminal law, family law in Shari'a and laws aimed at producing and upholding gender segregation and controlling women's sexuality articulate social norms and moral values, which need cultural justification and legitimation if they are to be applied across society. However, the idea of 'legal culture' goes beyond the mere study of the cultural embeddedness of certain legal practices or how laws are legitimized. Instead, it seeks repeated patterns of legal behaviour, which are reproduced in a taken-for-granted manner by officers of the law or by ordinary citizens. Thus, the concept of legal culture could be used to describe why the majority of people normally follow certain laws or to explain why they collectively ignore them, as in the widespread disregard for traffic rules in Iran.

Iranian (legal) culture demonstrates a number of specific properties, some of which are rooted in the country's long history. These will be discussed in terms of the Iranian sense of individualism, the relationship between civil society and the State, and the Iranian notion of permanence in human relationships. According to a socio-historical thesis developed by Katouzian (2009), dynasties which have historically ruled over Iran and its people have done so through the exercise of arbitrary power (or *estebdād*, as it is called in Farsi) as opposed to the rule of law, or rule by law.[19] As a result, the relationship between Iranian society and its rulers (or the 'state'[20]) has always been defined by degrees of hostility. This hostility, which may also be described as the State's lack of popular legitimacy or the 'stifling despotisms' of the Iranian rulers (Bausani 1971: 32), played as decisive a role in the sudden collapse of the first Persian Empire in 330 BC as it did in the 'astonishing downfall of the restored empire of Iran' (Bausani 1971) in the face of the Islamic invasion in AD 700 and the collapse of the Pahlavi regime in 1979. This hostility may also be viewed from the standpoint of Shi'ism, i.e. the branch of Islam that has played a significant role in the formation of Iranian culture and society since the beginning of the sixteenth century. As we shall argue in Chapter Eight, Shi'i Islam does not recognize the legitimacy or authority of any temporal government during the occultation of the 12th Imam, a fact that has historically enhanced the Iranian ruler's lack of legitimacy.

Iran's cultural heritage is partly pre-Islamic and partly 'a product of centuries of Islamic social and cultural experience' which, as Katouzian (2009: 12) points out, influences Iranians' social and psychological behaviour even in instances when they do not regard themselves as religious believers. However, the form of religiosity embedded in the cultural practices of Iranians is neither inherently political nor necessarily the same as the ideology propagated by the Islamic government. This point is discussed in Chapter Nine in terms of various competing discourses and centres of normativity and authority, which constitute the intellectual and political life of Iran.

The Layout of the Book

This book is presented in two parts. Part One consists of eight chapters, which together describe how the research for this book was planned and carried out, and the empirical material collected and analysed. Chapters Two to Seven present the results of interviews, and analyse them by searching for key concepts, ideas, images and discursive patterns that occur repeatedly. Each of these chapters develops a central theme, such as *estebdād*, education, trust, social class or gender. Chapter Eight explores the interrelatedness between the cultural keywords identified in the interviews, and Chapter Nine sums up the results in a final analysis against a broader literature review of studies of Iranian society, culture and politics. Part Two concludes the book by providing two supplementary chapters, one taking an in-depth look into the role of gender in the production of cultural meaning in Iranian society, the other offering a critical overview of the Iranian legal system, its concepts, institutions, sources and procedural mechanisms.

Chapter Two begins by discussing how the Islamic regime's sceptical attitude towards the social sciences has affected the development of empirical social studies, in general, and the discipline of sociology, in particular. It then goes on to reflect critically on methodological and ethical aspects of doing fieldwork in a politically hostile environment. Moreover, it explains how this study was planned and carried out in two separate stages, including a pilot and a larger study, how access to interviewees was secured, what type of empirical material was collected and how this material was analysed against the backdrop of other recent studies of Iranian society and politics. The chapter ends by critically reflecting on the scope and limitations of this study, by drawing attention to the ethnocultural and linguistic diversity of the population of the country.

Chapter Three presents a pilot study consisting of 20 open interviews conducted in Shiraz and 15 semi-structured interviews conducted in Tehran – all in 2010. This initial study aimed at examining the feasibility of carrying out this research, and the possibility of using interviews for collecting relevant empirical data. Its results were used to generate a number of research questions for a larger study, which was subsequently conducted in Tehran in 2012. This chapter also constructs a preliminary framework for the study based on the distinction between 'descriptive' norms, which refer to how people behave in actual fact (or to de facto existing patterns of social behaviour), and 'injunctive' norms, which refer to how they *ought* to behave (or to normative behavioural expectations). This distinction is employed in this book to analyse some of the responses from our interviewees. For example, when we asked our interviewees if they normally stop at a zebra crossing to let pedestrians cross the road, many replied by saying that 'one *should* stop [...]'. The gap we find in our interviews between how interviewees employ descriptive and injunctive norms is viewed against the assumption that Iranian society consists of two separate spheres of action, one restricted to the family, kinship and network of friends, which we shall refer to as the individual's immediate 'peer group', and one defined in terms of a larger 'society of strangers'. These two spheres, and the gap between descriptive and injunctive norms, exist in most societies. However, they take on special significance in Iran, which we shall unfold gradually as we analyse our interviews against the backdrop of Homa Katouzian's conception of the 'short-term society' and the prevalence of *estebdād*, or the arbitrary exercise of power and authority by successive Iranian 'states' (Katouzian 2009). Iranian dynasties and 'states' have ruled without popular legitimacy throughout the ages, and their forms of government, laws and legal orders have normally lasted a few hundred years at a time. This has affected the way Iranians view their government as well as society at large and its institutions, all of which are experienced as short-term constructs. By contrast, the individual's 'peer group' is experienced as enduring and capable of providing socio-economic security. Following Katouzian, we shall argue that this socio-historical development has exercised a profound influence on how Iranians conceive rights and responsibilities. Moreover, the historical tension between the Iranian 'state' and society has created a unique form of individualism – a particular sense of community and legal culture.

The next four chapters present the second stage of this study, which was conducted mainly in Tehran in 2012. They contain brief descriptions of the interviews carried out with specific groups – such as taxi drivers, lawyers and doctors – followed by an analysis that searches for repeated discursive patterns in the way our interviewees express their ideas and put forward their arguments and thoughts.[21] Taxi drivers were chosen because of their general experience of the traffic and their daily exposure to the problems it causes, while lawyers were interviewed because of their familiarity with law and law enforcement. Other professionals, such as medical doctors, were selected because of their extensive experience of researching road traffic injuries, while insurance managers were interviewed because of their insight into the economy of RTAs. Three questions guided the analysis in these four chapters: (1) which discursive patterns can be identified in the interviews; (2) which key ideas, images and concepts do these patterns signify; and (3) are the key ideas related to each other? As discursive patterns are identified in the interviews, they are briefly discussed and explored against the broader concerns of the study. As we return to certain ideas such as Iranians' form of individualism, their belief in *farhang-sazi* (literally 'culture building', but also used to refer to the top-down deployment of public policies to educate people about the traffic and the law), their non-compliance with the law and their distrust of the authorities, we develop them by searching for their interconnectedness.

Chapter Four presents 11 interviews with male taxi drivers, which reflect how they experienced the traffic problem and conceptualized the role of law and culture in respect to driving behaviour. These interviews allow us to form an understanding of why many Iranian drivers disregard traffic norms and safety rules, an understanding that slowly takes us beyond the results of our pilot study. Our interviewees demonstrated an awareness of the complexity of the causes of RTAs, saw and described them in cultural terms, and often sought the solution in educating Iranians from an early age to respect the law and traffic rules. Although repeated references to culture and education were also made in the pilot study, it was during these interviews that we became aware of education as a key concept in Iranian culture. We also found that many of our interviewees moved from discussing culture to *farhang-sazi* (in its 'culture building' sense), a post-revolutionary idea reminiscent of the Chinese 'Cultural Revolution', which we shall develop further in the context of other interviews with lawyers and other professionals. Other issues that were highlighted in the interviews with male taxi drivers included Iranians' excessive individualism, often expressed as *zerangi*, which means being smart or acting in a clever way, often by beating the system. These ideas and concepts gained in significance as they reappeared in other sets of interviews.

The idea of *farhang-sazi* looms large in Chapter Five, where we present 11 interviews with lawyers using largely the same semi-structured questions as we had put to the taxi drivers. Whereas some of the male and female taxi drivers supported the idea of more severe traffic fines to penalize reckless drivers, the lawyers we interviewed dismissed it as ineffective. They justified their stance against severe penalties by arguing that the primary cause of Iranians' disregard for traffic rules lay in their culture. They stressed the part that education (*amoozesh*) had to play in shaping people's driving conduct and respect for the law, and went on to emphasize *farahang-sazi* as a solution to the traffic problem. Several other insights were gained in the interviews with the lawyers, who generally expressed politically liberal views on law and punishment. One concerned their concept of law, which they generally expressed in legal positivistic terms as a function of a 'social contract' between citizens and the State. Several lawyers argued that in a situation where the authorities fail to honour their obligations to the citizenry, we cannot reasonably expect the ordinary 'man in the street' to uphold his or her legal and civil duties. The failure of the authorities to respect and uphold the law, and enforce it impartially and effectively, according to our lawyers, gave rise to widespread *mistrust* of the government and the legal system. This point draws our attention once again to the hiatus between individual Iranians and their rulers, defining it in terms of the absence of trust in their relationship. Finally, the lawyers expressed concern about the way the legal profession was being depicted in the official media, particularly in popular soap operas, wherein lawyers were portrayed as untrustworthy and immoral characters at the service of criminals. This systematic undermining of lawyers' standing in society coincided with the Iranian Government's plans to integrate the Iranian Bar Association, which enjoys a degree of autonomy from both the legal and political systems, into the judiciary.

Chapter Six presents eight interviews with different professionals, including four medical doctors who have carried out research on road traffic injuries and published numerous research papers in international journals. We also interviewed two insurance managers working at Tehran's largest insurance companies (and thus familiar with car accidents), one psychologist and one sociologist at Tehran University. These interviewees were more at ease and voiced politically sensitive viewpoints, either directly or through the use of metaphors and by making suggestive statements. One of the doctors said that he was trying to be 'politically correct' when drawing comparisons between people's attitudes to the law and to hospitals, explaining that Iranians believe that hospitals are mismanaged and therefore avoid visiting them unless they absolutely have no other alternative. Besides referring to a similar set of concepts, such as education and *farhang-sazi*, this group of interviewees highlighted the role of social class and gender in Iranian society. The image of Tehran that emerges out of these interviews is of a city divided into separate social spaces in accordance with a bewildering mixture of criteria, such as religiosity, tradition, loyally to the Islamic regime, modernity and social class. It is also suggested that the traffic problem appears differently in different parts of Tehran, according to where members of different social classes live.

The concern with social class continues to characterize our last set of interviews; however, while gender is mentioned in passing in

Chapter Six, it takes centre stage in Chapter Seven, wherein we present 12 interviews with female taxi drivers. These interviews take our study of driving habits into a new area, by compelling us to consider how gender translates into economic competition and provides a basis for the sociopolitical domination of men over women. At the same time, they show that social class and attitude to Islam have become instruments for perpetuating the tension between 'tradition' and 'modernity' and renewing the ideological conflict between the followers of the Islamic Republic and their opponents. Thus, social conflicts – whether defined as access to resources and income disparity, or in terms of gender differences and the denial of rights of women – become politically functional in the context of a society that maintains its precarious social, political and economic balance by renewing its revolutionary ethos on a daily basis.

The results of these four chapters are analysed in the search for a theoretical framework in Chapter Eight on Iranian culture, wherein we examine the interconnectedness of the key concepts and ideas identified in our interviews as *culturally* significant. We also explore the meaning of these concepts, and the patterns of behaviour that they generate, in a historical context, asking how and why they are related to each other, before relating them to law and society. The main argument of this chapter is that the Iranian sense of individualism (or 'personalism') is a distinct sociocultural entity rooted in the individual's 'peer group', and therefore it is different from the Western idea of individualism. This chapter argues that cultural norms, values and practices specific to Iranian society – as well as the cultural patterns of behaviour that embody them, ranging from *zerangi* and *taarof* (exaggerated civility) to driving habits – are ultimately dependent on Iranians' personalism. We shall also briefly explore the role of Shi'ism as a religion of protest (Dabashi 2011), which fosters a rebellious and potentially anti-state philosophy of life supportive of Iranian personalism.

Chapter Nine reflects on the nature of Iranian legal culture by exploring the types of law and social order that produce it, and asking how Iranian society is held together notwithstanding the sense of distrust that permeates people's relationship to the State. It brings together some of the ideas and insights that we gained from the analysis of our interviews and discussions on Iranian law and culture, in order to outline an empirically sensitized framework that may serve further studies of the interconnectedness of Iranian law, culture and society. We discuss the transformation of Iranian society, with its young population structure, and the repressive sexual policies of the government aimed at controlling women's sexuality. We also examine the sociopolitical implications of the growing number of educated women, who claim equal rights, and the gender and class policies of the Islamic Republic, which aim at maintaining the status quo by denying women their rights. We also posit that Iranian culture, which is rooted in Shiʿi Islam, remains a conservative force with respect to issues of gender and class, and, on certain points, finds itself at odds with the policies introduced from above by the government. The Islamic values and traditions that are embodied in the country's day-to-day social and cultural patterns of behaviour are not necessarily the ideological Islamic values of the state apparatus and the ideologues of the Islamic Republic, but rather the customary rules and the traditional, conservative values of ordinary Iranian families.

In the second part of the book, we provide two supplementary chapters that are directly linked to this study and are aimed at providing further background information. Chapter Ten discusses how 'meaning' is generated in order to uphold and reproduce certain gender relationships. This will be done through a further analysis of the interviews with female taxi drivers in Tehran. Chapter Eleven provides a brief description of the Iranian legal system, defining its main institutions and sources of authority. It also locates a number of key concepts, such as *urf*, which are used in the interviews and discussed in the text, in the broader context of the Iranian legal system. This chapter does not claim to cover all aspects of Iranian law, and is provided here only to assist the reader to follow some of the legal concerns voiced in the interviews with lawyers and others. It argues that the legal system of the Islamic Republic is lacking in legal autonomy, and that instead of unifying its institutions through the 'rule of law' it holds them together through the overarching authority of the Supreme Leader and an ideologized interpretation of Shariʿa – or the 'Islamic criteria' – which is implemented in accordance with the regime's expedience. The chapter ends by arguing that after 35 years of living under the Islamic Constitution, the overwhelming majority of Iranians we interviewed regarded parliament, and not the Leader or Shariʿa, as their primary source of law.

PART I

THE STUDY OF IRANIANS' LAW, CULTURE AND DRIVING HABITS

CHAPTER 2

CONDUCTING RESEARCH IN IRAN

Reza Banakar

Conducting social science research in Iran is associated with a number of particular challenges characteristic of societies where the right to freedom of expression is restricted. These challenges are discussed below, under the section on 'Interview Effects', in terms of trust. Collecting empirical data through interviews, for example, could pose a difficulty if the interviewees do not sufficiently trust the interviewer or have confidence in the interview situation. It must be emphasized, however, that Iran is not a totalitarian state, and the Iranian Government, which might appear from the outside as one single entity, is internally fragmented and composed of several competing centres of power and authority. As we argue in Chapter Nine, this political fragmentation does not allow for the total monitoring of political thought and action in the country, and between the centres of power and authority we find social spaces where public discourse flows spontaneously. Although Iranians generally avoid making politically sensitive statements in a formal setting (such as when they are being interviewed and recorded), they do make their critical voices heard in public spaces, where the context is non-ideological and the gathering is spontaneous rather than politically organized (see Bayat 2010).

This chapter will start by briefly discussing how the attitude of the Islamic government to empirical social research has influenced the

Figure 2.1   A Junction in Tehran © Hamid Shojaee.

development of sociology in Iran. It will then discuss the methodological and ethical aspects of conducting fieldwork in Iran, generally, and the research conducted for this book, in particular. The chapter ends with a discussion on the ethnocultural and linguistic diversity of the Iranian population, and how this diversity limits the scope of the study presented herein.

Attitudes to Social Science Research

In a recent review, Tavakol and Rahimi Sajasi (2012) argue that sociological research in Iran has stagnated and that Iranian sociologists have difficulty engaging with social problems in an effective manner. One main reason for this lack of progress, they argue, is the sociologists' dependency on state funding, which, together with the authorities' intervention in the research process, causes conservatism and discontinuity in the development of theory and methods (Tavakol and Rahimi Sajasi 2012: 208). The Iranian authorities have been suspicious of social sciences, which they see as inherently 'colonial' and, in their secular format, incompatible with their ideal of an Islamic society. According to Mahdi (2003 and 2010), the decline of social sciences began with the country's 'Cultural Revolution' of the 1980s and the resulting attempts to 'Islamicise both university curriculum and staff' (2003: 33), which coincided with the bitter war of attrition between Iran and Iraq. The conflict with Iraq was used to unite the country behind the Islamic regime, to legitimize an intensification of political repression and to cleanse public institutions of un-Islamic ideas, lifestyles and behaviour. Thus, the war provided a golden opportunity to politically consolidate the Islamic regime in the country, partly by carrying through the Cultural Revolution aimed at producing what Bayat (2010: 121) calls an 'ideal Muslim man' but also to eliminate the regime's political opponents. In the spring of 1980, 'universities were shut down for two years, Islamic associations were set up in schools, and all public places came under the watchful gaze of morals police and pro-regime vigilantes' (Bayat 2010).[1] During this time, many professors and lecturers were purged, thousands of students were expelled and a whole new curriculum was drawn up to implement the Islamization of higher education. The Cultural Revolution was sustained for a decade by using the war to fuel revolutionary zeal among the masses. It was also used to purge the regime's political opponents, to stifle free expression and repress the secular intelligentsia. Such a political climate, which does not tolerate dissent or critique, cannot be supportive of social sciences, which encourage questioning received wisdom and scrutinizing the intended and unintended consequences of public policies, laws, regulations and societal developments. As Mahdi (2010: 271) explains, during the Cultural Revolution, social scientists were targeted and 'accused of desacralizing religious knowledge and mythical beliefs and were thus subjected to harassment, loss of employment and public denunciation'.

The Iranian authorities' distrustful attitude towards secular social sciences continued after the Iran–Iraq war, as the regime struggled with internal dissent and external discontent towards its Islamist ideology. According to Asghar Kazemi, a law professor at Tehran University, Western social science books and materials, promoted by Western-educated and/or -oriented teachers and professors within Iranian higher education, have been blamed for contributing to public demonstrations and protests following the presidential elections in 2009 (Kazemi 2010). In a recent speech addressed to university professors, delivered on

2 July 2014, the Supreme Leader described the religious authorities' conception of 'humanities', which includes social sciences, thus:

> One other problem, which has caught our attention for some time [. . .], concerns humanities. We have a genuine need to bring about a fundamental change of humanities in our country. It does not imply that we have no need for the intellectual, scientific and research-based work carried out by other people [. . .]. However, some fields of humanities are products of Westerners. They have studied and worked on them and we should benefit from their studies. Our issue is that Western humanities are based on non-divine, materialistic and non-monotheistic assumptions. These [assumptions] make them incompatible with Islamic principles and with religious ethos. Only when humanities become based on divine principles and world views, they also become good and beneficial and may be employed to educate human beings and to help individuals and society. Such an approach to humanities does not currently exist within social sciences.

Sociology ranks high among the Western materialist (secular) disciplines considered 'incompatible with Islamic principles and with religious ethos'. Its continued existence could be justified only if it supported the Islamic regime's world view and let itself be employed as a tool for solving state problems.

The Iranian authorities, who are the primary funders of sociological research in the country, regard quantitative studies, which make use of large amounts of data and present their results through glossy statistical diagrams and charts, as 'proper science'. Bayatrizi (2010: 823), who has interviewed six prominent Iranian researchers who have secured significant state funds for their work and two grant administrators working for cabinet ministers, explains that the state-sponsored research 'favours policy-oriented research at the expense of disinterested, basic and theoretical research' (Bayatrizi 2010: 816). Moreover, it 'glorifies empirical sociology, especially quantitative methods like surveys, over all other types of sociological enquiry' (Bayatrizi 2010: 823). In her discussions with the six Iranian researchers, she finds that 'only one had expertise in qualitative research methods, while historical or textual analysis remained episodic' (Bayatrizi 2010: 823). What makes matters more complicated 'is the absence of arm's length government funding agencies and the weakness of private foundations and think tanks' (Bayatrizi 2010: 817). This state-sponsored research promotes applied studies with narrowly defined remits and empiricist methodologies, is not subjected to systematic evaluation, seldom made public, and 'researchers with the right connections can get their proposals and final reports approved without serious scrutiny' (Bayatrizi 2010: 822). It can happen that the authorities sponsor qualitative studies that require in-depth interviewing techniques, but even these are often carried out within a strict empiricist framework.

Research Permits

This positivistic and empiricist understanding of research is reflected in the requirements for obtaining research permits. To conduct quantitative social research, such as surveys, one requires an official permit, and if it is to involve members of governmental departments or institutions one must obtain a special permit from the internal security section of these departments, which are known commonly as *harasat*. Conversely, in order to carry out qualitative research, such as conducting open interviews, within the private sector, one only requires permission from the businesses organizations whose members are being interviewed. One does not require a permit to interview ordinary people in public spaces; however, researchers are advised to obtain a permit even in this respect. A matrix of forms of research permit is presented below (it was kindly drawn up in Farsi by Mr Keyvan Ziaee, who has worked as a researcher in Iran).

As the matrix shows, quantitative research aimed at studying governmental organizations is more carefully regulated in Iran, and is subjected to closer official scrutiny, than qualitative research. We must emphasize that the matrix provides a very rough approximation of official requirements and does not tally with our experience of conducting fieldwork in Iran. In order to conduct our fieldwork, we obtained a general permit from one of the main state universities in Tehran, which endorsed our project and allowed us to carry out interviews with various groups of people. We also obtained a permit from a taxi agency in Tehran and from the Iranian Bar Association in order to carry out interviews with their respective members. Although we had a research permit from a state university, neither the traffic police

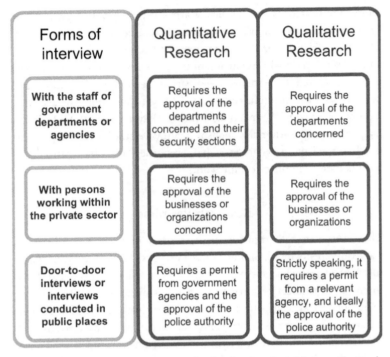

Forms of interview	Quantitative Research	Qualitative Research
With the staff of government departments or agencies	Requires the approval of the departments concerned and their security sections	Requires the approval of the departments concerned
With persons working within the private sector	Requires the approval of the businesses or organizations concerned	Requires the approval of the businesses or organizations
Door-to-door interviews or interviews conducted in public places	Requires a permit from government agencies and the approval of the police authority	Strictly speaking, it requires a permit from a relevant agency, and ideally the approval of the police authority

Figure 2.2   Official Requirements for Conducting Social Science Research in Iran.

nor the automobile manufacturer Iran Khodro granted us interviews. The traffic police passed on our request to their internal security, and our contact with Iran Khodro was cut short by their internal security staff (we shall discuss these matters below). Thus, official letters from the concerned organizations, whether governmental or private sector, can in theory facilitate access and help to establish a sense of confidence in the interview situation, but they do not *per se* guarantee access.

Several experienced researchers explained to us that it was improbable that the police would interfere with our fieldwork. The requirement to obtain permission from the police to conduct open interviews with ordinary people should be regarded as advice, rather than a strict obligation. However, if one is conducting surveys in public places, or door-to-door interviews, one will require specific permits from the police or the Ministry of Culture and Islamic Guidance. It is unlikely that researchers based outside Iran could obtain such permits.

Looking at a range of empirical studies conducted in Iran during the last few years dealing with a variety of questions – ranging from family law, domestic violence and women's rights to youth culture and trade – we find that access to interviewees and participants has been often established informally and through personal connections of the researcher. Keshavarzian (2007), who interviewed *bazaaris* (traditional merchants), does not, for example, mention that he had any official permit to conduct his interviews, but instead emphasizes that establishing interpersonal trust and relationships was crucial to getting access to the *bazaaris*. Keshavarzian (2007: 31) writes that 'through previous contacts [he] established six independent entries into the bazaar', but does not explain who these 'previous contacts' were, although he mentions in passing that he 'was directed through networks of relatives and commercial partners':

A simple mention that I was so-and-so's friend would usually solicit cooperation. On some occasions my interviewees would call on my behalf to arrange for an appointment, write a letter of introduction, or personally take me to their colleagues.

(Keshavarzian 2007: 31)

Zahra Tizro, a British-based researcher studying domestic violence, describes in more detail how she secured access to her participants in Iran:

Overall, I did not experience any major obstacle to my work and enjoyed high levels of cooperation. My personal background and connections played a large part [in] paving the way for my smooth landing in the research field. I approached people informally through friends and explained the nature of my research and academic interests and intentions. However, since I was dealing with a non-western culture, I was unable to use the guidelines for Western academic research in the forms of codes of conduct and ethical procedures. I was unable to present the interviewees' rights or to present these rights in the form of consent letters. This carried the risk of losing interviewees' trust, or of making them uncomfortable, while putting them in a formal setting could damage the interview or even mean losing it all together.

(Tizro 2012: 70–1)

Several ethical issues related to conducting research in politically unfavourable environments are forced to the surface in the above quotation, and they lie outside the scope of our discussion here. Tizro's argument that she suspended the codes of ethics of the British Sociological Association because she was doing fieldwork in a 'non-Western culture' is unsatisfactory. Nevertheless, her approach reflects the reality of carrying out research in Iranian society, where the state authorities are suspicious of social research generally, and where participants in research are wary of expressing to strangers views that might be deemed political or critical of authorities. Tizro (2012: 75) refers to the role of 'friends and family' in introducing her to some of her male interviewees, suggesting that (1) as a woman she could not otherwise interview men, and (2) this method of accessing interviewees is safe for the participants and the researcher. Her account reflects the dual 'architecture' of Iranian society, wherein networks based on family kinship and friendships are formed as enduring social units, which are separate from the State and society at large. While Iranians trust their personal networks of family and friends, which constitutes their 'peer group', they distrust the State and the social order of society at large. At the same time, the separation of the public and private spheres is gendered, mirroring the duality of veiled/unveiled, which as we shall argue, is central to Iranian culture. The public sphere is 'veiled' because it is constituted by 'outsiders', people who are not 'related' or trusted, and thus it is unsafe there to reveal one's true face or inner self (this applies to both men and women, albeit in different ways). In contrast, the private sphere is constituted by 'insiders', those who are 'related' and trusted, and is therefore safe and 'unveiled' – here one may reveal one's inner self. This duality, which is materialized in the architecture of Iranian houses, does not correlate with the dichotomy of traditional and modern or religious and secular. The 'unveiled' can be as traditional and repressive as the 'veiled' can be modern and secular.

Two Stages of the Study

This study was carried out in two stages. Stage One consisted of 20 in-depth interviews, each about one-hour long, conducted in Shiraz,[2] in June 2010, and 15 semi-structured interviews, each about 45 minutes, conducted in Tehran in December 2010. The interviews were recorded, transcribed and analysed, and the results were published as a research paper entitled 'Driving Dangerously: Law, Culture and Driving Habits in Iran' (see Banakar and Nasrolahi Fard 2012). A revised and developed version of this paper is presented in Chapter Three. The results of the pilot were used to construct a more comprehensive study based on a list of semi-structured questions, divided up into several sections, each focusing on various aspects of driving, such as experiences of traffic, the causes of reckless driving behaviour, attitudes to safety and the perceptions of the law and legality (see Appendix). These were then employed in a larger study which was conducted in Tehran with four groups: male taxi drivers, female taxi drivers, lawyers and other professionals including doctors who researched road traffic accidents (RTAs) road traffic accidents. Some of these doctors were initially trained as surgeons but had decided to turn to epidemiological research in search of preventive public health policies that could reduce RTAs. The methodological issues of the pilot study will be discussed in the next chapter. In the remaining part of this chapter, we shall instead focus on the methodological concerns of Stage Two, which provides the main empirical material used in this book and presented in Chapters Four, Five, Six and Seven.

Those who were interviewed for the pilot were initially introduced through personal networks of family and friends, whereas those interviewed in the second stage of the study were strangers. The first set of our interviews flowed naturally, and we were surprised by how openly most of the interviewees expressed themselves. The second part of the study, where we were not introduced to the interviewees by a trusted

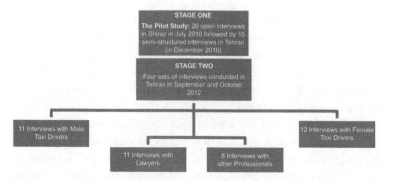

Figure 2.3   The Two Stages of the Research Process.

person, functioned differently in the sense that some of the interviews did not flow naturally from the outset. However, as we shall explain below, certain groups of interviewees perceived the interview situation differently and felt more at ease than others.

The Interviews

The interviews started by handing out to the interviewees a Participant Information Sheet in Farsi, explaining the aim of the research project as clearly as possible. The sheet underlined the fact that participating in this research was entirely voluntary, and that if they decided to take part they were still free to withdraw at any time and without giving a reason for doing so. The interviewees were assured of their anonymity and told that information collected about them would be kept strictly confidential (subject to legal limitations), and that in the transcription of the interviews and research reports all participants would be anonymized. This procedure, as noted by Tizro (2012: 70–1), impacts directly on the process of the interview, formalizing the exchanges between the interviewee and the interviewer.

We treated the interviews as a learning process. As they progressed, we noted that some questions concerning the causes of accidents and safety were soon exhausted, in so far as predominantly similar answers were given by most of the interviewees. We also noticed that some questions, such as those dealing with traffic safety and the causes of accidents, worked better in the sense of engaging the interest of the interviewees. These were also politically neutral questions, which nevertheless guided the interviewees to reflect on the cultural aspects of driving. Other questions that dealt with law enforcement and the sources of the law worked very differently in different interview contexts. Some questions proved to be unsuitable as points of departure for discussion for some interviewee groups, while others needed to be fine-tuned. However, the majority of the questions performed effectively in the course of the interviews.

The interviews were not limited to the questions posed at the outset, and so each interview situation was treated as a unique meeting in its own right and with its own potential, which could give rise to discussing new aspects of driving habits, safety and the law. The questions we had were used to set the primary contours of our concerns with the interviews, and were then utilized to keep the discussions running along one line of enquiry. In the course of the interviews, we added new questions, but we were also wary of making the interviews overly long.

Interview Effects

Eleven semi-structured interviews were conducted with male taxi drivers employed by one of the local taxi agencies in Tehran in September 2012 (for a list of interview questions, see Appendix). These interviews were associated with a number of 'interview effects', all of which were taken into consideration when analysing the results. Three factors – the premises where the interviews were conducted, the 'interviewer effect' and the potentially political, and therefore sensitive nature of some of the questions posed – were duly noted. The interviews were carried out on the premises of the taxi agency, where the interviewees were likely be overheard by their colleagues. Furthermore, the interviewer might have appeared as an 'outsider' to some of the interviewees, who, as a result, replied reticently to some of the questions. Some interviewees appeared to be on their guard when questions that could be interpreted politically were raised. In one instance, the interviewee stated that he did not wish to discuss certain questions related to law enforcement because he did not want to get into 'this type of discussion'.

Iranians as individuals, and even as representatives of government agencies, are normally accommodating and usually find it difficult to turn down an interview request; to say 'no' would be impolite. The fact that they might not turn down a request, does not however mean that they will necessarily participate in it. The Farsi word for 'interview' (*musahebeh*) has certain connotations that might unsettle some Iranians who wish to stay out of trouble, thereby discouraging them from participating in social science studies. Taking part in a recorded interview can amount to giving testimony that might be used against you later. Iranians tend to talk politics and discuss political issues openly within their 'peer groups' and, as mentioned above, criticize authorities in spontaneous gatherings in public spaces. Nevertheless, they are often wary of discussing with strangers specific issues that might have political implications for them. Consequently, interviews would work very differently if one had been introduced to the interviewee through a familiar and trusted channel. Lack of trust, combined with the fact that the interviews were carried out in a public space, left a perceptible mark on the interviews with the male taxi drivers. This does not mean, however, that the material collected through these interviews has no empirical value; instead, it means that when analysing the content of the interviews, we should consider their constrained nature.

The subsequent interviews conducted with women taxi drivers were, on the whole, more relaxed and some of them flowed more naturally. One explanation for this difference is that while the men were interviewed on the premises of the taxi agency, which did not offer privacy, the women were interviewed in their taxi cabs, where they could not be overheard. Similarly, the interviews with lawyers and other professionals were also conducted in their own personal offices and flowed effortlessly.

As mentioned above, we were planning to interview the traffic police, the traffic planning agency and representatives of the Iranian car industry. Despite submitting several lengthy applications to the police authorities, we were unable to obtain interview permits to speak with them. The authorities did not reject our application, but they did not grant us interviews either; instead, they passed us from one department to another, where more documentation was required. Throughout this lengthy process, the authorities treated us with cordiality and gave the impression that they wished to grant us permission. Nevertheless, no one within the traffic police was prepared to take the responsibility for putting their name to the research permit. Finally, our request was passed on to the *harasat* (the police's internal security organ), where the application remains unprocessed to this day. This was unfortunate, because the views of the traffic police and their experience of dealing with the traffic problem and enforcing traffic laws were important for this study. We were admittedly offered informal talks with various officers in Shiraz, but we decided not to carry out the interviews without a research permit from the authorities.

Our contacts with the public relations (PR) office of Iran Khodro, which is the largest car manufacturer in Iran, was by contrast more promising, and we were even granted an appointment to meet with the members of their PR office to discuss our study. Once we arrived at the Iran Khodro offices on the day of the appointment, members of their internal security informed us that none of their managers was available to speak with us. However, the staff of the PR department received us warmly and spoke with us while we were waiting at their offices. We shall not, however, make use of the discussions we had with them in the following pages.

Other Interviews

All the taxi drivers, and most of the lawyers and other professionals whom we interviewed in September and October 2012, were men. To address this gender imbalance in our data, we arranged 12 interviews with female taxi drivers, which were carried out later the same year, in December 2012, by Behnoosh Payvar. Such a comparison was necessary if we were to examine the role of gender in the study of the Iranian law, culture and driving habits. Some of the insights that we gained from this comparison are in line with mainstream feminist studies, which underline working women's concerns with, and responsibility for, the well-being of the family. By contrast, men appeared to various degrees free from such considerations or expressed themselves in other terms when family-related considerations were raised. Such a comparison also allowed us to explore how the interconnectedness of gender, politics and class conflicts are employed in Iran to perpetuate social and gender conflicts.

Women taxi drivers were generally open and willing to answer the questions, albeit in a cautious fashion that enabled them to stay within the correct parameters of Iranian public political discourse. As we noted above, one reason for their relative openness and willingness to talk was that they were interviewed in the privacy of their taxis. The tone of the interviews with the women was also more informal, and as a result many of the interviews flowed more naturally. Another factor that played a role in the quality of the interviews with the female drivers concerns their level of education. Only one of the male cabbies suggested in passing that he had studied at university (he did not, however, say that he had graduated), whereas, by contrast, many of our female cabbies had a university education.

Finally, 11 interviews were conducted with lawyers in addition to six interviews with medical doctors and other professionals, largely using the same questions and the same interview structure as we had used for the taxi drivers. Additional questions were asked regarding the role of lawyers and legal services in Iranian society. Discussions about traffic behaviour and law flowed more naturally and, with one exception, the lawyers came across as more engaged than the taxi drivers we had interviewed. As a result, the interviews became longer, averaging 1 hour 30 minutes, and legally more extensive than those with the taxi drivers. At least two main factors contributed to the fact that the interviews with the lawyers worked better and were associated with less interviewer effect. First, the interviewee and the interviewer were largely speaking the same type of professional language and could therefore easily establish mutual trust, while second, the interviews with the lawyers were conducted in the privacy of their offices.

Content Analysis

This study is based on a qualitative approach that aims at exploring Iranian legal culture by examining experiences of traffic rules, law and legality. The interviews were carried out in order to examine how Iranians viewed and experienced traffic, and how they felt about their own experiences and other people's conduct. Put differently, our objective was to see how our interviewees constructed socioculturally meaningful ideas about issues, ranging from traffic rules to law and legality, by attaching values to events, people, relations, places and conducts. Moreover, how did they use these ideas in order to make sense of their social environment and to generate normative representations of the world in which they lived? Thus, how they talked and reasoned – rather than the factual correctness of their statements – constituted the primary focus of our analysis. For example, when we asked our interviewees how the introduction of more severe penalties for traffic-related offences had influenced the behaviour of drivers generally, some replied affirmatively; however, the scope of our interviews does not allow us to generalize their responses, i.e. our interviewees can only express a personal view about such matters, a view which might or might not be valid. The question for us is how they argue their point of view. Looking more closely at the way our participants discussed the efficacy of penalties, we note that many of them contradict themselves. On the one hand, they state that the introduction of more severe penalties has had a favourable effect on traffic behaviour, while, on the other hand, they argue that traffic has not improved and that higher fines affect only those people who belong to the low-income section of society.

The experiences of our interviewees and our analysis thereof were then examined in the context of previous historical and sociopolitical research on Iran, which in turn let us to ask a different set of questions. Are the driving habits of Iranians related to their individualism, or personalism? Are they related to their concept of law and their experience of the State and authority? How do Iranians understand society at large as an abstract entity, and do they feel responsibility for the unknown people who constitute it? How do Iranians' driving habits relate to their perception of modernity and technology? Why, in a relatively short period, have Iranian drivers changed their attitude to wearing seat belts, while in the face of higher fines they do not change their careless driving habits or disregard for traffic rules? These are the broader set questions which define the concerns of this study. Some of these concerns were developed through the pilot study, while the last question emerged out of the interviews with the taxi drivers. The interviews conducted as part of Stage Two of this project aid us in reflecting more systematically on these questions, while also allowing us to fine-tune some of the enquiries and theoretical arguments that were formulated in the initial pilot studies.

When reading and examining the interviews, our focus was on the key concepts our interviewees employ to express their ideas, to describe their experiences, present their thoughts and articulate their values when describing problems related to the traffic situation in Tehran or when explaining the causes of traffic accidents. Expressed differently, the words, ideas, images, concepts and terms they use to problematize the traffic situation, reckless driving, the law and law enforcement are the primary objects of our study. For example, when one of the male taxi drivers (see interview 1:3:7, page 63, in Chapter Four) states that drunken driving is a frequent cause of accidents in north Tehran, our focus is not on the factual accuracy of his statement, as it might or might not be true; instead, we concentrate on his use of the adjective 'drunken', which indicates conduct in breach of Islamic law (he is therefore referring to people who do not live in accordance with proper Islamic laws, norms and values), and his use of the notion of 'north Tehran'. We cannot possibly prove or disprove the validity of his statement using the data from our interviews, but we can argue that 'north Tehran' has sociopolitical as well as economic connotations in the public political discourse of people who live in the city – it is where the more affluent and secular section of Tehranis lives. Thus, the interviewee is suggesting that many accidents in the affluent area of Tehran are caused by non-Islamic behaviour or by people who do not live as proper Muslims. To make matters slightly more complicated, the fact that the interviewee expresses this idea does not imply that he is a devout Muslim and lives his life in accordance with Islamic laws. He is simply articulating an injunctive norm in tune with the religious values of the political establishment. Finally, by mentioning only the 'north' as the area where drunk driving occurs, he is also implying that it does not happen in the 'east' or the 'south'. This means that in order to capture the discursive properties of the interviews, we need to pay attention not only to the concepts and ideas that they employ to express themselves but, equally, to those that they consciously or unconsciously exclude from discourse.

In the case of drunk driving in the north of the capital, the question then becomes whether there are identical or similar references in other interviews indicating north and south as two opposite, spatial, sociopolitical poles. Here we see a further, somewhat different, reference to the 'north' of the city by another driver:

> I think only those roads which are used by authorities and government officials are in a good shape and regularly attended to. And the officials all live in the north of the city. Roads in the other parts of the city receive very little attention.
>
> (Interview 1:2:49)

References to the 'north' have a different connotation in this context ('the north' is used here to refer to the part of the city where politically influential people live), and the 'south' is conceptualized differently through its absence (as a neglected area of the city). None of the male taxi drivers made explicit references to the south of Tehran; however, as we shall see in Chapter Seven, wherein interviews with the female taxi drivers are presented, female cabbies refer to the south of the city as a place where 'some people throw themselves in front of cars to cause accidents and collect *diyah* [blood money]', thereby suggesting a place of socio-economic depravation. References made to the 'north' and 'south' become significant once the other aspects of the interviews reveal them as politicized entities, which uphold an ongoing tension in Iranian society. This is one of the main issues that we shall gradually develop through reference to our interviews.

Translation from Farsi

All the interviews with the female drivers were first transcribed in Farsi before being translated into English. Other interviews were directly translated and transcribed into English. Special attention was paid to capturing the meaning expressed by the interviewees. When people speak normally, they often use broken sentences or leave many of their sentences incomplete, hanging in the air, as they pick up the threads of other thoughts and move in a different direction. This happens more regularly when they are arguing or looking for solutions than when they are describing something they know well. In the case of some of our lawyers, we noted that they could at times utter several sentences without actually saying something significant, before they said something important. We therefore excluded many of these utterances from our presentation of interviews.

In order to make the quotations reader-friendly, we also removed some of the fragments of sentences where we could see that they did not play a decisive role. As a result, the parts of interviews we quote appear more coherent than they were in reality.

Cultural Limitations of the Study

The fact that all our interviews were conducted with Farsi-speaking Iranians living in Tehran and Shiraz delimits the sociocultural scope of this study. Iran is a linguistically diverse country, consisting of a number of ethnocultural groups, including Persians (who constitute the majority, about 51 per cent of the population), Azerbaijanis, Kurds, Lurs, Arabs, Baluchis, Turkmen, Turkic tribal groups such as the Qashqai, Armenians, Assyrians, Iranian Jews, Georgians and other small ethnic groups. What we conclude about Farsi-speaking Iranians living in urban areas should not be extended automatically to national groups such as Turks, Baluchis, Turkmans, Kurds, Arabs or even many Farsi-speaking nationals who continue to live in small towns and villages across Iran. Although it might be possible to identify the 'contours' of certain values, practices and historical experiences that are shared by the majority of the people living in the country, it is doubtful that we could, as an increasing number of Iranian studies do – see, for example, Manavipour (2012), Hadizadeh and Assar (2008) and Nazarian et al.

(2013) – speak of Iranian 'culture' in singular terms.[3] Iranian political life and its administration have been dominated by the Farsi-speaking majority, but this political domination has not eradicated the cultural differences between various national groups. The continued existence of Iranian ethnic groups, with their own languages and religions, is a testimony to their cultural uniqueness and the fact that their world view differs from that of the Farsi-speaking majority. I should, however, hasten to add that all these languages – including Baluchi, Kurdish, Azari, and even Pashtun – are classified as Iranian languages (see Windfuhr 2009), underlining their shared linguistic sources.

To avoid generalization about the national groups living in Iran, one could consider using 'Farsi culture'. The word 'Fars', however, is associated with one specific area of Iran, which was the centre of ancient Persia, and carving out Farsi culture as a separate, supposedly discrete, object of study is associated with a series of other problems. Not only does Farsi-speaking culture have a great deal of internal diversity itself, but historically Fars has never existed independently of other parts of Iran. Moreover, despite the existence of separatist movements among the Kurds and Baluchies, as well as Arabs, most of the people living in Iran define themselves as Iranians and, arguably, share a sense of nationhood that can be traced back to the pre-Islamic era (for a discussion, see Holliday 2011: 24).[4] We shall therefore continue to use 'Iranian culture' in the following pages, albeit in an empirically restrictive sense, to discuss the cultural aspects of our interviews with the Farsi-speaking Iranians in Tehran and Shiraz.

Finally, this study does not approach Iranian society from the standpoint of religion, although it recognizes and discusses the role of Shi'ism. Islam, and Shi'ism in particular, are socio-historical and cultural constructs of the utmost importance, which are rooted in the deep structures of Iranian society, world views, cultural practices and the Iranian mentality, and can affect individuals and group behaviour at an unconscious level (see Katouzian 2009: 12; Arasteh and Arasteh 1964: 40; Kamali 2007: 387). They also constitute an integral part of the Iranian version of modernity. The rise of Islam as an ideology, and its revival as a form of polity and governance during the 1970s, provided an opportunity for Iranians to establish their own discourse on modernity, a discourse which aimed at transcending Western-centric modern/ traditional and secular/religious dichotomies (Mirsepassi 2000; also,

Figure 2.4   Iranian Languages by Area, Wikimedia Commons.

see Jahanbegloo 2004). The relationship between Islam and Shiʿism, on the one hand, and Iranian culture, society, law and politics, on the other, constitutes a set of highly complex issues and topics of discussion in their own right, which we shall use *ad hoc* in several chapters (see Chapters Eight and Nine in particular) in order to interpret the results of our interviews.[5]

CHAPTER 3

ESTEBDĀD: PILOT STUDY IN SHIRAZ AND TEHRAN

Reza Banakar and Shahrad Nasrolahi Fard

Cambyses was enamoured of one of his sisters and presently desired to take her to wife; but this intention being contrary to usage, he summoned the royal judges and inquired whether there were any law suffering one, that so desired, to marry his sister. These royal judges were men chosen out from the Persians to be so till they die or are detected in some injustice; it is they who decide suits in Persia and interpret the laws of the land; all matters are referred to them. These then replied to Cambyses with an answer which was both just and safe, namely, that they could find no law giving a brother power to marry his sister; but that they had also found a law whereby the King of Persia might do whatsoever he wished. Thus they broke not the law for fear of Cambyses, and to save themselves from death for maintaining it, they found another law to justify one that desired wedlock with sister. So for nonce Cambyses married her of whom he was enamoured.

(Herodotus, *The Persian Wars*, Book III, Chapter 31)[1]

Reckless Driving and Legal Culture

The ancient city of Shiraz, located in the southern part of Iran and near the ruins of Persepolis and Pasargadae, is the capital of Fars Province,

Figure 3.1 One of the Main Streets in Central Shiraz © Sirus Banakar.

known throughout its history for its poetry, literature, architecture, wine and gardens.[2] Shiraz, with over 1.5 million inhabitants (in 2009), has a severe traffic problem, and the driving habits of the people there are believed to be worse than, for example, in Tehran.[3] Twenty in-depth interviews were conducted in order to explore how people living in Shiraz perceived road traffic accidents (RTAs), and how they conceptualized and expressed their experience of driving habits and the traffic situation. Although no claim is made herein that the interviewees are representative of the population of that city, attempts were made nonetheless to ensure the spread of interviews across sociological categories such as class, age and gender. The interviewees include professionals, such as doctors, teachers, lawyers and civil servants, as well as students, taxi drivers, shopkeepers and shop assistants. The interviews began by asking why Iran had a disproportionately high rate of RTAs, and what the interviewees thought of Iranians' driving habits – no question was asked regarding law or the legal system. The interviewees were encouraged to account for their personal experience of RTAs and driving, how it affected their everyday life and to explain in their own words what driving a car meant to them.

The majority of our interviewees saw and described various aspects of traffic from the point of view of the driver, while a few people who did not drive saw it instead from the standpoint of pedestrians. As we shall explain in the next chapter, there is an old distinction in Farsi between the word *piyadeh*, which means pedestrian, and *savareh*, which means the rider of a horse but in modern Farsi also refers to the occupants of a car (see Shahshahani 2006: 86). The former connotes low status, while the latter suggests high standing, power and being in control – especially when the *savareh* is the driver (for a discussion, see Chapter Four). Thus, it is hardly surprising if in the context of our interviews we find a tendency to see the world from the standpoint of the driver rather than the pedestrian. Moreover, the car itself is a powerful cultural artefact that influences attitudes to driving in favour of the driver rather than the pedestrian. In these initial interviews, some emphasized driving's social and cultural dimensions, while others focused on its technological aspects. One male taxi driver, for instance, blamed women drivers for their incompetent driving, while a female driver blamed male taxi drivers for their aggressive and reckless driving. Various interviewees also touched in passing on a large number of disparate issues which, according to them, ranked amongst the causes of RTAs. These ranged from the general stress associated with living in large cities to the refusal of many drivers to wear seat belts (driving without wearing the seat belt was more common in 2010), and to the impact of increased migration from rural to urban areas. Despite all these differences, the overwhelming majority of these interviews overlapped to varying degrees, suggesting certain commonality in attitudes towards driving and the experiences of RTAs and traffic regulation. This commonality took two forms but used exactly the same words, such as 'lawlessness' or 'individuality', or various terms such as 'lack of culture' (*bi-farhangi*) or 'lack of the culture of driving'. In this section, we shall identify and describe these common points, hereon referring to them as the *recurrent themes* of the interviews, which were raised or emphasized by at least 17 of the 20 interviewees. Three of the interviewees diverged from the mainstream by not talking about disorder, one explanation for which is that they identified themselves with the political order in Iran and speaking of disorder would have implied criticizing the law-enforcement agencies. Once they were pressed to explain the causes of the high levels of RTAs, they blamed the public's disregard for traffic rules.

Law enforcement, or the lack thereof, recurs in 17 interviews. On the one hand, the interviewees blamed the police for their ineffective enforcement of traffic rules, while, on the other, they criticized both drivers and pedestrians for not respecting or obeying the law. One other persistent point raised by most interviewees concerned the culture of driving, whereby the majority implicitly or explicitly said that Iranians did not have a 'culture of driving'. This lack of driving culture, in turn, was linked to another recurrent issue regarding the excessive individuality of Iranians, namely that they drive for themselves, oblivious to other drivers or pedestrians. Similarly, those who saw the problem from a driver's point of view pointed out that pedestrians follow no rules – they cross roads wherever they like, causing chaos and accidents in the process. When they were asked about their experience of being a pedestrian, they simply repeated that there were no rules – one of the problems was that no traffic rules applied to pedestrians or protected their rights. Finally, more than half of those interviewed made passing remarks on the role of the car as a status symbol, by referring to the 'new rich with their expensive cars', who think that they own the roads. The following excerpts from the interviews illustrate the recurrent themes and the main concerns of the interviewees.

Theme One: The unreliability of laws and the inconsistency of law enforcement:

Pilot:1: A 60-year-old (male) civil servant: 'The police often don't enforce the traffic rules, but when they do enforce them they discriminate in favour of certain groups [...]. Iranians will obey the driving regulations, but only if they know that they will be caught and penalised if they break them [...]. Police don't enforce the law, and people don't respect it. [...] But there is another "law" that people follow willingly. You know, *urf* is more powerful than laws and ordinances made by Parliament.'

P:2: A 20-year-old (female) student: 'You know, the traffic rules aren't taken seriously by most drivers [...]. Driving to Iranians means pressing the gas pedal, it isn't about knowing the traffic rules or following the traffic signs [. . .]. Anyway, the traffic rules aren't enforced effectively and we know that there is one law for ordinary people and one law for those who are connected [. . .]. To be quite honest with you, I can't imagine how anyone could enforce traffic laws in this chaos.'

P:3: A 25-year-old (male) taxi driver: 'These people need to be educated and taught how to drive. The authorities [. . .] should take away their driving licences and force them to relearn the driving rules and retake the driving tests. But then, of course, you also must make sure that the laws are obeyed. There is no point in having traffic rules if they are neither followed nor enforced [. . .]. They need to make better use of the media like the television, to teach people the proper rules of driving.'

Theme Two: The excessive individuality of Iranians:

P:4: A 51-year-old (female) nurse from Shiraz: 'The problem with us Iranians is that we all want to get ahead of each other, no matter what. That is why we don't show any consideration when driving and cannot give way or show patience. Not only do we not show consideration, you know that a lot of people think they are smart [zerang] when they manage to break the rules and get ahead of other drivers.'

P:5: A 20-year-old (male) shop assistant: 'When I'm driving, I have to get through the traffic the best as I can. I'd never get where I'm going if I started giving way to others [. . .]. You cannot follow the traffic rules when everyone else sets them aside [. . .]. Anyway, no one respects your rights.'

In the follow-up interviews that we conducted at a later stage, the notion of *zerang* was identified as one of our key concepts, which emphasizes the Iranian form of individualism. However, it also throws light on how the individual relates to society at large and formal regulation (such as laws introduced by authorities). Often, to be able to circumvent rules and regulations, in order to beat the system, is admired as *zerangi* even though the action is ethically unjustifiable.

Theme Three: Culture and Technology:

P:6: A 35-year-old (female) teacher: 'We Iranians pride ourselves on being courteous, but we turn into the most inconsiderate and selfish people as soon as we get behind the driving wheel [...]. Something happens to us which makes us blind to other people, whether drivers or pedestrians [...] we just don't see them anymore as human beings. But the truth is that it has happened that I have stopped to let people cross the street. You feel sorry for some people, like old men and women. They remind me of my parents [...]. Otherwise when I am driving I have to be very careful not to hit pedestrians. They can be so careless walking in the traffic. They can jump in front of your car at any time. Pedestrians don't respect any rules and walk where they like. [...] In a sense, you see, there is no point talking only about reckless drivers and how to fix them. We also need to teach people how to cross the road.'

P:7: A middle-aged (male) medical doctor: 'The car was imported more than a hundred years ago [...], but the culture of driving couldn't be imported with it. You might think a hundred years is long enough to develop a culture [...]. But we haven't developed a culture of driving yet. There are traffic rules but they are set aside by everyone and enforced selectively and ineffectively by police [...]. We need to teach people the culture of driving.'

Comparing these excerpts, we notice that they are not exclusive. The way these themes are expressed shows the interconnected nature of law enforcement, driving culture, individuality and technology within this context.

The first interviewee (see Pilot: 1) made a reference to *urf*, which should be highlighted here. *Urf* refers to customary practices and usages prevalent among ordinary people; these have been developed gradually by Islamic jurists as a secondary source of law – the main sources of Shari'a are the Qur'an, *sunna* (tradition), *qiyas* (analogy) and *ijma* (consensus). *Urf* has played an important role in forming certain areas of law, such as those relating to family and trade. We shall return to *urf* in Chapter Nine, where we contrast it with state law. It was later, in the context of our second set of interviews, that we noted the important role of *urf* in forming the Iranian legal culture.

Preliminary Reflections: Descriptive vs. Injunctive Norms

Driving habits are shaped by a variety of social norms and cultural values learnt in childhood, including our attitude to society at large, to rules and to other people's rights (see Durkin and Tolmie 2010), as well as by peer groups, personal experience and psychological factors such as personality and temperament (Lupton 2002). All of the interviewees regarded Iranian driving habits as a social problem, and they also discussed, directly or indirectly, the importance of a 'culture of driving'. Here are two typical examples:

> P:8: A 50-year-old (male) shopkeeper: 'The way we drive is based on bad habits we have picked up over many years. Now it is so entrenched that we can't change it. Perhaps by educating our children from an early age to respect the traffic rules, and by using the mass media to inform people about correct driving culture, we could change our ways.'

> P:9: A 35-year-old (female) teacher: 'I don't say everyone, but most people I know understand that the way they drive is not right. They know we shouldn't behave towards each other in this way, but they still do it.'

The first interviewee contrasts actual driving habits against a set of standards of driving (a culture of driving) to make a value judgement, which suggests that there are behavioural expectations (prescriptive social norms) at the level of society regarding a 'culture of driving' or orderly driving behaviour. The second interviewee suggests that there are general prescriptive norms that should ideally be applicable to driving. These norms, which belong to the category of injunctive norms, are defined by Kallgren et al. (2000) as what should be done or what is commonly approved and disapproved of, while Elek et al. (2006) describe them as people's perceptions about what ought to be done. Injunctive norms regularize and bring to bear the normative force of discrete social values existing at the level of society on social action at the level of the individual. The decision to obey or defy them involves making a conscious or unconscious value judgement in regard to social goods. These 'ought norms' concern prescribed patterns of behaviour, reciprocity (expectations), a sense of responsibility and obligations. When they operate effectively, they generate shared expectations and mutual trust among the members of a social group by indicating the desirable form of conduct, while at the same time they influence the actor's conduct accordingly and promise 'rewards or punishment externally imposed by others, such as the society at large, parents or peers' (Venkatesan 1966: 384). These injunctive or ought norms should be contrasted with 'descriptive norms', which indicate 'what is commonly done' (Kallgren et al. 2000: 2002), or standard de facto behaviour (Elek et al. 2006). Descriptive norms capture a social group's standard ways of doing things, in contrast to *what* the social group might think it *should* be doing. Furthermore, they can mediate practical knowledge, social habits, usages and experience gathered through generations on how to perform a particular task effectively or make a decision in a specific situation. Descriptive norms lay the basis for customary practices and usages in everyday, collaborative activities, such as trade and exchanges between ordinary people. These customary practices become legally significant in Islamic contexts once they are recognized as *urf*.

There is normally a gap between injunctive norms and their corresponding descriptive norms. In instances in which this gap causes social dysfunction, the legislature introduces laws, backed by sanctions, to add to the normative weight of the injunctive norms and reduce the gap between what people ought to be doing and what they actually do in reality. Laws that are introduced to bring greater conformity to injunctive norms often fail or only partially succeed (see Griffiths 2003). One reason for this partial efficacy of laws is that the law as a body of rules, decisions and principles is dependent on institutions that implement and enforce these, as well as officials who interpret and apply them to individual cases. This means that the law itself can be divided into 'ought' (prescriptive legal norms) and 'is' (what the courts and law officials actually do) – what Pound (1910) characterized as the difference between 'law in books' and 'law in action'. It also implies that law itself suffers from the gap between injunctive and descriptive norms.

When the interviewees in this study complain that Iranians do not have a 'culture of driving', they indicate that there are certain standards of driving, i.e. injunctive or ought norms, shared by the majority of Iranians, which, to judge from the way they drive, are disregarded by individual drivers. These injunctive norms are defined vaguely in terms of standards of conduct. When the interviewees were asked to elaborate on what they meant by 'a culture of driving', only a few translated it into tangible traffic rules; others instead referred to the need to show consideration for others' safety and, above all, to recognize pedestrians and drivers as individuals. We find similar discrepancies between injunctive and descriptive norms of driving in Western countries, but what distinguishes the Iranian situation is the almost total break between them, i.e. between what is prescribed at the level of society as orderly driving, and how drivers commonly drive their cars and behave in traffic.

The interviewees also suggested that the rampant individuality of Iranians interfered with and undermined the development of a 'culture of driving'. When considering the importance of the tension between individualism, collective behaviour and state regulation, we should also remember that we are dealing with a form of behaviour that is mediated through the automobile, with its own specific form of domination and discipline (Urry 2007). Various studies that have been conducted in Western countries indicate that the car brings out a sense of individualism in people, generates certain cultural values, transforms our experience of time and space and stimulates the driver's longing for freedom (Redshaw 2008). These are partly products of systematic advertising and partly because automobiles generate a sense of control over our physical environment (see Urry et al. 2005; Miller 2001; Neal 1985; Lewis 1980; Dettelbach 1976). Moreover, driving is experienced as an inalienable right even though it is, arguably, a privilege granted by the State through its issuance of driving licences. The important point is that the car is much more than a means of travel or transportation, and driving is much more than a set of skills or driver performance (Evans 1991). The car is also a powerful cultural artefact, representing modern men's and women's desire for autonomy, freedom, power, control, status and identity. This sense of freedom and power, admittedly, is largely superficial and, at least in Western countries, constrained by injunctive norms that are upheld with the help of formal rules of driving and legal rules of traffic.

The rising levels of RTAs in Iran, and concerns about Iranians' sense of individualism and (lack of) driving culture, as voiced by the interviewees, suggest that driving clearly fuels the individualistic side of the Iranian identity. This, however, is not a problem unique to Iranians, but what is unique to the Iranian situation is the inefficacy of the injunctive norms of driving, which in most other countries exert the minimum degree of constraint on driving habits, thus maintaining a relatively orderly and safe driving environment. One question begs to be asked: why do injunctive norms, which ultimately concern social goods that benefit everyone, fail to exert any perceptible regulatory impact on the rampant sense of individualism of Iranian drivers?

Interviews in Tehran

Partly to explore this question, and partly to broaden the empirical scope of this study, 15 further in-depth interviews were carried out in Tehran between December 2010 and January 2011. These interviews had more of a structure, in the sense that they involved a number of themes related to law. Each interview consisted of two main parts, the first of which aligned with the interviews previously conducted in Shiraz and explored: (1) how the interviewees experience the traffic situation, (2) in what terms they conceptualize it, (3) their perception of the causes of the collective disregard for traffic laws, for human life and for the rights of other people, such as the collective disregard by drivers of the rights of pedestrians, (4) attitudes to traffic rules and conventions, (5) if and how they thought driving was related to law and social order, and (6) what they thought of the enforcement of traffic regulations. The second part examined the interviewees' perceptions, attitudes and conceptions of law and social order. A number of broadly formulated questions were raised in order to allow for probing into legal issues voiced during the interviews in Shiraz.[4] The interviewees were asked to explain: (1) what images the word 'law' conjured up in their mind, (2) who they regarded as the primary source of legal authority, (3) to whom they would turn if they needed legal advice and protection or sought to resolve disputes, (4) whether they felt that laws made by the government and parliament addressed their needs, (5) how these laws were enforced, (6) whether they trusted the courts and other legal authorities, and (7) their conception of justice.

The first part of the interviews, which focused on driving habits, matched those conducted in Shiraz. Besides finding identical keywords,

such as 'arbitrary enforcement', we also found broadly identical forms of
expression by both cohorts in Tehran and Shiraz. For example, a 30-year-
old (male) taxi driver from Tehran complained about those who used
their car as a symbol of status ('just because they are driving an expensive
car, they think they own the road and everyone should give way') and
went on to cover almost all the main issues raised by the interviewees in
Shiraz. He touched on the issue of individuality, saying that:

> P:10: 'All they [the drivers] care about is driving their cars. They
> pay no attention to traffic signs. We should not need the police to
> watch over us all the time to obey the rules [. . .]. You cannot
> respect the traffic rules when nobody else does.'

He saw 'the absence of law and legal regulation' as the main cause of the
traffic problem, and he distinguished between the law and its
enforcement, arguing that not only was it lacking in strength (saying
several times, 'our law is weak'), but also that its enforcement was
inadequate and arbitrary. Effective enforcement of the law was crucial,
because, as he put it:

> P:11: 'We will not follow the law if there is no force and threat
> behind it [. . .]. Everyone has his/her own set of rules [. . .].
> Authorities plan a lot of improvements but don't carry them
> through – like the rule to wear a seatbelt, which isn't enforced
> [. . .]. Laws are enforced, but they are not the same for everyone.
> The law doesn't see or treat everyone in the same way.'

For him, 'law' conjured up the image of courts and police, and he
regarded parliament as the primary source thereof. However, when he
was asked about his attitude to the law he said, 'law means trouble'.
He explained that he had had firsthand experience of legal processes and
would 'avoid the law and the courts' as far as he possibly could do so.
If he had a legal problem, he would instead turn first to the community
elders to resolve it, for 'law and courts have no effect'.

Another interviewee (a 35-year-old male interpreter) also expressed
misgivings regarding the law and the courts. He stressed that 'people are
not equal before the law', and 'when ordinary people are brought before
the court, they are treated as guilty till proven innocent' (a similar point

was also made by most interviewees, including a female defence lawyer). Thus, in so far as people were able, they would avoid the courts and resolve their disputes either by negotiating themselves or with the help of elders. However, when there were issues which could not be settled in this way, they had no alternative but to turn to the courts.

A (second) female lawyer, on the other hand, indicated that the law itself was up to scratch and satisfied all international standards of draftsmanship. However, referring to how her own car was once towed away, despite the fact that she had parked it legally in a permitted zone, she admitted that the law was not enforced correctly, uniformly or effectively by the police. Moreover, it was not obeyed by the people. She was one of the few interviewees to link the way the law was enforced with the way it was obeyed: 'The arbitrariness of the law turns ordinary people away from the law'. She also drew attention to inconsistencies in the implementation and enforcement of legal rules and principles, which, according to her, undermined ordinary people's belief and trust in the legal system:

> P:12: 'They [the legislature] tell us that we must obey the law because it is based on principles enshrined in Islam. But they are inconsistent in implementing the rules of Islam. Where the rules of Islam do not serve their ends [...], they circumvent them by arguing that they don't fit today's society. But when it suits them, for example, when they want to dismiss the rights of women, then they insist that certain rules must gain the force of law because they are part of the principles of Islam.'

She also stated that Iranians did not have a culture of driving and added that 'we are individualists, and as long as we get our way we don't care about other people's rights'.

It is of interest that all the interviewees saw law in terms of 'positive law', i.e. legislation made by parliament rather than laws emanating from divine sources,[5] and regarded parliament as the primary source thereof. The lawyer quoted above referred to Islamic law but regarded law and its sources in terms of parliament, legislative organs and the executive. As the quote suggests, she is sceptical of the way in which Islam is used to justify (man-made) laws. It is worth noting that the point made by this lawyer regarding Iranian authorities' inconsistent implementation of the rules of

Shari'a can be observed particularly in respect to their often draconian sexual policies. In connection with Iran's birth-control campaign between 1986 and 1996, when reducing the birth rate was deemed necessary for improving the country's economy, the government adopted an uncharacteristically liberal view on sexuality, because, as Afary (2009: 15) explains, 'it suited its purpose'.[6]

Three other interviewees connected the sources of law to Shari'a and Islam. A female medical doctor mentioned in passing that the source of law was partly religious and partly parliamentary (she did not, however, refer to the Qur'an or Shari'a as a source, and she used the word 'religious'). An advertising agent also recognized the religious aspect of Iranian law, but he referred to 'customs and traditions' as equally important legal sources (for a discussion on *urf*, or customary law, see Chapter Nine). Finally, a 50-year-old shopkeeper, whose answers deviated on many points from the other interviewees, said that the law of the land was rooted in Shi'i Islam. When asked what constituted justice, all the interviewees defined it in terms of equal treatment before the law. None described justice in religious terms or defined it in phrases that implied any awareness of what justice means in Shari'a. This could, arguably, suggest a deep-rooted secular understanding of law, or equally it could imply that Iranians regard Shari'a as being embedded in their legal order (see Arjomand 2008: 37).[7]

To sum up, although some of the interviewees suggested that driving habits had deteriorated over the last few decades, none of them stated or suggested that RTAs constituted a recent problem. The interviewees in Tehran, who were asked directly about the increase in the number of vehicles over the last few years, did not regard it as the main cause of the problem. However, although some suggested that many people used their cars excessively, consequently causing unnecessary congestion, they were concerned primarily with the poor and arbitrary enforcement of traffic rules, the public's disregard for these rules and the lack of what they called a 'culture of driving'. All of the interviewees either touched on or discussed at some length what we could broadly term 'excessive individualism' as a problem, hence suggesting Iranians' inability to follow rules and respect other people's rights. Finally, most of the interviewees expressed misgivings about the legal system and courts of law. Some felt that the laws were fine, whereas a 35-year-old shopkeeper wondered, 'what is the point of having good laws when the lawmakers don't follow the laws they have made?' The main point emerging out of the second set of interviews is that injunctive norms fail to curtail the rampant sense of individualism of Iranian drivers for two reasons: first, the enforcement of traffic rules is experienced as arbitrary and the legal system as hostile, and, second, because the disregard for norms and the rules of traffic is widespread.

Driving Habits and Legal Culture

Differences between road traffic safety in different countries are often analysed using a combination of factors such as the quality of infrastructure, driving conditions, the culture of driving or the efficacy of how traffic rules are enforced (McAndrews 2010). Only a handful of the interviewees mentioned the poor quality of roads and the conditions of cars as one of the causes of RTAs. Most of those questioned, including one interviewee who mentioned 'dilapidated vehicles', instead emphasized the role of the culture of driving and (the lack of) enforcement of traffic rules in this respect. The remaining part of this chapter will therefore concentrate on the cultural and legal dimensions of driving that are reflective of how people interact with each other at the micro level and with society at large, in order to create a form of social order. As mentioned above, this interaction is mediated through mobility technology, which in some respects constrains and forms behaviour – one important aspect discussed above regarding cars is that they stimulate the sense of individuality of drivers and their yearning for freedom and control. In the case of Iranian drivers, these effects on behaviour take on disproportionate dimensions because injunctive norms fail to exert the minimum degree of constraint on their behaviour. This point is linked intricately with the external legal culture of Iranians, who, as the interviews suggest, perceive the law and the legal system in a negative light, and with the internal culture of the police force, which (again, according to many of those that we interviewed) does not enforce traffic laws uniformly or effectively.[8] To understand Iranian legal culture, we must analyse the views and sentiments expressed by the interviewees in the historical context of Iranian society. We shall therefore draw on the historical thesis elaborated by Katouzian (1997, 2009) regarding the relationship between the Iranian state and society.

Iranian State, Law and Society from a Historical Perspective

A Qajar king, Fath Ali Shah, told a British diplomat, John Malcom, in 1800 what it was like to be a Persian king. Unlike the British king, who had to rule by law, he enjoyed unrestricted power and on the slightest whim could have his most important ministers executed. Yet he admitted that his power had no permanency and realized that when he died his sons would fight over the throne. Fath Ali Shah's remarks aptly described his own and the proceeding dynasty. Trustworthy court officials lost their lives for momentarily displeasing the king. Court intrigues and rivalries led the king to distrust everyone, even the members of his own family. [...] The honorary titles given to the king and the nobility reflected their unlimited power. The king, from earliest times, has always been known as Shah-in-shah, the King of Kings.

(Arasteh and Arasteh 1964: 36)

State and Society in Iran

Iranian states (or, to be more accurate, Iranian rulers)[9] and dynasties have existed without popular legitimacy, and their forms of governments and laws have never lasted more than a few hundred years at a time. A rule of law similar to that which developed in ancient Greece (see Salehi-Esfahani 2008), or one resembling Roman law, which has prevailed throughout the history of Europe, has never existed in Iran, where systems of laws devised during various periods have proved as ephemeral as the states that introduced them. In the Islamic era, Shari'a came close to providing a more permanent legal basis; however, even the enforcement of these rules was restricted in that they 'could be applied only in so far as they did not conflict with the wishes of the state' (Katouzian 2009: 6). The State would find ways of legitimatizing its rule in the short term, but the long-term rejection of state rule by the people left a mark on the formation of Iranian society and affected, for example, how rights and responsibilities were developed and employed: *'Since the people had no independent or intrinsic rights, they did not accept any independent and intrinsic responsibility'* (Katouzian 2009: 7 [my emphasis]). This could potentially explain Iranian drivers' disregard for the rights of pedestrians and other drivers, and throw light on the disjuncture between the injunctive and descriptive norms of driving.

Katouzian (2009) stresses the point that *estebdād* should not be confused with absolutism or totalitarianism in the European sense. He writes (2009: 208), for example, that it would be misleading to compare Reza Shah (who ruled Iran from 1925 to 1941) with Atatürk or Mussolini, for he wielded arbitrary (personal) power over his subjects' lives and property, while the above-named rulers were dictators who worked within certain impersonal political/ideological and even legal frameworks.[10] One way to distinguish Iranian arbitrary state rule from other types of dictatorship is by defining it in terms of short-term states and societies that do not allow for the development of social, political and legal structures into long-term institutionalized practices. Arbitrary rule creates an arbitrary state and a form of government not constrained by legal frameworks, existing independently of the State or outside its sphere of power. This, in turn, creates an arbitrary society, which tends towards social disorder and political chaos whenever the State loses its control. Lastly, an arbitrary state and a short-term society give rise to a particular form of individualism that privileges the core and the extended family. Daniel and Mahdi (2006: 157) stress the centrality of the institution of family in Iranian society:

Family gives individuals social status, determines their life chances, protects them against all threats, and ensures their emotional health. Social life also revolves around the family and its kinship. Elders are the backbone of the family and garner the most authority and respect [...]. Family gatherings are the most important aspects of social life.

We shall argue (see Chapter Nine) that Iranian society is in transition and that, as a result thereof, the family is changing character in large cities such as Tehran, where divorce rates soar. Nevertheless, family remains the cornerstone of Iranian society and one of the primary sources of normativity and religiosity, but also of patriarchy. In a society in which the individual's moral conduct and identity are defined by reference to family and kinship, being concerned with the good of society – a society which is incidentally short-term, unstable and unreliable – becomes a nonsensical behaviour.

Iranian Individualism

Iranians pride themselves on being cordial, courteous and hospitable. Some of these cultural traits – like *taarof* (*tæ'arof*), which we shall discuss at some length in connection with our interviews in the coming chapters – have roots in the nation's long history and are probably thousands of years old. These ancient customs are also ill at ease with modernity, and they show the bewildering complexity of contemporary Iranian culture. As one of the interviewees explained:

P: 13: 'Three Iranians can spend several minutes standing at a door imploring each other to be the first to step out [. . .]. But as soon as the same three people step out of the door and into the driving seats of their cars, they change. Once behind the wheel of their cars, the last thing crossing their mind would be to give way to other cars or, God forbid, brake at a zebra crossing to allow a pedestrian to cross the road.'

One explanation is that when these three Iranians are 'imploring each other to be the first to step out of the door', they meet and perceive each other as individuals. Later, when they are driving, they perceive each other as strangers – as abstract entities towards whom they have no responsibility. The first situation involves concrete face-to-face interaction, while the second is mediated through the use of the automobile. The car as a modern technological innovation has what appears to be an alienating effect on drivers, which applies as much to Iranians as to North Americans, Africans or western Europeans. The major difference is that neither the injunctive norms of driving nor the traffic rules introduced to close the gap between injunctive and descriptive norms have any perceptible effect on Iranians' driving behaviour. That is also why they do not recognize the strangers driving the other cars, walking on the pavements or trying to cross the roads as rights holders. The question that has to be asked is thus: why do Iranians feel no sense of responsibility towards these strangers, while drivers in other countries do?

Political and legal short-termism combined with *estebdād*, which have characterized Iran's history and its legal culture from antiquity to modern times, have produced a particular form of individualism. Katouzian calls it 'personalism', arguing that it is an old historical phenomenon that 'has been part of Iranian social psychology and attitudes for centuries and affects modern and traditional Iranians alike' (Katouzian 2009: 16). Personalism lays the basis for a particular form of community and legal culture, the significance of which becomes apparent once it is explored in the context of Iran's political history. Katouzian (2009: 16–17) explains that personalism manifests itself in two ways:

> First, Iranians who are not related by family bond or friendship are unusually detached from one another: the sense of social cohesion and regard for *unknown individuals* among Iranians at large is not very strong. That is why collective activity, such as party politics, voluntary social institutions and so forth, does not have strong roots in the country [...]. This side of Iranian personalism is most readily and clearly observed in Iranians' driving habits, where everyone behind the wheel is anonymous and virtually every driver cares little about traffic regulations and the rights of other drivers. Nor does any driver apparently care about the rights of pedestrians, even at designated pedestrian crossings [...]. The second characteristic of personalism runs in the opposite direction and results in an unusual care for and attachment to others. Iranians are unusually attached to members of their own family, extended family, clan and close friends, and will help, defend and even make sacrifices for them when they are in need.

Katouzian's thesis can be challenged in many ways. For example, Iranians, as he readily admits, do act collectively and with regard for 'unknown others' under certain conditions. The Islamic Revolution in 1979 was an example of such collective action, as were the demonstrations in June 2009, when mainly middle-class urban Iranians took to the streets collectively to challenge the outcome of the presidential election (see Dabashi 2010). Moreover, traits similar to personalism occur in other societies, including Western ones, and Iranians are hardly the only people with reckless driving habits or a lack of consideration for people outside their immediate 'peer group' – i.e. core family, extended family and networks of friends. The sociocultural specificity of Iranian personalism therefore appears too thin, too subtle and too tenuous to be taken seriously as a keystone of Iranian identity. Yet, returning to the interviews, we see that every interviewee raised the issue of Iranian individualism as one of the main causes of RTAs. The same individualists do not turn to the courts when they have a legal problem but to community elders. They do not identify themselves with the courts and state law – as one interviewee quoted above put it, 'law means trouble', and as a female defence lawyer said, 'the court officials humiliate you' – while they regard their community as a source of dignity, security and support. Analysing the data collected through the interviews in the context of the political history of Iran, we can find support for the hypothesis that the failure of injunctive norms to regulate the driving behaviour of Iranians is largely the outcome of a form of individualism that is disconnected from society at large. The excessive individualism of Iranians, which is enhanced through the technology of the automobile, is part and parcel of the arbitrary state and legal culture of *estebdād*.

Some General Observations on the Pilot Study

The results of the pilot study were used to construct a more detailed list of semi-structured interviews, which we then employed to conduct a larger study in Tehran in 2012. The results of this second study will be presented in the following chapters, but it might be useful to mention very briefly and to relate the results of the pilot study to the later interviews. The notion of culture, generally, and the idea that Iranians have not developed 'a culture of driving', in particular, as well as an emphasis on Iranian personalism, came to the fore in all the subsequent interviews. As we conducted more interviews, we discovered education (*amoozesh*) and the related post-revolutionary notion of *farhang-sazi* as two key concepts in our study, and although references were made to education in the pilot interviews, we overlooked their centrality as cultural concepts. Moreover, direct references to 'lawlessness', or statements amounting to Iran being 'a lawless country', which were made in our pilot in Shiraz, took a more subtle form in the later interviews. Only two of our interviewees in Tehran referred directly to *estebdād*, while others talked about the arbitrariness of law enforcement. This may be explained by the fact that the initial open interviews in Shiraz were conducted in a less formal fashion.

In the remaining chapters of this book, where we present our second set of interviews from Tehran we find an emphasis on the role of social class, gender and religiosity – or the tension between 'tradition' and 'modernity' – that was not articulated clearly in the pilot. These interviews also provide a basis for developing a sociologically more complex picture of Iranians' personalism, i.e. by explaining how their sense of individualism is linked to their 'peer group'. This allows us to explore their relationship to society at large, on the one hand, and to the State and authorities, on the other. As we form a more complex understanding of the way Iranian individualism is related to its peer group, society and the State, a more multifaceted picture of Iranians' attitudes to law and legality takes shape. Although most of the Iranians we interviewed later also described the law and its sources in a secular fashion, some of their discussions related law, through culture and custom (*urf*), to religion. However, we shall also argue that this form of religiosity is not ideologically forged, and is a product of the lifeworld rather than the administrative apparatus of the ruling Islamic Republic.

CHAPTER 4

FARHANG-SAZI: INTERVIEWS WITH MALE TAXI DRIVERS

Reza Banakar and Shahrad Nasrolahi Fard

Tehran is not an 'interesting' city. It is not like its regional counterparts Istanbul or Cairo, with their long imperial or colonial histories, pivotal geo-political locations, memorable architecture and natural charm. Tehran remains a provincial metropolis of some 12 million people, with streets chocked by 4 million vehicles and air pollution that kills 3,600 inhabitants per month; factors contributing to a 'liveability' ranking that places it among the ten worst cities in the world, between Dakar and Karachi. But it is a city with extraordinary politics, rooted in a distinctive tension between what looks like a deep-seated 'tradition' and a wild modernity. [...] Tehran has resisted being 'Islamized.' Secular resilience, ongoing socio-economic inequalities and political exclusion have turned the city's main squares and backstreets into political battlefields. Three decades on from the Islamic revolution, Tehran remains a dramatic space of contention over the legacy of 1979 and the claims of citizenship.

(Bayat 2010: 99)

Bamdad Taxi Agency is one of the hundreds of private taxi companies that operate in Tehran, providing a vital service for the inhabitants of Iran's overcrowded capital city. It has some 40 drivers, who are available on call from the early hours of the morning to the late hours of the evening. These drivers have diverse backgrounds, but they are often drawn to taxi driving not because it is their ideal occupation but because they have to make a living. Working as a taxi driver in the busy streets of Tehran, they will tell you, is very hard work – both physically and mentally. It does not bring them social status, but it does allow them to make a living in a city with a soaring unemployment rate estimated to be above 24 per cent (i.e. twice the official rate of 12 per cent).[1] Their ages also vary from early 20s to late 60s. Bamdad's offices are located in west Tehran, in a relatively quiet street, tucked away amongst a row of local shops selling food and household items in an unpretentious middle-class neighbourhood. Its manager is a friendly and accommodating man in his early 40s, who became our first interviewee.

This chapter presents 11 semi-structured interviews with male taxi drivers, which we conducted at the premises of Bamdad Taxi Agency in September 2012.[2] We can reiterate that the interviews were carried out to explore how Iranians view and experience traffic, and how they describe their own experiences and other people's conduct. Thus, our study's main focus was on how they constructed socioculturally meaningful ideas about traffic-related problems, rather than the factual accuracy of their statements. In the following pages, we start by discussing how the causes of road traffic accidents (RTAs) were described and discussed by male taxi drivers, before we move on to other topics such as culture, education, law and family, which were identified as key concepts.

In the following pages, we shall mark each quotation with a specific number, which will indicate: the set of interviews (if it is, for example, from interviews with male taxi drivers, lawyers, other professionals or female taxi drivers), the number of the interviewee in that set, and the number of the quotation in the chapter. For example, 1:4:1 indicates: 1st set of interviews (with male taxi drivers), interviewee 4, quotation 1 in this chapter.

The Causes of RTAs

Our interviewees generally agreed about the state of traffic in Tehran, describing it as 'scandalous', 'chaotic' and 'unbearable'. One of the drivers explained that 'there are traffic jams from six in the morning until late at night' (1:4:1); another told us that traffic was very heavy, particularly in the afternoons when a 'journey which normally takes 45 minutes in the morning, could then take three hours' (1:8:2). As interviews progressed, the drivers linked the idea of chaotic and stressful traffic to other issues such as the selfish behaviour of drivers, their skills, experience and reckless driving. Recklessness and disregard for traffic rules were then connected to other factors, ranging from attitudes to the law, law enforcement and safety, to culture, how the city is divided up into various spaces, class divisions and the rural/urban divide. The quotes below show how discussing traffic unfolded a number of wider social problems:

1:10:3: 'Tehran's traffic is appalling [...]. It affects my work a lot. When I am driving, I must concentrate hard all the time to avoid accidents with cars and motorcycles. So I am constantly stressed when driving my taxi. [...] Reckless driving and ineffective traffic laws are the main causes of many accidents. Over the last 37 years I have been driving, I have learnt that we don't have proper rules for driving, like the ones you find in Western countries. In countries like England and Sweden, for example, it is much harder to get a driving licence.'

1:11:4: 'Some people don't have a culture of driving and think that driving is all about speeding and following their own rules. They are selfish and reckless. Speeding is another cause of accidents: some drivers are absent-minded and they also use drugs.'

Our interviewees agreed that most accidents were caused by reckless driving, which was in turn related to drivers' disregard for traffic rules and other factors such as Iranians' individualism. However, various drivers mentioned other causes, ranging from the poor construction of roads, potholes and inadequate signposting, to the poor standard of cars manufactured in Iran and drunken driving, which also generate accidents.

1:2:5: 'Accidents happen because people ignore the traffic rules, or because of poorly constructed roads, or busy traffic. [...] Certain places, such as junctions in town, create a lot of accidents [...]. In some places the roads are badly signposted [...]. Eighty per cent of accidents on the motorways outside the cities are caused by carelessness [...] because drivers are in a hurry, they are tired or stressed. A lot of people are stressed for personal reasons. People who are stressed drive badly.'

1:5:6: 'One of the main causes is the lack of standards; you know that our cars don't have any standards. The other problem is speeding. A lot of younger people have accidents because of that, or because they don't have good driving skills or enough driving experience. [...] Besides speeding, some people have accidents because they drive under the influence of drugs. Some have accidents because they are stressed or are tired. Some cars cause accidents for mechanical reasons. [...] In my opinion about fifty per cent of accidents are caused by carelessness.'

1:3:7: 'Seventy or eighty per cent of the accidents are caused by the drivers who don't pay enough attention to traffic rules, or because they are bad drivers [...]. Some people just enjoy speeding [...]. Some people drive under the influence of drugs [...]. Especially in the north of Tehran drunken driving causes many accidents [...]. They drive while intoxicated, because they know no one is going to stop them.'

The above reference to drink driving in north Tehran should be placed in the context of how the city is divided into four sections (or spaces) of north, south, west and east, each with its own socio-economic characteristics. As Khosravi (2008) has shown, spaces in Tehran are classified in terms of the dichotomy of modern and traditional; for example, Shahrak-e Gharb and the Golestan Shopping Centre in the north of the city epitomize modern Tehran, while Javadieh or the Bazaar in the south represent the traditional part of the city. At the risk of making a sweeping generalization, the more affluent and secular part of the middle classes have usually lived in northern and western Tehran (*balaieh shahr* – the upper part of the city), whereas the poor, the more traditionalist groups, the working classes and migrants have lived in the south (*payineh shahr* – the lower part of the city) or the east.[3] The spatial division of Tehran is not new and may be traced back to the 1930s when, according to Asef Bayat, the city was redesigned to reflect the desired image of the new Persia as 'a modern, unified, secular nation state':

The city walls were demolished once and for all [. . .] and attempts were made in the following decade to end the *mahalleh* [local neighbourhood, or community] system through the adoption of a zoning pattern based largely on class segregation. A new urban model took shape with modern buildings and boulevards designed by Europeans and European trained architects. Nevertheless, many aspects of the older urban structure and social organisation persisted, now juxtaposing with the emerging realities of the city of petro-dollars.

(Bayat 2010: 102)

In contemporary Iranian cities, *mahalleh* has lost much of its socially unifying force, although neighbourhoods continue to play an important role in how the life of the city is organized, and group-based identities and forms of social order are developed locally. However, the normative force exerted by these neighbourhoods varies considerably depending on whether we are in south Tehran, where the poor, more traditionalist and working classes are, or in north Tehran, where the more affluent and secular sections of society live. We shall discuss the sociopolitical significance of this spatial/class division, in the coming chapters, but it

Figure 4.1 North of Tehran, Wikipedia, Public Domain.

suffices here to point out that the above interviewee (1:3:7, page 63) was making an implicit reference to different classes, lifestyles and behaviours associated with the social division of the city space, when he made the point that the people in north Tehran are prone to drink driving.[4]

Another historically related issue, which reappeared in the interviews (and was emphasized in the pilot study), concerned the urban/rural divide. The overwhelming majority of those living in Tehran have either moved to the capital from the provinces and other large cities or are second- or third-generation migrants. The 'mass rural-urban migration', which began in the 1960s and 1970s, swelled the population of the city significantly within just a few years (Bayat, 2010: 103), and the majority of migrants, who often had little resources, came to live among the underprivileged in the suburbs of southern Tehran. Our interviews reflected a dividing line between those who have always lived in large cities and those who have migrated there from the provinces.

1:7:8: 'Some of the accidents are caused by people from the provinces, who are not used to driving in large cities or driving on highways.'

The rural—urban divide is one of the themes we confronted in many of our interviews, and we shall discuss it further in the coming chapters.

Let us return for the time being to the causes of RTAs in Tehran. The manager of the taxi agency, at different stages of the interview, mentioned assorted factors as the primary causes of RTAs in Tehran. Although at first sight he might appear to be contradicting himself (in different parts of the interview, he states different causes for traffic accidents), he gradually provided a comprehensive list of factors, to which other drivers only partially referred. The manager started by arguing that most of the accidents were caused by drivers who were under the age of 30, suggesting that youth *per se* was a factor. This is, of course, a valid argument because Iran has a young population structure, and a large part of the drivers in Tehran are also under the age of 30. International studies have also demonstrated that age correlates with the propensity to high-speed and careless driving, both of which can result in serious accidents — in short, younger people are accident-prone. He also referred to those who drive under the influence of drugs and alcohol or those who are stressed (because life in the city is stressful), and then he went on to say that there were also drivers who are simply reckless. Later in the course of the interview, in a different context, he added that dilapidated vehicles and new cars (which are manufactured in Iran) with faulty brakes were a source of accidents inside and outside the cities. Moreover, some roads were also badly planned, and certain places in town, where heavy traffic met from various directions, generated accidents.

> 1:1:9: 'Many accidents are caused by the poor conditions of our vehicles [...], which are made in Iran and are often faulty. There are also many dilapidated cars which cause accidents [...] on the motorways, and many of the accidents are caused by speeding and because people are reckless or tired [...]. People disregard traffic rules for many reasons, for example because they are in a hurry or stressed [...]. I have seen several serious accidents which have been caused by people who have been driving under the influence of drugs.'

In addition, he stated that as many as 60 per cent of accidents were caused by drivers' recklessness and their disregard for traffic rules and regulations. Finally, he mentioned that many drivers were stressed, either by the traffic itself or generally by life in the capital city.

Farhang-sazi

Taxi drivers frequently referred to *farhang* (culture) in their interviews in order to describe the traffic behaviour of other drivers or the causes of traffic accidents. Once they started considering how to deal with the traffic problem, they referred to *farhang-sazi*. As we shall see in the following chapters, this idea is also used repeatedly by other groups of interviewees such as lawyers and doctors. As a concept, it consists of two parts: *farhang*, which means culture, and *sazi*, which means making, constructing or building. It may therefore be translated literally as 'culture building', or, depending on the context it may be also interpreted as attempts to use public policies to re-socialize people, in order to 'reform' their social behaviour. Some of the taxi drivers mentioned it several times in the course of their interview, especially when they were searching for explanations for, or solutions to, reckless driving. Here are two examples:

> 1:1:10: 'The most pressing problem in our society today is, unfortunately, related to traffic. A large part of our time is spent every day coping with the city traffic. This problem also goes back to the inability of policymakers to do *farhang-sazi* in respect to driving.'

> 1:9:11: 'The traffic situation in Tehran is very chaotic [...] because we have failed in our *farhang-sazi*; a culture of driving has not been implanted in the minds of people and the current behaviour is based on poor driving habits.'

In taxi drivers' discussions, *farhang-sazi* has positive and constructive connotations, in that it refers to a cultural process that may be adopted and developed to reform social behaviour and thus improve social conditions. Their argument is that through education, or by teaching people to respect the law and by informing them of, or enlightening them about (i.e. providing them with *agahi*), the consequences of disregarding the rules of traffic, one can bring about *farhang-sazi*. Put differently, *farhang-sazi* is a cultural process through which the authorities can reshape and mould values, norms, perceptions, attitudes and, ultimately, people's behaviour with respect to traffic. This concept suggests a shared belief in some form of social engineering, a top-down intervention by policy makers, but as we shall see it is also linked to Iranians' attitude to education.

The Power of Education

Closely linked to the idea of *farhang-sazi*, we find a widespread belief in the role of education (*amoozesh*) and the importance of informing people (*agahi*) about laws and rules of driving – and the dangers of disregarding these. In fact, *farhang-sazi* can only be realized through education and by providing *agahi*. Most of those we interviewed argued that by educating Iranians from an early age one could change their attitude towards driving and traffic rules. This point is expressed in the following three quotations:

1:1:12: 'This [the traffic problem] has to do with insufficient training and education, which isn't provided in a systematic way. Admittedly, the authorities have been paying more attention to traffic [...] over the last two years. It has had some impact, but it hasn't improved the traffic, because to make a difference we need *farhang-sazi*. We have to start with children's education [...] at the primary and secondary school. This will take a long time.'

1:10:13: 'Laws are not enforced properly. However, I think one should not start with the law but instead try to educate the people, because they don't know about the rules. [...] Not only do we need good laws, but we need to train and educate our drivers from day one.'

1:3:14: 'Mass media, such as the radio and television, can play a very important role in improving traffic conduct. Moreover we need to ensure *farhang-sazi* from an early age. Children should become familiar with the law and learn to respect it from an early age at school, so that following traffic rules becomes second nature to them when they grow up.'

It is likely that *farhang-sazi* emerged as a discrete idea during the Cultural Revolution of the 1980s, when attempts were made to Islamise Iranian society partly by remaking the system of education (see Hunter 2014: 128–9), which is perhaps why our interviewees also linked it to learning and education. As we shall argue, the Islamic regime has also made an almost unconditional commitment to education as a good in itself, and although Iranians do not trust their officials generally they nevertheless appear to be prepared to trust *farhang-sazi* through education. Another related idea is the lack of a 'culture of driving', which was also mentioned by many of the interviewees in the pilot studies conducted in Shiraz and Tehran.

1:3:15: 'It is because of our culture. I mean, in a way we don't have a driving culture [...]. Many tools and technologies have been introduced into Iran gradually [...] like first we had television, then DVDs [...] and people have learnt to use them; people's culture has developed in line with the development of technology. But it has not worked with driving. It is as if they have woken up one morning and found themselves behind the wheel of a car, without having the slightest idea of what the car is for. The only thing they know is how to press the gas to drive it'.

1:4:16: 'Traffic hasn't improved, because of people's culture. They don't have a culture of driving. They don't show consideration for each other. [...] You have to coerce Iranians and threaten them before they change their ways. Since they have increased the penalties, they respect traffic rules a bit better. But the traffic situation has not really improved, because their culture has not improved.'

The notion of culture lies at the heart of our interviewees' understanding of driving behaviour, although it is unclear what this culture consists of. The remaining part of this chapter, together with the next three chapters, will partly aim at unfolding the concept of culture by placing it in relation to a range of other ideas that were expressed during the course of the interviews, but also by considering how the Iranian identity and sense of individualism have developed historically and in relation to the State and society.

Attitude to Penalties

With a few exceptions, the male taxi drivers expressed positive views on the increased traffic penalties and fines, while at the same time many of them also stated that in their opinion the new traffic fines had not made a significant difference in the way people drove their cars. This belief in using penalties as a deterrent was also prevalent among female taxi drivers, which may suggest a cultural property in Iranian society that approves of taking harsh measures in order to ensure social control. However, it is also important to point out that a few of our male taxi drivers clearly stated their disapproval of penalties:

1:5:17: 'The new laws are forced on people, without trying to improve public services [...] or to improve the quality and safety of the roads [...]. On the whole I am against attempts to force people through the threat of penalties.'

1:11:18: 'The new increased fines have perhaps had an impact on thirty per cent of drivers, amongst those who have received their driving licence more recently. But the drivers haven't changed their ways. The penalties have not had any impact on wealthy people, because they can afford to pay it, while they do affect people like us.'

Others underlined the importance of education and the limits of penalties (see quotation 1:10:13 above). It should also be noted that more severe penalties did not have any support among the lawyers, who almost unanimously argued against punishment and the threat of sanctions as primary methods of regulating and reforming behaviour.

Although Iran has been moulded socially, culturally and economically by the revolutionary ethos of the Islamic Republic for 35 years, it nevertheless remains a divided country with huge social and economic disparities between various groups. An awareness of the socio-economic disparities in Iranian society was clearly expressed by many interviewees, especially in connection with the introduction of the new penalties. As mentioned above, many of those taxi drivers we interviewed were positive towards increased traffic fines, but they were critical of the fact that the policy did not make any difference to wealthy drivers who could afford to pay them.

1:1:19: 'In my opinion the introduction of more strict fines for driving offences affects the behaviour of about thirty per cent of drivers. In our capital city, there are many people who are very wealthy, and to them increased penalties make no difference [. . .]. It makes no difference to them if they pay 10,000 or 100,000 Tomans [100,000 or 1 million Iranian Rials] in penalties. But it makes a difference to economically weak classes, to those who cannot afford to pay heavy penalties.'

1:7:20: 'The increased penalties affect only poor and economically vulnerable people. It has no effect on the wealthy and well-to-do sections of society who can pay the penalties. I don't think that the increase in traffic fines will improve the situation. The solution is not in penalising people. They have to find another solution.'

As we explained, Tehran was redesigned in the 1930s, from a traditional city that was divided into religious and ethnic quarters into one where the inhabitants were segregated according to their socio-economic class (see Bayat 2010). The idea of 'class' is used often in the interviews to refer to economic disparity, but also to different lifestyles, cultural attitudes and religious values. This classic division, which was initially used to redesign Tehran about 80 years ago, appears to be in force in Iran even today.

Iranians' Sense of Individualism, or 'Personalism'

Most interviewees referred to Iranians' sense of individualism, or 'personalism' as we shall call it following Katouzian (2009). They did so either by referring to selfishness and disregard for the rights of others or by explaining that everyone is only interested in what he or she is doing and not in other people, who constitute an abstract, collective entity. When asked if there are informal rules that affect the conduct of drivers in traffic, one of the interviewees stated that informal rules are those personal rules that individuals make up as they go along, thus causing chaos and accidents:

> 1:11:21: 'It is because of our individuality and selfishness, and because we only consider ourselves and don't respect other people's rights. This is reflective of people's personality, and one can't object to their selfish behaviour, because one most probably ends up quarrelling with them. All of this goes back to our selfishness and individuality. [...] The reason for this is that drivers do not have respect for others and pay attention only to their own self-interest and needs.'

We find similar ideas about people disregarding the rights of others in almost all our interviews. References to rights are made either in an implicit fashion, as in the next quote, or explicitly, as in the second quote below:

> 1:5:22: 'People learn to drive because they need to use the car to get them to work [...]. They don't learn to drive systematically and according to the principles of good driving [...]. It doesn't occur to them that driving has certain rules and laws. All they care about is using the car to get to where they are going.'

1:1:23: 'Some drivers disregard traffic rules because they are inexperienced, like the younger drivers who lack experience. Others drive badly because they have been drinking or taking drugs. There are also those who just don't care. They don't care about other people's safety. They have no respect for other people's rights; they believe they may do whatever they like.'

Rights and obligations are potentially moral and legal ideas, which are linked in our interviews with the Iranians' sense of individualism. Those who do not respect the rights of others are unlikely to respect the law unless they are compelled to do so by the threat of punishment. These are then related, through intelligence (*sho'ur*) and awareness or knowledge (*agahi*), to one's family:

1:6:24: 'The traffic situation has not improved in Iran, because people do not obey traffic rules [. . .]. Part of the problem, however, is rooted in family values and education, which do not teach people to respect themselves or other people in society.'

In the course of the interviews, the individual's family and close circle of friends, which we called their 'peer group', revealed themselves as the social foundation of this Iranian personalism.

Pedestrians: *Savareh* versus *Piyadeh*

In an online travel guide to Iran we read:

HOW to cross a busy street? Look for a pedestrian crossing, step out a short distance and wait for traffic to stop? Not in Tehran. Traffic never halts, so you must do as the locals do – step out when there is about a 5m gap between oncoming vehicles and spin like a whirling dervish; hopefully traffic will go around you. Iranian drivers are adept at missing pedestrians, but only just. There may be close calls, but no one is aiming to kill you.

(Life 2013)

Iran has one of the highest rates of pedestrian fatalities worldwide – three and half times higher than countries such as Belgium and Holland.

According to the Global Burden of Road Injuries (GBRI) report (2011), as many as 26 per cent of all traffic-related fatalities in Iran involve pedestrians, and according to Shahshahani (2006), a host of various factors contribute to this high rate of fatalities among pedestrians, some of which have to do with poorly designed city spaces and crowded pavements that force pedestrians to walk in the road. However, Shahshahani also points to the attitude of drivers to pedestrians, and the opposition between the word *piyadeh*, which means pedestrian, and *savareh*, which refers to either the rider of a horse or the driver of a car. She writes:

> In the Persian language, there is a dichotomy, a binary opposition, in the worth of human beings depending on whether they are riding a horse or driving a vehicle, or going on foot. *Piyadeh* also means illiterate, ignoble, incapable; such persons are treated dismissively and considered as marginal and, as a result, lose their pride. To make someone *piyadeh* means to make them lose their position of power. In popular language, to *piyadeh* someone means to steal their money or to denigrate them. On the contrary, *savareh* is someone riding respectfully in a position of power.
>
> (Shahshahani 2006: 86)

The current relevance of this binary opposition remains an empirical question, which has become socially and psychologically complicated by the impact of automobile on behaviour, not to mention the role of automobile as a cultural symbol. This binary opposition was employed in the Iranian driving laws and regulations of 1968, whereby the pedestrian was defined not as a subject in his/her own right, but in passing and almost as a function of driving. Symbolically, writes Shahshahani (2006: 88), 'only six out of the 137 signposts related to driving concerned pedestrians'. Even in the recent global statistics on road traffic injuries, presented by the GBRI report, we read:

> Most road deaths (42%) in Iran occur among car occupants [...]. Pedestrians and motorcycle riders account for another 26% and 14% of all deaths, respectively. The large number of deaths among motorcyclists in Iran is of special concern. Motorcycles are among the most risky modes of transport.

Figure 4.2   Pedestrian Crossing, Amir Kabir Street, Tehran © Gustaf Öhrnell.

Although the rate of fatalities amongst pedestrians is almost twice that of motorcyclists, the GBRI only regards death rates amongst the motorcyclists as being 'of special concern', thereby ignoring the fact that over one quarter of all traffic-related fatalities are among pedestrians.[5]

It should come as no surprise, therefore, if the subject of pedestrians represents a thorny issue and makes some of our male taxi drivers uncomfortable (as we shall see, female taxi drivers have a somewhat different way of talking about pedestrians). Asked if they stop at crossings to let pedestrians pass, they all responded affirmatively, but anyone who has tried to cross the street in central Tehran (or any other Iranian city) knows that taxis and cars normally do not brake to let pedestrians cross the road. One interesting point that arises here is that once the taxi drivers are invited to talk about pedestrians, they often make use of injunctive, normative statements (which emphasizes what they ought to do, rather than what they normally do) in order to express themselves. Here is an example:

1:6:25: 'From a driver's perspective, I ought to respect pedestrians. I should show respect to them, and vice versa they should show respect for drivers [. . .]. I always stop to let pedestrians cross the road,

but I should also add that it was the reason why I had an accident.
I stopped to let an elderly couple cross the road and a minibus
crashed into the back of my car causing a great deal of damage.'

The respondent states that he 'ought to respect' pedestrians, but he does
not go as far as to say that he does in actual fact respect their rights.
He thus recognizes the traffic rules, or the laws of society at large, which
expects drivers to behave in a particular way. Similar injunctive
statements are used in respect to pedestrians in other interviews. Here
are two more examples:

1:1:26: 'When I am driving and come across a pedestrian who is
crossing the street in the designated place, then I should try to
stop the car at the safe distance to allow him/her to pass.
We should care about pedestrians.'

1:2:27: 'When we are driving, we should treat pedestrians with
consideration – that is the way we would like to be treated ourselves,
if we were walking along the road or trying to cross the street.'

This type of response is not necessarily culturally specific to Iranians, but
it nevertheless demonstrates the existing gap between descriptive and
injunctive norms in the context of traffic behaviour, but with respect to
pedestrians generally.

Safety

In the course of the interviews, the notion of safety was raised in relation
to road safety (whether the roads are safe), vehicle safety standards
(whether the cars are safe) and personal safety (do the drivers and their
passengers wear seat belts?). The drivers generally regard the safety of
the cars made in Iran as very low:

1:3:28: 'The cars which are made in Iran have very poor safety;
they are made of flimsy and unreliable material. Many Iranian cars
don't have an inbuilt airbag or functioning ABS.'

Attitudes to road safety varied. Some regarded the roads as generally safe,
while others stated that the roads and highways were poorly designed and

poorly maintained. When it came to wearing seat belts, they all stated that they always wore their seat belt and also made sure that their passenger sitting in the front seat did so, too. One reason for this was that they would be fined if the passenger seated in the front was not wearing a seat belt. They did not, however, insist that other passengers, who were sitting in the back, wear their seat belts, because it was not required by law. When it comes to wearing seat belts, none of the taxi drivers made an injunctive statement. We should add that over a period of less than ten years there has been a change of attitude in Iran – especially in Tehran, where most drivers comply with the law in this respect – which is why the interviewees did not use injunctive statements.

This leads us to another question: why has the combination of fines and information succeeded in changing the behaviour of drivers with respect to seat belts but not generally with respect to other rules of driving? Why have Iranian drivers not become more considerate of each others' rights? One possible hypothesis is that, while wearing seat belts concerns *personal* safety, does not require much effort, does not interfere with a driver's planned journey and does not involve other people, the other rules of driving are *relational*, i.e. they are defined in relation to, and in interaction with, other people (potentially, unknown strangers). This hypothesis is in line with Homa Katouzian's socio-historical theory that Iranians attach a great deal of weight to their 'peer group' – i.e. family, kinship and friends – but that they are nonchalant towards strangers.

Self-respect (*Šæxsiæt*)

One of the insights gained from the second set of interviews – which had not been identified in the pilot study – concerns the central role of self-respect (*šæxsiæt* or *shakhsiyat*)[6] in the way our interviewees understand a host of issues, from the law and obeying the law, to how one behaves in traffic.

1:11:29: 'Law (*ghanon*) means to have self-respect.'

1:6:30: 'A good driver shows self-respect and therefore respect for other people [...]. The traffic situation has not improved in Iran, because people don't obey traffic rules [...]. Part of the problem is, however, rooted in family values and education, which do not teach people to respect themselves and other people in society.'

1:8:31: 'People should respect themselves while driving. Those who respect themselves also show consideration towards other people.'

Although *shakhsiyat* was duly noted at an earlier reading of the interview transcripts, we decided to highlight it as one of the key concepts at a later stage once we had begun comparing interviews with male and female taxi drivers. As we shall see, the idea of self-respect looms larger in the interviews with female cabbies. *Shakhsiyat* operates at the level of social interaction, as an individual's 'public face', but a 'public face' which does not require for its validity interacting with unknown social actors or recognizing strangers' autonomy and rights (for a discussion, see Koutlaki 2002). Instead, for its affirmation, it is dependent on one's 'peer group'. Iranians who refer to *shakhsiyat* mean that respect for other people's rights will automatically emerge once the individual recognizes his/her own value and behaves with dignity. Thus, the idea of *shakhsiyat* becomes related to Iranian personalism.

Zerang

The word *zerang*, which in Farsi means 'smart' or 'clever' but may also imply 'sly' or 'cunning', is used by several interviewees to refer to calculating people who manipulate every situation to their own advantage. Iranians have an ambivalent attitude towards this concept, showing both tacit admiration for *zerang* people and at the same time moral disapproval of their methods. The adjective 'smart' in the English language can mean 'keen', 'cool' or 'clever', although these different meanings are often clearly demonstrated by the context of the discussion. *Zerang*, on the other hand, can simultaneously imply contradictory meanings irrespective of the context. Iranian culture and the Persian language harbour many similar contradictory ideas and social attitudes.

1:3:32: 'Most people do not follow the law; they prefer to side-step it, even when they know that to obey the law would benefit them and society at large [...]. Why do they do that? Because they would like to appear as *zerang* in the eyes of other people [...].

By doing so, they also present themselves as different from the masses and emphasise their individuality.'

In the quotation above, the interviewee uses the idea of *zerang* to connect Iranians' unwillingness to follow the law and their sense of individuality (personalism).

Taarof (*tæ'arof*) in Traffic

Taarof is a specific national trait of Iranians, through which they express their culturally inherited sense of exaggerated civility, modesty and consideration for 'the other'. Etymologically, writes Koutlaki (2002: 1, 740), '*tæ'arof* is an Arabic word meaning "mutual recognition," thus an indication that *tæ'arof* functions as a tool for negotiating interactants' relationships'. It is hardly surprising if frequent references are made to *taarof*, often in relation to Iranians' exaggerated individualism:

> 1:2:33: 'When in traffic, drivers don't see each other as human beings, their eyes don't meet; they only see each other's cars. They only see the cars and don't think that another human being is behind the wheel of the other car [...], so they disregard each other's rights. When these two very people want to step in through the door, then they treat each other like human beings – with consideration – and spend time doing *taarof:* "after you".'

According to Taleghani-Nikazm (1998: 4), *taarof* is a shared cultural trait, 'a system of formality composed of stylized and ritualized linguistic patterns', which characterize interpersonal interaction amongst Iranians. It is an essentially linguistic game – one party offers, while the other refuses to accept at first but eventually gives in – which regulates daily interaction in various situations, from entering a room, where several people can offer each other to be the first to step across the threshold (which means that the person[s] who offer lower their status, or raise the other person's status), to shopping (where the shopkeeper will start by saying, 'No, please, you don't need to pay...'). *Taarof* can take many forms, and is used by all Iranians constantly when encountering acquaintances as well as strangers. A person who knowingly or unknowingly (in the case of non-Persian visitors) fails to engage in this linguistic game can be regarded as rude and uncivilized. Two important characteristics of *taarof* are: (1) it is a linguistic game, and (2) it seemingly – even deceptively – lowers the social status of the person who offers through flattery and compliments. The fact that *taarof* is a language game explains why it does not work in a traffic situation where social conduct is mediated through the medium of the automobile rather than linguistic exchanges.

References made to self-respect (*shakhsiyat*) can also throw light on *taarof*. If our assumption regarding the centrality of self-respect in Iranian culture is correct, then we could describe the significance of *taarof* also as part of the attempt to establish one's self-respect in the first place, rather than acknowledging other people's rights or recognizing their identity, autonomy or singularity. By showing excessive respect to the other, Iranians exercise their need to demonstrate their self-respect in face-to-face relationships. Another way of looking at it is by focusing on the person who lowers his/her status by making an offer – by lowering one's status, one indirectly establishes self-esteem (one cannot lower one's status if one does not have high status in the first place).[7] This point will be developed further in Chapter Eight.

The Arbitrariness of the Law

Another idea that we confront in our interviews concerns the arbitrariness of the way in which laws are enforced, and a distrust of authorities. This point was expressed clearly by the male taxi drivers despite the fact that they were generally on their guard and mindful of what they said in regard to the authorities. It was made more forcefully in other interviews, when the interviewees demonstrated greater trust in the interviewer.

1:9:34: 'The enforcement is entirely selective here, which means that if our traffic officers dislike someone they penalise them. For instance, they can fine different people differently for the same traffic offence. They give a fine to one person, exempt the other or reduce the penalty of a driver from 300,000 Rials to 150,000 Rials.'

The arbitrariness of the law can also be expressed in a different way, by emphasizing law's lack of autonomy:

1:2:35: 'People generally follow the law. Those who do not follow the law either see themselves above it or have enough money to buy their way out of trouble, or they get away with breaking the law because they have the right connections.'

Some of the interviewees (such as interviewee 2 in the above quote) stated that Iranians generally followed the law. However, their general tone indicated that they probably feel obliged to say so, because it was the 'politically correct' response. The following examples are less guarded, and also engage with the idea of law enforcement.

1:1:36: 'Half of people obey the law – half do not. Laws are often not enforced [...]. About 60 per cent of the time the law works and is enforced properly, while the remaining 40 per cent of the time it fails and leaves much to be desired. Although the authorities work to bring various activities under the rule of law, once the law is introduced, it is not sufficiently enforced.'

1:5:37: 'Most people do not follow the law for many reasons. But I don't want to go into why people don't follow the law or why laws are not enforced. I don't want to discuss politics.'

The question 'do you think the majority of people follow and obey the law?' was politically loaded, and as a result made some of the male taxi drivers uncomfortable. Other groups, such as lawyers, who were interviewed in the privacy of their offices (see the next chapter), engaged with the questions of law to a much greater extent, and expressed themselves more openly.

The Source of Law, and Resolving Disputes

All the male taxi drivers who were interviewed defined the sources of law and legal authority in terms of the Iranian Parliament (the *Majlis*) and the judicial system. An ostensibly secularized conception of the law and legality emerged out of the interviews, which is at odds with how Iranian law is otherwise defined in terms of the Qur'an, the *sunna* or *ijma* as a religious law. Even when the interviewees were asked about justice, they often described it in terms of the way that 'positive law' is enforced, and even their notion of justice was not related to a higher form of natural law.

As we shall see in the next chapter, not even the lawyers we interviewed defined the law in terms of Shari'a, although some of them emphasized the role of *urf* – which refers to customary laws and codes of conduct (treated as a secondary source of law in Shari'a).

Among those interviewed, the majority stated that when facing a potentially legal dispute they would first attempt to resolve it themselves through personal contacts. If they did not succeed in negotiating their way out of it, then they would turn to the courts and the police. A few people mentioned that they would use mediation centres, and a few admitted using community elders. Here is one such example:

> 1:10:38: 'I try to resolve the issue through personal contact. If I fail, then I ask friends and neighbours to intervene and help to resolve the dispute. If that fails too, then in the end I turn to the law and lawyers.'

However, the younger interviewees stated that they would turn to legal authorities directly to resolve their disputes. This was perhaps because they have had little or no experience of disputes, or it could indicate a change of attitude among younger Iranians who do not see elders as the centre of their community. As we shall see, it could also depend on which part of the city one finds oneself in. In the south of Tehran, for instance, where the more traditionalist population lives, mosques continue to play a role in creating a perception of community, and people still turn to elders to resolve disputes.

Concluding Remarks

The first two parts of our semi-structured interviews, which enquired into the causes of traffic accidents and safety issues, were exhausted very quickly. Most of the interviewees referred to a host of factors, ranging from the young constitution of the Iranian population to poorly designed and maintained roads, as the causes of accidents. Nevertheless, they all mentioned the reckless behaviour of Iranian drivers as the main reason for road traffic collisions. Reckless driving was, in turn, related to drivers' disregard of traffic rules, on the one hand, and their inability to respect other people's rights, on the other. The interviews suggested that

Iranians' inability to meet each other in traffic as rights holders or individual citizens who are worthy of respect has to do with their personalism. This should not, however, divert our attention from the point made above, in that their driving behaviour is mediated through the technology of the automobile, which brings out the driver's sense of individualism irrespective of culture.

The taxi drivers interviewed in this chapter believed that *farhang-sazi* offered *the* solution to the problem of traffic: the authorities, with the help of the mass media, were to inform people of the dangers of disregarding traffic rules and the importance of respecting the law. At the same time, many of those we interviewed were distrustful of the authorities, and regarded the law as an arbitrary instrument at the service of the wealthy and the powerful. This brings us back to our starting point regarding the class-ridden character of Iranian society, but it also underlines the paradoxical approach of Iranians to social problems, in that, on the one hand, they believe in the force of *farhang-sazi* and education, while, on the other hand, they distrust those who are (and will be) expected to plan and carry it out.

In regard to the source of law, almost all of those interviewed referred to man-made laws and institutions such as parliament, but the younger interviewees did not state that they would turn to community elders to begin with in order to resolve their disputes. This is one of the points that diverges from the pilot study, and it could suggest a change of attitude amongst the younger generation as well as a weakened awareness of community amongst the more non-traditional sections of the Iranian population. References were also made by male taxi drivers to mediation centres, which have been set up by the government in order to resolve minor civil disputes.

Turning our attention to the cultural aspects of the interviews, the male taxi drivers brought into focus a number of other concepts, such as *zerang* and *shakhsiyat*, which we had not identified in our pilot as key cultural ideas. One initial suggestion is that *zerang*, *shakhsiyat* and *taarof* are positive and negative expressions of Iranian personalism. We shall return to them in the coming chapters as we search for a theoretical framework that can incorporate all these key concepts.

CHAPTER 5

TRUST: INTERVIEWS WITH LAWYERS

Reza Banakar

Introduction

In this chapter, we present 11 interviews that we conducted with members of the Iranian Bar Association in Tehran, employing largely the same set of questions and the same interview structure as we used when interviewing the taxi drivers. Additional questions were, however, used to explore the role of lawyers and legal services. As we explained in the methodology chapter, the lawyers showed a greater sense of trust in the interview situation than did the male taxi drivers, and thus spoke with less restraint about the law and its enforcement in Iran. Unlike the male taxi drivers, several lawyers made reference to the pre-revolutionary era, which could be regarded as a politically sensitive topic in conversations with strangers. According to a former judge of the traffic courts:

2:11:1: 'Since the revolution, not only have our driving habits not improved, they have in fact deteriorated.'

Another former judge went somewhat further in his comparison of the two eras:

2:2:2: 'Before the revolution, driving had respect. If you broke the rules, people would look at you disapprovingly. In those days, society didn't tolerate reckless driving. Today, nobody cares. First, we have to change the way people regard driving. Second, we have no traffic police worthy of the name. [. . .] We need police who can intervene while drivers are breaking the rules – and not police who can only write fines after the event.'

The judge's account of pre-revolutionary driving is probably tinted by nostalgia for 'the good old days', and should not be taken at face value. Although the traffic situation has deteriorated due to a range of factors, including the growing number of cars and an increase in the number of younger drivers, there is no evidence to support the statement that Iranians were more rule-abiding drivers before the revolution. The point made here is that the judge felt more relaxed when talking to the interviewers and ventured to express politically sensitive views, while the male taxi drivers were generally on their guard.

When asked if they had the time to be interviewed, most lawyers told us that they knew nothing, or very little, about traffic regulations, but once the interviews started, some of them could not stop talking about the traffic problem. In the course of these interviews a number of interesting topics, such as *diyah* (blood money) and *urf* (customary laws) were discussed. In addition, the lawyers raised new issues that threw light on the role of the law and the legal profession in Iran. In the following pages, we shall discuss a number of ideas – including the culture of driving, *farhang-sazi* (culture building), education, *shakhsiyat* (self-respect), respect, *zerangi* (smartness or slyness) and *taarof* (exaggerated civility) – that we identified as key concepts in the previous chapter. These concepts were employed by all interviewees as a set of interwoven ideas to discuss Iranians' driving habits and their attitude to the law. Finally, a concern with 'rights' and 'obligations' loomed large in the interviews with the lawyers. Rights were discussed both as a relational, moral idea that ought to shape Iranians' behaviour towards each other and as a legal concept that should set the parameters for the interplay between citizens and the State.

The Culture of Driving

When the lawyers were asked about Iranian drivers' disregard for traffic rules, several replied by using almost the same sentence, namely:

'It all goes back to our culture', and then went on to talk about Iranians not having developed a 'culture of driving'. This was one of the main discursive patterns identified in the pilot study and also in the interviews with the taxi drivers. One of the lawyer interviewees, for example, stated repeatedly that the traffic problem could be traced back to Iranian culture in that although drivers knew the basic rules of traffic, they nevertheless broke them because they did not have a culture of driving:

> 2:7:1: 'In principle, this [how we view traffic accidents] goes back to the way we behave, our knowledge, awareness and culture of driving. For me, the culture of driving is about respecting the rules and laws of traffic. [...] A person who has not learnt to follow the rules of traffic lacks a culture of driving. [...] People who disobey the laws of driving know the basic rules of traffic; they know, for example, that they should not exceed the speed limit in certain areas. Yet they break the laws because they lack a culture of driving.'

This interviewee goes on to emphasize the importance of education, arguing that one should teach the culture of driving to children at an early age and that driving should be treated as an indicator of one's personality, personal dignity and 'self-respect' (*shakhsiyat*). In contrast to the above interviewee, another lawyer saw the 'culture of driving' as more than just following the rules:

> 2:11:4: 'To understand why Iranians drive badly, we need to look at their culture. From the time when they first started to drive, they received formal training and were taught the traffic rules as part of their driving test. They know how to drive a car, but they don't have the culture of behaving in traffic. It doesn't occur to them that they aren't alone in the traffic and there are other people whose rights need to be respected. Also, there is a group who might want to follow the driving rules but can't do it because of the prevailing culture. This is because laws and rules haven't been institutionalized. People aren't familiar with ordinary laws and driving rules, and the authorities have neglected to carry out *farhang-sazi* in this respect.'

The same interviewee then went on to define what he meant by *farhang-sazi*:

> 2:11:5: '*Farhang-sazi* involves establishing a norm amongst the people and institutionalising discipline and procedures about how to do things. One example is the use of seatbelts [...] compared to 10 years ago, people do it because the idea of wearing your seatbelt is now institutionalised.'

According to many of those we interviewed, the culture of driving varied from place to place in Iran, and, although people in Tehran drove badly, the driving habits in other large cities were even worse.

> 2:11:6: 'The traffic situation affects my work badly, particularly in the morning. I prefer not to take my car out. The traffic and the way people drive have been normalised for us who live here, and perhaps we might not notice how strange it is. But I regularly have visitors from other countries. They find the driving here bizarre and extremely dangerous. Visitors also point out the driving habits in other large cities, in Shiraz in particular, where it is much worse than in Tehran. In Tehran people have learnt to follow certain rules, to some extent, but in other cities, Iranians' driving truly frightens away any visitor.'

Ironically, many of our interviewees in Shiraz (see the pilot study) referred to the urbanization process and complained about the poor driving of people who had moved to the city from rural areas. Occasional references to 'outsiders' as a source of the traffic problems in Tehran were also made in the interviews with the male taxi drivers, while, as we shall see, it surfaced more frequently in the interviewees with female cabbies. This attitude to 'outsiders', sometimes referred to in Farsi as *dehati* (peasant or bumpkin), which is a denigrating word suggesting a culturally unsophisticated person, has several dimensions, one of which is related to opposition between traditional behaviour and a modern lifestyle.

> 2:9:7: 'We have many people who continue to think and behave traditionally despite the fact that they live in a modern, albeit not

quite civilised, society. Since they remain rooted in traditional society, they refuse to employ the laws which are brought about for the use of the automobile and other forms of modern technology. [...]. This causes tension between them and society.'

Another lawyer discussed the process of urbanization and the people from the provinces in a different context, and he went on to refer to 'self-respect' (which we shall discuss separately below, as one of our key concepts) and the growth of the 'new rich', who have no principles:

2:11:8: 'Many formerly poor farmers in rural areas, for example in the north of Iran where I have visited regularly over the years, have more recently become wealthy, as land prices have gone up. The first thing they do is to buy a car. They have a driving licence and know the basic rules of driving, but they have no idea about the principles and the culture of driving. We find a similar development in large cities, where the unstable economic situation allows certain types of people, who have no self-respect, to make billions within a few weeks. These people have no respect for other people's lives and don't care if they kill someone in the traffic, because they can afford to pay their *diyah* (blood money – discussed below).'

'Peasants' from the provinces are thus not only described as traditionalists and non-modern, but they are also disliked because at least some of them have become wealthy. A concern with the tension between modernity and tradition exists in many of the interviews we conducted, but the view of 'outsiders' as a source of traffic problems was voiced more frequently in Shiraz than in Tehran. One possible reason for this slight difference of attitude is that unlike Shiraz, which, despite growing dramatically over the last three decades has in many ways maintained its traditional and provincial atmosphere, Tehran has become a cosmopolitan city, where people from different cultural and linguistic backgrounds have shared the same space for decades and have therefore developed a greater acceptance of cultural diversity and difference. Also, the overwhelming majority of people who live in Tehran are either migrants themselves or else the children or grandchildren of people from the provinces.

Rights and Obligations

2:9:9: 'The law is a social contract requiring everyone to follow the appropriate set of rules and processes.'

In the course of the interviews, the lawyers often referred to law, society and social relations in terms of a 'social contract', reflecting their shared moral and political philosophy, and one which is often associated with Enlightenment philosophers such as Rousseau, Hobbes and Locke, who saw the origin of society and the legitimacy of the State in contractual terms. Somewhat oversimplified, according to the social-contract theory, we acquire civil rights by agreeing to surrender parts of our personal freedoms in return for a well-organized government and a good society. As part of this contract, we need to recognize and respect other people's rights and freedoms. The social-contract theory is rooted in the tradition of Western liberal democracy, which assumes the social and legal autonomy of citizens, and it also treats legal and political institutions as human creations. Although the first part of the theory, which requires the partial surrendering of one's freedoms in return for an effectively governed society, might be attractive to Iran's Islamic government, its overall positivistic methodology is potentially at odds with the central tenet of Islamic law, according to which the Qur'an is the primary source of law.[1] Moreover, the social-contract theory also underlines the duties of the State, i.e. it postulates that the State is accountable under the law and must honour its obligations to its citizens. The State's duties to its citizens were on the minds of most of our lawyers, who repeatedly referred to 'rights' and 'obligations', arguing that the Iranian authorities tend to emphasize citizens' obligations but without ensuring their civil rights. Their argument was that under circumstances in which the individual's rights are neither upheld by the authorities nor respected by other fellow citizens, we cannot expect the ordinary person in the street to keep his or her side of the social contract. This widespread indifference to the rights of others has, in turn, a detrimental impact on all walks of life, including traffic and driving behaviour, which are governed by rights and duties.

2:9:10: 'The authorities have become used to placing obligations on people, without giving them any rights. [...] Law is a form of social contract, and I would behave according to the law as long as my rights are respected. I would not follow the law when my rights are not recognised and respected. [...] Most Iranians are unaware of their rights – they have no idea that the government has certain obligations towards them in terms of providing security, healthcare, work and housing [...]. These rights are defined in the Constitution. When the government doesn't acknowledge people's rights, many of them end up in confrontation with the state. In the traffic situation, this reveals itself as confrontation with the police. [...] They [Iranians] say, "In this country we only have duties, but no rights".'

2:10:11: 'I see the laws of the land, including traffic laws and regulations, in terms of the social contract, which requires all parties to honour their obligations. [...] It means that the state also has duties towards its citizens which by law it is required to fulfil. It's no good if laws only express duties for citizens, because if the state fails to fulfil its duties, it will force people into confrontation.'

Both lawyers quoted above approached rights from the point of view of the State's obligations to the people, arguing that the authorities' disregard for the rights of citizens was a source of 'confrontation' between the people and the State. Another lawyer provided a somewhat different understanding of rights by focusing on how Iranians honoured their obligations to each other:

2:10:12: 'Iranians tend to see only their own rights and their personal needs, but not their obligations to other people. [...] Their interpretations of the law and their understanding of their rights become personalised; for example, I may violate your rights when I am in a hurry. It is a very personal interpretation of my rights, which justifies all actions which I might take to ensure my own personal interests.'

The third lawyer, interviewee 10, by describing the difficulties inherent in upholding rights and obligations against the backdrop of Iranians' sense of individualism, provides two possible explanations for (or hypotheses about) the logic behind their behaviour. First, in a sociopolitical setting in which one's rights are respected neither by fellow citizens nor by the authorities, one might react by attending only to one's own rights and needs. After all, rights are not realized by making one-sided commitments to honouring other people's claims but through social relationships based on reciprocal respect and mutual commitment to the fulfilment of duties to the rights holders. Second, in a socio-historical setting in which the individual's duties are to his or her 'peer group', i.e. family and a close circle of friends, one might not feel a moral obligation towards 'strangers', thus disregarding their rights. These two explanations are not exclusive, and operate as two parallel processes that directly and indirectly reinforce each other, thereby widening the gap between ordinary Iranians and the State while fuelling the formers' individualism and disrespect for the rights of strangers.

Shakhsiyat and Taarof vs. Zerangi

The word *shakhsiyat*, which we defined in the previous chapter, emerges from our interviews as an important cultural idea:

> 2:7:13: 'The way you drive and behave in the traffic is an indicator of your *shakhsiyat*.'

> 2:2:14: 'In the previous regime, drivers of private cars had *shakhsiyat* – they didn't carry fares illegally.'

The latter interviewee then goes on to contrast *shakhsiyat* with *zerangi* (we also discussed *zerang* – which refers to a 'smart' or 'sly' person – in the previous chapter), stating that 'the disregard for rules is seen by some people as *zerangi*',[2] i.e. they think they are being clever just because they break the rules, 'while in fact they are violating other people's rights'. Finally, towards the end of the interview, he states the following:

> 2:2:15: 'To follow the law, means to respect yourself. If you disrespect yourself, you can't expect others to respect you.'

An identical idea also surfaced in many interviews with the taxi drivers. One of the female cabbies went as far as to say, 'Law means self-respect'. The emphasis on self-respect, as expressed by Iranians, should be compared to the way the notion of 'respect' is normally understood in

Western cultures. Whereas in the West respect is understood in terms of acknowledging and upholding other people's dignity and rights, the Iranians we interviewed conceptualized it in relation to oneself, i.e. in terms of one's own dignity and maintaining one's own rights. This is, admittedly, paradoxical, because one cannot maintain one's rights outside a relationship based on mutual respect for rights and obligation. It is suggested herein that the point of departure for our interviewees was not other people's rights but their own rights. This can also be explained by referring to their sense of personalism, as discussed in the previous chapter. A tentative interpretation of this apparent paradox is that the interviewees' references are not so much to their own person but to their personal community network.

The idea of *taarof* was also present in the interviews with the lawyers and was similarly contrasted with *zerangi* – for example:

> 2:8:16: 'We Iranians use *taarof* in all walks of life, with the exception of driving. Unfortunately we think that we are *zerang* if we ignore traffic rules and regulations. As long as the rules are not enforced forcefully, very few people will take them seriously and follow them.'

Interviewee 8 contrasts *taarof* with *zerangi*, which may, depending on the context of discussions, operate as the opposite of self-respect. It is important to reiterate that Iranians have an ambivalent attitude to *zerangi*, and in a situation in which it is employed in an emphatically negative tone it then becomes the opposite of *shakhsiyat* (a person of honour and self-esteem does not manipulate every situation to his or her personal advantage).

The 'Tribe' of Pedestrians

The negative attitude to pedestrians, which we discussed in Chapter Four by contrasting *piyadeh* (a person who is on foot) and *savareh* (a person riding on horseback) was also present in the interviews with the lawyers. When asked about their views on pedestrians (How do you see pedestrians when you are driving?), many answered in injunctive normative terms. A female lawyer, for instance, stated, 'When driving, the person behind the wheel should treat pedestrians in a way which he

would like to be treated by drivers had he been on foot', and then she
went on to add:

> 2:9:17: 'A pedestrian should be treated with great care. But they
> also abuse traffic rules. When you stop for a pedestrian to cross the
> road [...] you feel that they regard you with disrespect, and also
> the drivers in the cars behind you, who also had to stop, can behave
> disrespectfully towards you. Women drivers are subjected more to
> this type of disrespectful behaviour than men. Let me add this as a
> footnote [...], that unfortunately, in our society, women drivers
> are seen differently just because they are following the law [...].
> This is an important point that men cause more fatal accidents
> than women. [...] It happens often that pedestrians abuse their
> rights. Even in places where there are pedestrian bridges, many
> people continue to cross the roads.'

The lawyer, a 40-year-old woman, underlines the gender aspect of driving
by stating that women are treated differently in traffic. She also hints that
there is tension between drivers and pedestrians – this tension was
expressed, in different ways, in many interviews. Although most
interviewees admitted that one should treat pedestrians with care, they
also emphasized that pedestrians too had duties and should follow the
rules of the traffic. Perhaps because of the socioculturally negative
connotations of *piyadeh*, and the positive connotations of *savareh*, the
interviewees often saw the problem from the standpoint of the driver, as if
they themselves could never be a pedestrian. Expressed differently,
pedestrians belong to one 'tribe' – to the tribe of *piyadehrow* – and drivers
to another – to the tribe of *savareh* – and they only meet under the
stressful conditions of the streets of Tehran.

Lawyers and Legal Services

Three points regarding legal services emerged from our interviews with
the lawyers. First, the idea of obtaining legal counsel was not rooted
among Iranians, who have a low opinion of legal knowledge:

> 2:1:18: 'Even when their business is in trouble, they don't turn to a
> lawyer straight away, but go round asking the advice of their friends

and acquaintances [. . .] – asking their friends and family how they should handle their problems legally. Finally, when they are completely stuck and forced to realise that they have no way of getting themselves out of their situation, only then do they seek a lawyer's council. But then it could be too late to do much about it.'

Second, only the more knowledgeable and well-to-do sections of Iranian society engaged the services of lawyers:

2:6:19: 'You know, those who are aware of the technical developments know that for each type of problem or dispute they need specialised advice. They also value the lawyers' counsel and are prepared to pay for it. But ordinary people aren't willing to pay the fees and don't make use of the legal services. They believe they can manage their cases on their own and don't need to be represented by a lawyer. It means that they often don't turn to a lawyer, unless they are confronted with a very serious problem which practically forces them to engage the services of one.'

Third, the public's attitude to lawyers was rather negative and simplistic:

2:2:20: 'People do not have a very high opinion of lawyers' services. They just want to get things done – they don't care if it is done through the assistance of a lawyer or with the help of the grocer round the corner. If they know that the grocer knows the judge who is deciding their case, obviously they turn to the grocer for help [. . .]. Ordinary people want to get their legal problems resolved; they couldn't care less if it is done through the proper channels of the law or not. In a country where the law is not employed correctly, lawyers have no role to play.'

According to our lawyers, many people thought that they were only interested in charging fat fees while doing the bare minimum for their clients, and therefore people tried not to turn to them for advice when they encountered a legal problem. This was then linked to 'a wave of negative publicity directed at lawyers,' which we shall discuss separately below.

Lawyers' Legal Autonomy

Several lawyers discussed the independence of attorneys and the fact that many people, and even the authorities, do not understand that as officers of the court they are required to represent the accused irrespective of the charges brought against him or her. That is why many lawyers who have represented political prisoners have themselves ended up in prison.

> 2:9:21: 'When you represent a political prisoner of the Bhai faith, it doesn't mean that you share his religious beliefs. In fact, you might defend him despite the fact that you abhor what he stands for. As a lawyer you defend his rights to a fair trial and due process. [...] Once I told the former President of the Bar that we lawyers were the victims of our clients, because people judged us by the crimes committed by our clients.'

This interviewee then went on to explain that this lack of understanding of lawyers' professional neutrality is related to ordinary Iranians' conception of the law as an institution that is not free from political influence or the exercise of power. There are also many clients who do not quite understand the limits of their rights, which is particularly striking in family cases where women seek separation.

> 2:9:22: 'Sometimes clients come with some expectations and plans that I can't support and have to advise them against. For example, some women come here and tell me that they want to do certain things through the law. I have to remind them that they are women. I tell them that their gender makes no difference to me, but the law treats them differently by giving them half the rights of a man. I explain to them that I am forced to work within a legal framework which denies them equal rights. So I can't take on their husbands legally, because I won't have a chance of winning.'

Discussions on the role of lawyers in Iranian society – whether Iranians trust lawyers and make use of their services – were linked by some interviewees to the arbitrary character of the law in the country. Here are four examples:

2:1:23: 'The laws aren't properly interpreted and enforced. They are instead interpreted and enforced in an arbitrary fashion to serve personal interests. In the context of traffic and driving, this interpretation of law can be clearly seen in the way insurance companies behave, in that they often deny people's rights.'

2:5:24: 'Unfortunately, unfortunately, unfortunately the public mistrusts lawyers, the judicial order and the legislature [...]. The law is unpredictable and can change without warning or logic [...]. I have personally been harmed by the law, because it lacks stability. [...]. Should I trust a law and a legal system which doesn't defend my rights? [...]. You can't force people to trust your legal system. [...]. Nothing is more damaging in a society than a legal order which fails to protect ordinary people and their interests. We have laws which address all walks of life, from outer space to the bottom of the oceans [...]. But what is the value of a law which cannot be enforced? Can we trust a legal system which does not protect us?'

2:8:25: 'Sadly, our laws have become subjected to arbitrary interpretation and enforcement. In this country, in many instances, policy aims carry greater weight, and they are given higher priority, than laws [...]. The legal system presents us with policies that undermine the laws which clearly describe legal procedures, and we are told to realise these policies because they have higher priority than enforcing the law.'

2:9:26: 'When you mention the law, I think of the Iranian Constitution of 1357. Admittedly, the Constitution did not incorporate all the principles we find in the Convention of Human Rights; yet, it contains a solid basis for all the laws of the land. It clearly defines the legal rights and duties of the citizens and requires that all be treated equally before the law irrespective of race or religion. [...] The idea is that all legislation, legal measures and policies are constructed and introduced in accordance with the Constitution. For example, the Constitution categorically prohibits all forms of torture. But when Parliament has interpreted the Constitution in order to draft new legislations, it has introduced exceptions to the Constitutional principles, saying, for example, that torture is unlawful but allowed in certain situations. To give you another example, according to the Constitution, healthcare, education and sports are free and the state is obliged to provide these for all citizens. But they have introduced various fees for these public services. These exceptions undermine the contract which exists between the state and the people. It undermines the integrity of the Constitution and creates uncertainty in the role of the law and makes people distrustful of the judicial system. The state had a contract to provide free education, but I have to pay 2,000,000 Tomans per year for my son's school. When the state does not honour its contract, I feel obliged to oppose its laws.'

Our interviews with the lawyers supported the assumption made in the pilot study that Iran's law and its legal system were experienced as a form of arbitrary exercise of power. As long as people treat the law with distrust and find themselves in opposition thereto, lawyers in Iran will have a difficult time providing legal services in an effective or meaningful manner.

Punishments and Traffic Fines

Most of the lawyers we interviewed argued with conviction against punishment as the primary form of deterrence or as a basis for creating an effective criminal policy, generally, and for improving traffic behaviour, in particular. Instead, they underlined the role of education and the importance of *farhang-sazi* in altering people's behaviour.

2:9:27: 'If you wish to improve the traffic, there is no point in introducing new laws – as was done recently – with more severe penalties and higher fines. Even if we increase the fines tenfold, we won't improve the traffic situation. It all returns to how society and the government view and understand individuals. Before we resort to laws designed to penalise people, we need to inform them of why the behaviour in question needs to be changed. [...] The media can help with educating people in traffic and in other instances. *Farhang-sazi* has been shown to be a more effective way of dealing with these problems.'

The lawyers' stance against punishment is in line with their general liberal understanding of the law and society, which we discussed above in relation to their emphasis on rights and obligations. Moreover, most Iranian lawyers have experience of criminal-law cases, which has probably made them consider the logic of harsh punishments meted out by some Iranian courts.

That fact that most Iranian lawyers take on criminal cases is an interesting point in itself. There is an absence of specialization among them, which means that they accept a variety of cases across the legal spectrum, dealing with criminal cases as well as private law disputes in the course of a day's work. One of the female lawyers we interviewed was the exception to this rule, in that she only took on family-law cases. Another lawyer that we interviewed suggested that he could not make a living if he specialized, which is an interesting point because it suggests that the Iranian legal service is not utilized by the public. This notion is supported by other issues that the lawyers raised concerning the general attitude of people to their services.

The idea of large legal firms, which would allow for specialization, is not established in Iran, and many Iranian lawyers operate as sole practitioners. As a result, they often have to take on any case, irrespective of its legal grounds or aspects, that might be brought their way in order to make ends meet. International lawyers, who have a different clientele, are the only exception to this rule.

The Image of Lawyers in Iran

Several lawyers criticized the way in which the legal profession had been depicted in soap operas and films produced by Iranian state television. They also pointed out that the attempt to discredit the legal profession was extended to the judiciary, which has close ties to the political apparatus, and the court system could intentionally throw obstacles in the way of lawyers:

2:5:28: 'All government agencies disrespect lawyers. In my legal work, I am daily up against a set of problems which have nothing to do with the law; yet, they prevent me from doing my job as a lawyer within the court system, [...] the details of which I can't divulge here. Our people don't have a favourable view of lawyers. It started with a number of soap operas which depicted lawyers as corrupt, dishonest and cheats [...]. Basically, every time the television has presented a lawyer, this person has been a trickster [...]. Society starts expecting you to behave in that way. [...] Our legal system humiliates lawyers – it does not treat them with respect [...] despite the fact that a good and competent lawyer elevates the juridical order and the judges. Legally knowledgeable and competent judges treat lawyers with due respect and see them as on a par with themselves. But those judges, who don't possess these qualities, see lawyers in a different way and need to humiliate them.'

Another lawyer agreed that people's attitude towards the legal profession was not as good as it used to be, but this was also related to the rising number of inexperienced lawyers:

2:10:29: 'People respected lawyers in the past. At the moment, their attitude towards them is not as positive as it used to be [...]. This is partly because of the fragile foundations of the legal profession in Iran [...], for only if I uphold my self-respect and dignity will others respect me. The number of lawyers, particularly young lawyers who have been accepted to the Bar, who have entered legal practice has increased recently. To make a living in a difficult economic situation, they are forced to act in ways that are ethically questionable. Their inexperience in legal practice has undermined the dignity of the legal profession.'

The reference made to 'self-respect' in this context, which might appear at first glance to be misplaced, should be understood in the context of the lawyers' code of professional ethics. The growing numbers of inexperienced lawyers who are struggling in a rather lean legal market to survive economically do not always practise by the legal profession's code of conduct. It is also interesting that for this lawyer, to practice law ethically amounts to maintaining one's self-respect and dignity (*shakhsiyat*).

Law and Justice

Most of the lawyers interviewed stated that Iranians do not abide by the law, 'have no respect for the law and do not trust the system' (2:2:30), and saw it 'as a self-preserving mechanism at the service of the political system and not a mechanism which aims at preserving their rights and safety' (2:10:31). They also argued that the laws were not enforced in a satisfactory fashion, thus making the outcome of legal processes uncertain and unpredictable. They meant that this uncertainty discredits the role of law in society, undermined the rule of law and gave rise to negative attitudes towards the law.

> 2:1:32: 'In our society lawlessness is tolerated. Breaking the law doesn't cause a person's fall from grace. Far from it, in traffic, if someone breaks the law by, for example, driving through a red light or not stopping where he is supposed to, other drivers will not treat his conduct disapprovingly; instead, they will follow his example. It means that we need to prevent lawlessness through *farhang-sazi* – by way of propaganda through radio, television and newspapers we need to introduce the ideas which counteract lawlessness.'

> 2:4:33: 'We always take our cue from the Chaplain and follow him. In a society where the law is not fully enforced by the authorities, you can't expect ordinary people to abide by the law. [...] The role of law in Iranian society is just to keep people preoccupied. And Iranians are not law-abiding at all.'

Against this background, it is not surprising to find our lawyers distinguishing sharply between law and justice, arguing that legality did not necessarily entail justice, a fact of which the court and most judges were painfully aware.

> 2:1:34: 'Law and law enforcement have nothing to do with justice. The courts make a judgment on the basis of the facts and evidence provided to them. They don't know the truth [...]. Courts may make a decision which is legally correct, but it might or might not satisfy the requirements of justice. [...]. Never can a judge claim that his judgment is a representation of justice.'

That is also why people's conceptions and expectations of law and justice can vary across different jurisdictions.

2:10:35: 'For example, some believe that if someone murders another, justice would require imposing capital punishment, but others, like in Sweden, believe justice is served by rehabilitating rather than executing the murderer.'

According to this lawyer, justice transcended the personal needs of individual people and was realized differently in different places. This understanding of justice, which was shared by most of our lawyers, does not come across as a religious notion; it might be because they have a non-religious conception of justice, but equally because Islam has a rather down-to-earth and practical understanding of justice. Two of our lawyers (including one of the female lawyers) defined justice in terms of the *effort to place everything in its proper place*, which is an Islamic conception of justice. Whereas God *places* everything in its proper place, people can only *try* to place them in their right place. The effort to achieve this is 'doing justice', which also means that justice is a process rather than an end (also see the discussions on justice in the pilot study in Chapter Three and references to Krämer [2007: 25], wherein the Islamic understanding of justice is linked to the will of God).

The Sources of Law

In the pilot study, it was argued that Iranians defined law in terms of 'positive law', i.e. as laws promulgated by parliament rather than in terms of Islam or the divine sources of Shari'a. Once they were asked about the sources of law and legal authority, the majority either referred to parliament or to the legal system and executive. Some lawyers also underlined the importance of those who draft the laws and those who enforce them, and some even stated that Iranians regarded the judge as the ultimate source of authority (for it is the judge who decides their legal cases). However, the second set of interviews highlights the significance of religion in Iranians' understanding of the sources of law, although the picture which emerges is a sociolegally complex issue. Admittedly, very few people made any reference to Islamic law or Shari'a once they were asked about the sources of law; nonetheless, the idea of *urf* (i.e. customary law) loomed large in many discussions, and it was suggested that it played an important role in Iranian culture. The following interviewee – who has worked as a judge, an attorney and a law lecturer – explains this point without reference to *urf* as such, although he clearly argues that Iranians, in the first place, follow those rules and laws which are embedded in their religious and cultural beliefs.

> 2:11:36: 'Ordinary people show greater respect for those laws which are in accordance with their religious beliefs. Those laws which are in line with people's beliefs do not require police or other authorities to enforce them. When I teach, I give students two examples of tax evasion and marriage between blood relatives and close family, both of which are prohibited in law. [...] Whereas tax law would require careful enforcement to bring about compliance, the ban against marriage between blood relatives is followed by most people automatically [...], because it's embedded in their beliefs. People generally comply with certain laws, not because they are enforced by the police or other authorities but because the laws reflect their beliefs and religious convictions. Therefore, when a law is linked to people's belief, they tend to follow it, and those people who are not religious will value those laws which are morally justified. [...]. People have a nonchalant attitude to traffic laws, because driving rules are not seen as moral or religious laws and because they have no roots in their beliefs.'

Iranians do not experience the rules of traffic as morally binding, partly because they feel no obligation towards each other when driving (this point was discussed above). It should also be noted that they have different takes on Islam, i.e. there is a plurality of interpretations of Islamic rules and laws in operation in Iranian society, and not even within the Islamic government do we find total agreement on the interpretation of Islamic laws. Thus, various groups' religious beliefs may be at odds with those of other groups, as well with those of the government. Islamic law, in theory, does accommodate a degree of diversity in cultural practices by employing *urf* as a secondary source of law:

> 2:1:37: '*urf* is an integral part of the Islamic culture of our country, and the rules of *urf* are very powerful indeed. Not even the most

rigorous laws have managed to harness the force of *urf*. There were, for example, several attempts to remove *mehrieh*[3] – an attempt which in practice proved to be in vain, because it went against the prevailing rules of *urf*. [...] The fact that people follow *urf* demonstrates its force. [...] According to the law, women who appear in public spaces without an Islamic *hijab* – which means that their entire body except their face and their hands should be covered – will be disciplined. However, we see that this strict conception of *hijab* is not enforced in practice, because *urf* has a different and broader definition of *hijab*. According to the law, women's hair and feet should not be visible, whereas according to *urf* it is ok if some of their hair or feet are visible [...]. The prevailing *urf* has accepted that women need to wear sandals during hot summer days. In practice we see that women who appear in public in breach of the *hijab* rule, as defined by *urf* rather than by Islamic law, are reprimanded and punished.'

Again, we need to treat the factual accuracy of enforcement of the *hijab*, as stated by this interviewee, with care. Several people, with whom we discussed the issue of *hijab* laws, argued that the rules were enforced differently in different parts of the city, which supports the idea that there are different interpretations of laws in operation in the same city. For instance, while laws are only loosely adhered to in northern Tehran, where wealthy and Westernized Iranians live, they are strictly followed in the southern part of the city, where the more traditionalist sections of the population live.

Another interviewee, who also worked as a judge, referred to *urf* directly – albeit by distinguishing between the man-made law of parliament, Islamic Law, Shari'a and *urf* – and suggested that we are dealing with an obfuscated legislative process:

2:2:38: 'The law has developed a great deal since the revolution, but there is a lot left to be done. The fact that we are trying to implement Islamic law gets in the way. The laws which are introduced by Parliament are first sent to the Council of Guardians for approval – to see if they are in accordance to the principles of Shari'a.[4] The laws which are deemed incompatible with Islamic law are referred to the Expediency Council,[5] which approves 90%

of them – and it can only achieve that by setting aside Shari'a and going against the *urf*. It means that 90% of the laws are not compatible with Islamic principles [...]. These legal disagreements could be avoided if Parliament made legislations which were in line with the values of society today.'

The above description of the law-making process suggests four centres of normativity engaged in a political struggle against each other. In the struggle, the Council of Guardians and the Expediency Council represent two opposing political forces belonging to the Islamic regime. Shari'a and *urf*, however, are described in relation to each other and regarded as customary law and different from the Islamic law that the Iranian Government wishes to establish. As this jurist explains, 'Islamic law gets in the way' of legislating good laws which are in tune with *urf*. He also argues against *diyah*,[6] the Islamic doctrine which allows the payment of blood money, stating that, 'To remove *diyah* would be an important and positive move. The authorities must get rid of *diyah*'. He then goes on to argue that:

2:2:39: 'Iranians are not a law-abiding people. Over thousands of years, throughout our history, we have been ruled by despots who violated the rights of ordinary people. As a result, people have always tried to evade state laws [...]. I don't think that the distrust of the law is new – it has always existed. All over the world, people pay their taxes on time. We Iranians never do. [...] Our *bazaari* merchants, for example, keep two books, one for themselves and one for the tax authorities. However, when it comes to their religious duties, to paying their *khoms* and *zakat* [religious dues amounting to one fifth of their annual net profit], they do not have two books. They do not cheat when it comes to paying their religious dues, because they believe in the value and the legitimacy of these duties. They behave according to *urf*, but they become antagonistic in their dealings with the rulers and [...] try to circumvent state laws. It has been their attitude to the law in the past, and it is their attitude today. To change this attitude is very difficult, for they have avoided their rulers' laws throughout the ages. One can do something about it only through *farhang-sazi*'.

Finally, two of the lawyers stated that Iranians regard themselves as the primary source of law – to give one example:

> 2:10:40: 'In the context of today's society, Iranians regard themselves as the primary source of the law – they consider themselves as a source of unwritten law. Iranians see only their own rights and their personal needs.'

Thus, even the source of law is related to Iranians' sense of individualism and their one-sided understanding of rights. However, an individual can entertain a personal idea of legality in so far as it is accepted at the level of his or her kinship and community network.

Excursus: A Note on the *Bazaar*

The reference above to the *bazaari* merchants, who played an important role in bringing down the Pahlavi regime and subsequently benefited (at least initially) from the revolution, is also of interest. The *bazaar* is the centre of trade and commerce, as well as a social, political and religious space, in every Iranian city. Traditionally, each city had a main *bazaar* and each neighbourhood or city quarter had its own little *bazaar* (or *bazaarcheh*). The architecture of the *bazaar* linked the main mosques and other urban facilities such as the public baths (*hammam*) and government offices, thus integrating the local neighbourhood or community (the so-called *mahalleh*). At the same time, as Sharifi and Murayama (2013: 129) explain, it also provided a sociocultural site for developing a local identity and feeling of community. *Bazaaris* are socially conservative men with close ties with the *ulama* (Islamic jurists), the local clergy and the local mosques (*bazarri* and *ulama* families often intermarry, thus consolidating their political alliance).

One would expect that the *ulama's* rise to power after the Islamic Revolution benefited the *bazaaris* and brought them close to the Islamic state. However, *bazaaris* continue to pay greater attention to *urf* than to state law, which suggests otherwise (for discussions on the sociopolitical and cultural aspects of the *bazaar*, see Khosravi 2008; Tutan 2008; Keshavarzian 2007). The fact that many *bazaaris*, who, as a social class, include both petty traders and rich wholesalers – and even local bankers – pay their religious dues to their local clergy, as implied by our interviewee, may be a reflection of their religiosity and indicate that the rules of *urf* play a significant role in how Iranians organize their socio-economic activities. Equally, it could be a function of the merchants' sociopolitical standing in the *bazaar* community. By paying their dues to the clergy and supporting the local mosques and religious schools, they continue to uphold their strong ties with the *ulama* and show solidarity towards their local community. The *ulama*, in return, provide them with a degree of protection against state interventions, and uphold their interests at the level of policy making.

Notwithstanding the religious and political coalition between *bazaar*, *ulama* and the mosque, we find tension in the relationship between *bazaaris* and the Islamic state. The Islamic government has undercut the political influence of the *bazaar*, – albeit unintentionally, as Keshavarzian (2007) maintains – and, as a result, the *bazaaris* hold differing views of the Islamic state. *Bazaaris* seldom protest publically against the Islamic government, but there are signs that sections of the *bazaar* are disenchanted with the government's economic policies. In July 2010, the Grand Bazaar in Tehran went on strike in protest against Ahmadinejad's attempt to raise their taxes (*Economist*, 29 July 2010). Moreover, *bazaaris* know only too well that Iranian states, whether Islamic or secular, are, historically speaking, short-term constructs. Unlike political regimes and governments, which rise only to fall from power, the local community and the local clergy remain a relatively stable social and economic support for the *bazaar* and its merchants.

Reflections on the Role of Trust

Much of what we have discussed in relation to Iranian law and the legal system, and even with respect to the attitude of Iranians to the legal profession as well as to the judiciary, revolves around the concept of trust. One needs to trust in the government and believe that the state apparatus is on the side of its citizens, which requires officials to honour their obligations to the people. One also needs to trust in the political institutions and believe that their exercise of authority is legitimate, which means that these institutions must show that they operate within the constitution and are, in practice, accountable under the law. This in turn requires trust in the law and its institutions – such as the police, the courts and the judiciary – and belief in the correct and impartial enforcement of the law.

Trust is the 'glue' that holds together a functionally differentiated modern society consisting of various groups with conflicting social interests and diverse identities. Trust reduces the complexity of the totality of human activities and communications by increasing the potential of social relations and institutions to cope with uncertainty, and, in doing so, it reduces the need for total control of all human actions and social developments (see Luhmann 1979). In complex modern societies, we need to trust in money, which functions as the communication medium of the economic system; truth, which validates the correctness of many of our social systems, including science, and the legitimacy of political power (Luhmann 1979: 55). It is, above all, the third medium of trust, i.e. trust as it is communicated through the authorities and state institutions, that is clearly lacking in Iranian society. Iranians do not trust their rulers – a fact which is not historically new – and therefore they do not submit to the laws imposed on them by their rulers. As our interviews show, this simple point has many socioculturally complex ramifications, which we hope to unfold gradually through further interviews.

CHAPTER 6

SOCIAL CLASS: INTERVIEWS WITH OTHER PROFESSIONALS

Reza Banakar

In this chapter, we present eight additional interviews that were conducted with different professionals in Tehran. These included interviews with four medical doctors, who carry out research on road traffic injuries and who have published numerous research papers in international journals; two insurance managers working at Tehran's largest insurance companies, who are familiar with car accidents; one psychologist; and one sociologist at Tehran University. Of these interviewees, only the psychologist was female. Our first medical doctor was a neurosurgeon with many years of experience in researching road traffic injuries in Iran. He explained that a while ago he and his colleagues noticed a decrease in the rate of traffic accidents, and decided to investigate this finding by conducting quantitative research based on a representative sample of 2,200 people living in Tehran. As part of this study, they asked the respondents if the traffic situation had recently improved or deteriorated. In all, 40 per cent replied that it had improved while 46 per cent answered that it had deteriorated, demonstrating the difficulties in drawing factual conclusions on the basis of this type of research, which focuses on people's attitudes and opinions about social events.

We reiterate that the interviews we carried out did not aim at extracting factual data on traffic behaviour, but are instead part of an inductive search for discursive patterns. When analysing these interviews, we look for the form of arguments and how the interviewees experience traffic and the law and how they describe other people's attitudes. Factually, we find too many contradictions between what the interviewees say about certain aspects of the traffic situation to allow us to generalize some of our findings. Below, for example, we see that one of the insurance agents states that the authorities refuse to acknowledge that there is a serious traffic problem in Tehran. In contrast, the sociologist argues that the traffic problem has gained societal proportions and forced itself on the authorities, who are struggling to find solutions to the issue. Similarly, we come across contradictory statements about the role of traffic penalties. While some of the interviewees think that the introduction of more severe traffic fines has had some perceptible impact on the behaviour of drivers, others dismiss it as ineffective. Nonetheless, the way in which they all discuss the fines and punishment suggests a general conception of how punishment and behavioural reform are related in Iranian culture. They also throw light on Iranians' attitudes towards the authorities.

Like the lawyers, this group of interviewees are clearly more at ease than our taxi drivers, and voice politically sensitive viewpoints, either directly or by analogy, by making suggestive statements. One of the doctors says that he is trying to be 'politically correct' when comparing people's attitudes to law and hospitals, explaining that:

Doctor 3:3:1: 'In the same way that they [Iranians] hope to avoid ending up in a hospital, they also hope not to come into contact with the law. They think that if they end up needing the law, they will have no control over what happens. [...] I am being politically correct here. [...] There are countless stories about mismanagement and the abuse of power within hospitals in Iran, and people often believe that the hospitals don't help them. People have the same attitude to the law.'

Some interviewees continue to express their views very generally, leaving it to the interviewer to interpret what they are alluding to. For example, one of the doctors we interviewed said that problems related to driving, law and traffic rules were caused by 'the totality of society', and went on to add that 'What people say and do are two different things, and in my opinion the gap between these two is very large in Iran' (Doctor 3:2:2, the complete quote is found on the opening page of Chapter One). Although the interviewee does not explain what he means by 'the totality of society', the context of the discussion suggests that he is alluding to the significance of Iran's prevailing form of sociopolitical organization. It is noteworthy that this doctor also points to the gap between injunctive and descriptive norms in Iranian society as a social problem. In contrast, other interviewees in this group express their views more openly. When we asked one of them why Iranians had progressed in many walks of life but not in their driving, he first paused in reflection for almost a minute before saying:

> Doctor 3:1:3: 'We have regressed in several walks of life since the revolution; we have morally regressed in our development. When it comes to following the law, we have probably taken a backward step in our progress. [. . .] Religious scholars have paid a great deal of attention to the exegesis of holy texts pertaining to minor bodily functions and needs, such as how to use the toilet correctly. They have published voluminously on such matters. But they have neglected to analyse the significance of recent developments such as driving or information for our social life. [. . .] In this country, you get the impression that all human progress has come to a halt. Well, this is a grave problem which we [. . .].'

The interviewee does not finish his sentence, and after another pause he moves on to talk about a different topic. Another interviewee stated that he regarded the President as the least law-abiding person in the country, and then he declared that he had better not say more on that topic. The openness of the doctors, when discussing political issues, is in stark contrast to the male taxi drivers' cautious and distrustful replies. One possible explanation is that the doctors' social standing provides a degree of protection against the arbitrary nature of the political apparatus. Another reason may be found in the interview situation itself, in that the doctors were more trustful of the interviewer than the taxi drivers were. It is, however, more likely that this group of interviewees can voice critical views as a partial result of their professional standing in Iranian society. As in other societies, Iranian professionals, such as doctors and lawyers, have traditionally belonged to the elite and have enjoyed a degree of political influence compared with other groups. This is of course only part of the explanation, as the political standing and sympathies of various social classes and groups in Iran is a highly complex topic, which we shall discuss below as part of our interview with a sociologist.

Heightened Individualism

The female psychologist that we interviewed was in her mid-thirties and worked as a family mediator. She regarded rising materialism and individualism among Iranians – an individualism that is clearly different from, and a challenge to, Iranians' personalism – as a cause of dispute between family members. In her professional work, she came across many disputes caused by family members not wishing to share their material belongings, such as their cars. This forced those who could afford it to buy their own car, thus, according to her, leading to growing traffic congestion on the motorways and streets.

> Psychologist 3:6:4: 'Iranians are becoming more individualistic, which means they are becoming more independent of their families. In times of economic hardship and soaring inflation, these individuals don't wish to share their possessions, things like their automobile which they have worked to pay for. You know, they don't even want to share their things with their own family members. This creates friction between them and disputes within families. That is why each person tries to get his or her own means of transport. The increased car ownership of independent individuals is fine, as long as the motorways and roads in Tehran can accommodate the increased volume of cars manufactured by the car industry. But unfortunately, this is not the case in Iran. Parts of Tehran have such heavy traffic congestion that [they look] more like a car park than a motorway or road.'

Our psychologist suggests that the family, as a traditional basis for collective care and security, a union of individuals, is undergoing transformation in the increasingly materialistic environment of Tehran. The materialism she refers to play a more significant role in large cities such as the capital than in more provincial towns and in rural areas, where the culture of consumerism is not as pervasive and the economy remains tied to agriculture rather than trade and technology. This draws attention to the uneven socio-economic development of Iran, wherein significant differences continue to mark the lifestyles of people depending on where they happen to live. The psychologist then went on to emphasize that driving was extremely stressful in Tehran, even though in her opinion it varied in different parts of the city. According to her, you would have a different experience, and be confronted with different traffic problems, depending on whether you were driving in the north or south of the city.

The sociologist, a university professor in his forties, also considered the role of individualism, although he viewed it from a different angle by describing the traffic as a Bourdieusian social field, with its own actors, forms of competition and stakes:

Sociologist 3:5:5: 'Coping with the traffic becomes a part of everyday life for people who live in cities such as Tehran. They have no alternative but to get used to it, and this eventually generates its own subculture and rules and customs. The traffic operates like a "social field," with its own mechanisms and rules [. . .], where drivers interact with each other. We also have rules which are introduced into the field from above by the traffic authorities. It doesn't mean that social actors follow the rules, though, because this field is one of struggle permeated by social conflicts and contradictions. Drivers have their own interests and conceptions of what is at "stake," and this often produces a situation wherein drivers behave as if they are fighting for their survival, and without consideration, reminding us of social Darwinism where every person tries to get his own way by resorting to sheer force. In this field everyone attends to his or her own immediate interests in the traffic. [. . .] Not only does the field compel people to misbehave and break the laws, but it also makes them disregard moral codes.'

In this social field, the sociologist points out, the authorities and their traffic rules also play an important role. In fact, the authorities become one of the 'actors' competing for 'stakes'. However, it is not their rules or the need to uphold the laws of traffic which is at stake, but whether one can safeguard one's own personal interest. In this way, the traffic authorities are not representatives of the public interest but are one among many actors struggling for a stake in the field of traffic. This sociological description of traffic is in line with the lawyers' understanding of traffic chaos in Iran in terms of disregard for rights and obligations. While the lawyers viewed it normatively, the sociologist viewed it descriptively, albeit in social-theoretical terms. We find a similar description of traffic behaviour in our interview with the third medical doctor, who posited that two main rules governed Iranians' driving:

> Doctor 3:3:6: 'The first rule is called "fill in the gap," which means you simply drive forward in the traffic jam, if you can, you know, and into any empty space in front of you. The second rule is called "anything goes" and is used when following the first rule. It means that you may drive in any way you like, as long as you do not have an accident or damage your car. Most people in traffic behave individualistically and have one thing in mind: to get ahead of the other cars. How you do it doesn't actually matter, and when you do it, you don't feel bad about it, if nothing bad has happened and no one's been hurt.'

According to this interviewee, the unspoken rules of driving generate the perception of the 'skilful driver' as a person who can get ahead of other drivers in the traffic without an accident, which means without damaging *his* or *her* car. Although this doctor did not use the concept of *zerang*, he was nevertheless thinking in terms of the 'smart' individual: the one who gets away with breaking the rules. Although the context of the discussions indicates that the doctor does not approve of these 'smart' individuals, he nevertheless describes them in a matter-of-fact tone. In other words, although the context is critical of 'smart' people, his tone suggests an acceptance of their behaviour as a part of life.

Penalties and Punishment

According to the sociologist, attempts to reform social behaviour by introducing fines and the threat of sanctions only aggravate Iranians. Penalties fail to produce the desired effect, because ordinary Iranians do not see the police as representing their interests; instead, they see 'the police as an arm of the state, which is only interested in its own survival'

(3:5:7). Perhaps not unexpectedly, he also turned to the role of education as the way to tackle the traffic problem. Moreover, without using the notion of *farahang-sazi* he combines the role of culture and education:

> Sociologist 3:5:8: 'Each type of activity, such as driving, has its own culture. We need education to realise people's ability. But education works only if people understand how they personally benefit from what you are trying to teach them. It isn't enough to tell them that following the traffic rules is in the public interest.'

The psychologist argued, along the same lines, that increased fines had had an effect on drivers' behaviour, but that drivers needed to understand why it was vital to behave differently and to respect other people's rights, if we were to improve the traffic situation. Otherwise, drivers would follow the rules as long as they were in view of a traffic camera or they thought that traffic police were watching them:

> Psychologist 3:6:9: 'I think when something is forced on us without explanation, like when traffic fines are increased to change behaviour, without telling people why they should change their ways, then people react negatively. You can never reform people's behaviour by forcing them to follow blindly; and, mind you, nobody should be forced in that way. In principle, when you don't know why you are doing something, you won't be able to do it properly and satisfactorily. When you introduce strict penalties for traffic offences, you force drivers to follow the rules, but if they don't know or share your rationale, they won't do it with conviction and wouldn't understand why they needed, for instance, to stop at the pedestrian crossings. They don't consider that it might happen they too may be in the position of a pedestrian one day and might like drivers to respect their rights. We see that the heavy fines have forced people to follow the rules, but this obedience is not the result of their awareness and agreement. In our country, mutual respect is still not valued, and we can't put ourselves in other people's shoes.'

In the above quote, the psychologist makes a distinction between the driver (*savareh*) and the pedestrian (*piyadeh*), echoing a Persian proverb that 'the rider is oblivious to the plight of those who travel on foot'. But why is it so difficult for the driver of the car to imagine that one day he or she might be in the same position as the pedestrian? We shall return to this question in the coming chapters, where one of the female taxi drivers states that she stops at zebra crossings because the pedestrians could be members of her family trying to cross the road. However, here we should mention that the distinction between *piyadeh* and *savareh* can also refer to disparity in terms of wealth, and, ultimately, to social class and standing, which are deeply rooted in Iranians' understanding of how the individual is related to society. References to income and wealth were present in the previous interviews, where, for example, the male taxi drivers discussed traffic penalties. The first car-insurance agent repeats what many taxi drivers said in respect to the introduction of more severe traffic fines:

> Insurance agent 3:7:10: 'If we divide the drivers into three groups of 1) low income, 2) middle class and 3) wealthy drivers, in my opinion it has no effect on the wealthy drivers. It had some effect on the low-income drivers, forcing them to be more cautious.'

The second insurance agent had a different take on the role of the new fines, suggesting that official statistics had shown a decrease in the rate of accidents:

> Insurance agent 3:8:11: 'The increase in penalties, the campaign of impounding vehicles and the tightening up of the restrictions on speeding on the roads and motorways has slightly reduced the rate of damage to cars. According to annual official statistics, fatal car accidents have been reduced due to the increase in penalties.'

The two social scientists were concerned about the legitimacy of the fines and penalties in general, pointing out that people must understand (i.e. gain awareness, or *agahi*) about why they are being penalized; otherwise, they will refuse to change their driving habits. The two insurance officers expressed their views on the new penalties differently – one suggesting that they had had some effect on drivers with low incomes, the other arguing that they had had a 'significant' impact. We see here that the way in which penalties are viewed and experienced varies from group to group. The social scientists are concerned with the legitimacy of penalties and therefore take a potentially normative stance. The second insurance agent, who stated that the fines had had a 'significant' impact, could also be expressing a normative view in the sense that he hopes that fines will introduce new norms. Otherwise, as he points out, the only result of the new fines is a *slight* reduction in the damage reported to insurance firms.

Gender

In the first three sets of interviews – those with the male taxi drivers, the lawyers and the other professionals – the role of gender was neglected. Although we were aware of the central part played by gender differences in Iranian society, and that some of the topics such as *diyah* and *urf* that we discussed in the previous chapters do indeed have important gender dimensions, their significance was not expounded upon during our initial interviews. This eventually led us to interview women taxi drivers in Tehran, who placed gender at the top of our research agenda (see the next chapter). Nevertheless, discussions relating to gender and driving surfaced occasionally in other interviews. For example, in the course of her interview, the psychologist stated that women were harassed in traffic by male drivers, which in turn caused accidents:

> Psychologist 3:6:12: 'When a young woman is behind the wheel we see that most men would like to harass her. [. . .] Admittedly, this is on the decrease, and seeing women drivers has been somewhat normalised.'

Also, one of our female lawyers stated that women drivers were seen and treated differently in traffic because they were women (see interview 2:9:17, page 92). Gender came up in the interview with the second insurance agent (a 30-year-old man) in connection with the role of law and justice:

> 3:8:13: 'Law and justice should go hand in hand, but unfortunately this is not what happens in Iran. Law without justice is meaningless, although there is no justice in our laws in Iran. For example, in many cases laws confer rights on men or

fathers but not on women or mothers. In matrimonial contexts, men enjoy legal privileges which are denied women.'

The first doctor we interviewed also referred to gender, albeit in passing, and suggested that women's driving was different to men's, without explaining in which way. The third doctor discussed gender briefly in connection with a large-scale study that he had conducted in Tehran, which, amongst other things, mapped patterns of car ownership and use. According to his study, women owned only 1 per cent of motorbikes but 30 per cent of automobiles in the city.

The Law

Most of those who were interviewed in this section regarded parliament, the government and other authorities as the primary source of law. Only one of the doctors stood out as the exception, by stating that the highest source of legal authority was the *Velayt-e-Faghih* (the Supreme Leader) and then the president. Another doctor we interviewed dismissed both the holy scriptures and the constitution as sources of law:

> Doctor 3:3:14: 'I suppose those who are religious would regard the Quran as the primary source of law. [He then laughs ironically and adds:] But I haven't come across anyone who takes the Constitution as the primary source of law, even though I suppose some lawyers might mention the Constitution [he laughs again].'

This is yet another example of cautiously expressing politically sensitive views. In this case, the interviewee does not say what he personally believes to be the source of law, and instead he tells us what some religious people believe, before suggesting that the constitution is not a source of law even though some lawyers might treat it as such.

According to the fourth doctor, who was deeply concerned with the spread of immoral anti-Islamic culture, 'fidelity to the law [had] decreased', and there [were] groups of people who would circumvent the law, if and where they [could]' (3:4:15). The second insurance agent that we interviewed stated that the government and the police were the primary sources of the law in Iran, and then he went on to add:

Insurance agent 3:8:16: 'However, I often wonder why we feel afraid of the police instead of feeling secure.'

Although our interviewees did not use the notion of 'trust' in their replies, much of their concern can be expressed in terms of trust, or lack thereof, in authorities, professional bodies and social institutions such as the law. In 3:3:1, quoted above, one of the doctors compared people's attitudes to law and hospitals, explaining that in the same way as they avoided hospitals, where they believed mismanagement was widespread, they also avoided the legal system. A similar latent concern with trust was expressed by the (female) psychologist:

Psychologist: 3:6:17: 'Sitting in a taxi, you hear passengers talking spontaneously to each other about all sorts of things [...]. That is where you hear that people are dissatisfied with the type of laws which are made in Iran. They recognise that there are laws, but they are unwilling to follow them, because they think that the laws are either not enforced or, when they are enforced, they are not enforced to protect their rights. People do not have a positive attitude towards the law and the legal system, because they feel that it is driven by favouritism and nepotism [...]. In principle, the feeling in our society is that there are no laws.'

Here, the psychologist echoes the interviewees in the pilot study, who complained about 'lawlessness'. As regards the law, the sociologist distinguished between people's attitude to the law and their views of lawmakers. According to him, although Iranians generally have a favourable view of the law, they do not have a positive view of law makers, who, they feel, break the law with impunity:

Sociologist: 3:5:18: 'Since most social actors regard themselves as rational beings, they view the law positively and define themselves as law-abiding. [...] However, they might have views on those who make the laws. Traffic rules exist as part of general laws, and most people obey them if they recognise them as legitimate. [...] One issue which affects the public's attitude in this respect is discrimination in law enforcement. In traffic, you often see that official cars – it can be the traffic police itself – breaking traffic rules without being stopped or fined. This overt disregard of the law by officials negatively influences the ordinary people's perception of the law. My point is that law in itself has very little impact on behaviour. How it is enforced is, on the other hand, decisive and determines if people respect it. [...] We need to start educating people at school and do *farhang-sazi*.'

In short, according to the sociologist, you cannot respect laws, whether traffic or criminal laws, if those who make them and are responsible for their enforcement do not respect and follow them accordingly. The first insurance agent also argued along the same lines, stating that 'generally speaking, the law is not properly enforced, and where the law is not correctly enforced, we always find people who disregard it'.

Finally, a connection is made between law enforcement and corruption:

Doctor 3:1:19: 'We should distinguish between the law and the enforcement of the law. One of the research projects I was keen to set up, and it was first approved but then blocked, concerned factors which hinder the effective application of laws. What factors hinder the police's enforcement of the law? We asked the police why they do not enforce the law effectively and uniformly. We made an initial investigation and discussed it with them. The police meant that sometimes they did not enforce the law because they felt threatened. Fining some drivers might lead to physical confrontation. Secondly, some traffic offenders might be "connected," and if the police stopped them, the officer might be reprimanded and find himself transferred to some remote backwater of southern Iran. If these were the only causes, we could still do something about the problem. But there is more [...]. The police officer I was speaking with said to me, "Imagine there is another factor concerning corruption. Would you dare take it up and publish that corruption was a reason for poor enforcement of the laws?"'

This doctor suggests that corruption is one of the most important factors affecting the enforcement of traffic laws. However, it cannot be discussed publicly or researched openly. Although some of the interviewees in Tehran referred indirectly to corruption, in the informal discussions we had with various people it was mentioned regularly. Moreover, in two interviews conducted in Shiraz, corruption was discussed openly:

Taxi driver from Shiraz 5:3:20: 'The police do intervene and stop drivers who break the law. But what takes place between the traffic police and offenders is not as straightforward as you might expect, because people always negotiate these things on the spot. For example, if you are stopped for an offence which costs, say, a 40,000 Toman fine, you might be able to negotiate a lesser fine, say 20,000 Tomans, if you hand cash to the officer in charge rather than deposit it later into their account. The police will let you off the hook.'

A farmer, who lives in Shiraz and drives to work on the outskirts of the city in his old van every day, described his recent encounter with the traffic police in similar terms:

Farmer from Shiraz: 5:3:21: 'Last week, when I was driving to work, I was stopped by a traffic police officer for no reason. I asked him what the problem was. He replied that he had stopped me because I was eating while driving and my stop-light didn't work. The fine for these two offences came to 120,000 Tomans (about £40). I told him that I couldn't pay him such a fine and that it was more than what I would earn in one day. I put my hands up and admitted that I was eating a sandwich, and I also explained to him that I was a farmer on the way to work and I was eating behind the wheel because I hadn't had the time to have my breakfast that morning. But my lights worked fine. I said we can test them. The officer got very aggressive and shouted that I should stop the nonsense and instead show him my car registration. I went back to the car and fetched the registration. I put 20,000 (about £5) in the registration book and handed it to him. I thought he would be discreet about it, but once he saw the money he said, "You're bloody pathetic, aren't you? Your fine is 120,000 Tomans and you want to give me 20,000?" I said I didn't have any more money on me, and he replied, "Well in that case, you have to pay

120,000, don't you?" In the end, I took out my wallet and gave him another 20,000 and he let me off because he could see that it was all that I had on me.'

The farmer meant that the traffic police had stopped him arbitrarily (the part about his stoplight not working, according to him, was fiction), and the aim of this exercise was to 'shake him down'; in fact, he was not upset about it and told the story as if he were describing a game in which the two participants normally indulged. Not only does there seem to be tolerance towards petty corruption of this kind, but there is also a tacit understanding thereof because, as the taxi driver in Shiraz pointed out, people know that traffic officers are poorly paid.

The two aforementioned accounts of corruption are from Shiraz and not Tehran, and once again we need to emphasize that they are not produced here as factual data or evidence of police exploitation in Iran. However, they do exemplify the way in which many Iranians talk about system corruption and law enforcement. It should also be reiterated here that despite a great deal of effort made on our part, we did not receive permission to interview a traffic-police officer.

Arbitrariness and *Estebdād*

Corruption within the legal system and the arbitrary enforcement of the law are not necessarily the same thing, although both have a negative bearing on whether the citizenry trusts the law and legal-system officials. For example, one of the doctors explained that he could influence the way in which he was treated by using his social status. When he was asked how laws were enforced, he replied:

3:1:22: 'I can only tell you about my personal experience of law enforcement. It has happened on a number of occasions that the traffic police have stopped me for various offences, and each time I have told them that I am Doctor X and they back off. One time, a police officer told me that he couldn't care less, but once I took out my ID, he let me go.'

He then went on to argue that in order to improve the enforcement of the law, one needed to monitor the police's work. Needless to say, policing the police is somewhat problematic, but he meant that it would improve the way in which they work:

> 3:1:23: 'If we could introduce a system, where our police authorities who fail in carrying out of their professional duties know that they will be disciplined, then law enforcement will improve.'

The sociologist argued that, in his opinion, the majority of Iranians were in favour of the law in the same way that they endorse moral codes of behaviour (his notion of law is probably broad and includes *urf*). The problem is that there is a massive difference between what Iranians define as their moral standards of behaviour and how they behave in practice. In Iran we are confronted with the phenomenon of 'law avoidance', whereby people evade the law because they feel a considerable distance between themselves and the authorities.

> Sociologist 3:5:24: 'In societies where there is *estebdād* and the culture of *estebdād* prevails, we also find an aversion to the law. In such societies, people do not see the police as part of society – they see it as the representative of the state. [. . .] In the context of our society, any form of organisation which is linked to the state is automatically mistrusted, because people believe that the state operates only to ensure its own interests and security.'

He finally explains that different groups of people, depending on their resources and social background, resolve their disputes differently, in that they might mobilize their family and friends or alternatively turn directly to the police as representatives of the legal system; traditionally minded people tend to use the former method of dispute resolution, while the middle classes prefer the latter. But if their experience of state law and its institutions is negative – for example, if it takes too long or costs too much – or one has to bribe officials to get one's case processed, then one either accepts it for what it is or tries to find an alternative solution.

The third doctor did not refer to *estebdād* as such, but in an indirect way he emphasized the relationship between law's legitimacy and people's willingness to obey the law – interestingly enough, in reference to the 'social contract', which was also invoked by the lawyers:

Doctor 3:3:25: 'In Western democracies, laws are viewed as legitimate because they are based on social contracts with the people. To pass a red light is a breach of the law but also the breach of a social contract, and therefore it is an offence which is viewed disapprovingly. [...] In contrast, in societies which are ideologically [...] governed, the force of law has a difference source than a social contract with the people. When ideology operates above the law and at a different level [...], when it does not prohibit driving through a red traffic light, and according to the driver's own calculations there are no reasons for respecting the red light, then the result becomes a widespread disregard of the traffic light system.'

The 'ideology' concept is used by the interviewee to refer to the dominant political system in Iran, which, according to him, sits in contrast to Western democratic systems, wherein laws are based on a social contract with the citizenry. What is suggested here is that Iran's political system operates above the law.

Social Classes and Spaces

Most of the interviewees suggested that the traffic problem and the flow of the traffic vary in different parts of Tehran and during different hours of the day. One of the car-insurance agents that we interviewed described traffic in terms of time and space, but also suggested that the north and the west of the city provide different spaces compared to the rest of the municipal area:

Insurance agent 3:7:26: 'At different times of the day, such as during the rush-hours, different parts of Tehran [...] experience heavy traffic [...], but the traffic towards the west of Tehran feels less, considering the number of cars and [because of the] large streets which provide more space for the cars. I don't get stuck in a traffic jam when going towards these places at any time, but the centre is congested in the morning and afternoon. The streets in the north of the city will have traffic in the evening. There is a traffic jam every Thursday afternoon in Tehran. Indeed, Tehran is paralysed at these times, and you would do better getting around

on foot than trying to drive. However, they [the authorities] say
that there is no problem with traffic jams.'

The insurance agent did not refer to south Tehran, perhaps because he
never drives that way. In contrast, the sociologist referred to it
repeatedly. According to him, those religious groups who predominantly support the Islamic regime live in south Tehran, an area where the
working classes have traditionally lived (this is, however, not quite
accurate),[1] The Westernized portion of the city's population, on the
other hand, lives in north and west Tehran, where wealthy Tehranis have
always lived. In that sense, different sociopolitical groups occupy
separate spaces within the same city. Similar spatial segregation along
political lines can be seen in most other Iranian cities. Interestingly
enough, the traffic situation and driving habits in the capital can
deteriorate as one drives from the north to the south:

Insurance agent 3:7:27: 'If you compare the driving habits in
Tehran with other cities in Iran, you are bound to notice a
significant difference. Time after time I have heard visitors from
other cities saying that it is easier to drive in Tehran than in other
cities, because people in Tehran, relatively speaking, pay more
attention to the traffic rules. [...] I think that improving the
traffic and driving requires time, and also that people experience a
different type of driving behaviour. Also, if you compare various
parts of Tehran, you will notice that people drive differently in
different parts. Even social class has an impact on their driving
habits and how they behave in the traffic. [...] However, how
people behave generally in the traffic is often reflective of what is
going on in society at a different level. Sometimes the individual's
actions, disregard for the law and so on have their roots elsewhere.
They can mirror people's attitudes and reactions to other
developments in other fields, ranging from the economy and
politics to the social and cultural aspects of society.'

The sociologist also referred to cars as an indicator of income and social
class, and suggested that sometimes the traffic police (who belong to the
lower income group) target people who are driving certain types of cars.
The third doctor also expressed a similar idea:

Doctor 3:3:28: 'If we go back 25 to 30 years, owning a car was an indicator of your social status. [...] to own a car gradually became a necessity irrespective of your social class. [...] Now car ownership has spread, and the majority of those who drive professionally belong to socially disadvantaged groups with a different attitude to traffic and driving. Since they are the majority of drivers in the street, they leave their cultural mark on driving.'

The doctor is suggesting that socially disadvantaged groups, the members of which often live in south Tehran and are often religious, drive more carelessly than the more Westernized section of the population, which lives in the north of the city. Let us refer back to our interviews with one of the taxi drivers, who also made the distinction between northern and southern Tehran but meant that drink-driving incidents were more frequent in the north. The point made here is that our interviews, sooner or later, all turned to the problematic issue of social class and politics, or the income disparity between different sections of society.

Reflections on Social Class

Ongoing conflicts between the different sections of Iranian society, who live in different parts of the country's cities and behave differently, were discussed in every interview that we conducted. These conflicts were expressed in terms of income disparity (in relation to more severe traffic fines) or the tension between the 'nouveau riche' (who are immune to increased traffic penalties) and the ordinary hard-working masses, who are hit hard by various policy measures. Alternatively, we find frequent references to illegitimate power disparity (the arbitrary exercise of legal authority) and corruption – and, as some of our interviewees put it, certain people are simply 'above the law'. Yet another division exists between the city dwellers and 'peasants' from the rural areas, who have no culture but apparently do have money. More importantly, there is a division between supporters of the Islamic regime and others (this is a highly fragmented and diverse, but large, group of people with different backgrounds, beliefs and visions of the future). This is not necessarily the same as the separation between religious and secular groups, or the conflict between the traditionalists and modernists, which we shall discuss in Chapter Nine.

Prior to the revolution, class divisions were somewhat more distinct: the modernist section of society came predominantly from the wealthy and educated middle classes, while the traditionalists came predominantly from the economically disadvantaged parts of society. However, even at this time, there was not a clear-cut distinction, because the *bazaaris* (local merchants and traders) were traditionalists and politically conservative, but they were also wealthy, relatively well educated and politically influential at the community level. This means that class divisions were never based on wealth and education alone, and were defined also in terms of lifestyle and the role that religion plays in people's everyday life. Since the revolution, not only have class divisions not disappeared, but, as our interviewees pointed out time and again, they have also been employed (perhaps intentionally) as a constant source of social tension in society, which sets groups of people up against each other. One main difference between the periods just before and after the revolution is reflected in the politicization of religion and, by extension, the politicization of gender, which will be the focus of the next chapter. Social classes, which are a function of the economic relations and power structures in Iranian society, are now redefined in terms of religion and loyalty to the Islamic regime.

The divisions that we encountered are not new, and Iranian society has always been deeply divided along the lines of social class and status – a point reflected in the old distinction made between *piyadeh* (the pedestrian) and *savareh* (the rider), and perhaps, in more modern times, between *balaieh shahr*, or the upper part of the city where the wealthy live (the north), and *payineh shahr*, or the lower part of the city (the south and the east Tehran) where the poor and the working classes have traditionally lived. In contemporary Iran, these divisions take more complex forms as the traditional understanding of social status and class conflates with other factors such as political influence, religiosity, gender, wealth and income. Our interviews show that these sociopolitical and economic divisions have not been removed as a result of the Islamic Revolution, but been redefined in ideological terms that exacerbate the contrast between the 'haves' and the 'have-nots'.

CHAPTER 7

GENDER AND DOMINATION: INTERVIEWS WITH FEMALE TAXI DRIVERS

Reza Banakar and Behnoosh Payvar

'Ladies,' she [the foreign reporter] said, 'what would you say is your main motivation for choosing this career?'

Mrs Elahi [a sixty-year old taxi driver] immediately answered, 'Money, obviously.'

The reporter looked at her ... as if she had not given the appropriate answer and said, 'I really need more elaborate answers for my report. I have to...'

Mrs Elahi said, 'What do you want us to say? To lie?'

The reporter got closer to Mrs Elahi ... and ... said: 'You live in a country where you are denied many of the basic rights awarded to women. Yet you have taken up a profession that is generally considered a masculine occupation.'

'Well, you really fail to appreciate who we are,' said Mrs Elahi, 'and clearly you don't think much of us ... You come from a country where women are astronauts and pilots and you still think that it's amazing that we drive cars for a living!' And then she said, 'Listen, lady. You can ask as much as you like, but my motivation is still money ...'

(Internet blog describing a foreign journalist's interview with a group of female cabbies in Tehran)[1]

Introduction: A Typically Iranian Contradiction

Iran's first taxi company dedicated to driving 'female passengers only' was launched in the holy city of Qom in 2002, followed by the first radio-operated taxi service for women in Tehran in December 2005. Similar companies offering taxi services by women for women soon established in most large cities in the country. Women taxi drivers steering their green cars in the chaos of the traffic-congested streets of Tehran remain a suprising sight in the gender-segregated context of the Islamic Republic, thus creating contradictory messages.[2] Driving taxis might not be empowering women in the sense of ensuring their attainment of equal rights in law, but it certainly does not constrain their presence in the public sphere. It also acknowledges them as economically independent actors. Moreover, one cannot but wonder how Iranian women have succeeded in breaking into the taxi business, which is a male-dominated occupation in every country. Finally, although Iranian law allows women to drive any type of vehicle, custom and culture do not quite approve of them driving taxis. In that sense, women taxi drivers challenge not only a male-dominated occupation but also mainstream social norms and the cultural values of their society. To have female taxi drivers in the midst of a society preoccupied with gender segregation, paradoxical as it might sound to outsiders, is nevertheless a typically Iranian thing to do. The sight of women taxi drivers in Iran is an important sociocultural sign, albeit one which does not lend itself to simple interpretations. This chapter hopes to throw some light on this typically Iranian paradox, which exemplifies how modern socio-economic conditions merge with custom and tradition in a historical context.

Twelve interviews were arranged and carried out with women taxi drivers at the Banovan (Women's) Taxi Service in Tehran in November 2012, using semi-structured questions similar to those that we employed when interviewing their male counterparts. In addition to those questions that we put to the male cabbies, we also asked the following of the female taxi drivers: What does it mean to be a woman within a profession which has traditionally been dominated by men? How do people generally regard women taxi drivers? How do male taxi drivers regard you? This chapter will start by discussing how gender, class and social conflicts are employed in a revolutionary context in order to maintain a form of social control that, in turn, upholds the Islamic regime in Iran. We shall then account for some of the views expressed by female taxi drivers in respect of the themes we have already discussed in other chapters, but we shall also pinpoint issues that did not arise in other interviews. The chapter concludes by comparing the interviews between male and female taxi drivers, before we then reflect on their differences and similarities.

Class and Gender Conflicts in Iranian Society

One of our first woman interviewees emphasized that driving a taxi was not a 'good' job stating: 'I am not satisfied with my work and do it only because I have to' (4:2:1). Male taxi drivers would readily admit that their job was stressful and demanding, but they would not acknowledge that they drove a taxi because they had to. The phrase 'taxi driving isn't a good job' can suggest that it involves hard and stressful work, but it can also imply that it is not a socially *appropriate* occupation for a woman. For example, our second interviewee said that she works as a driver not because she wants to but because she has no other alternative. Others stated that 'in men's opinion, cabbies [were] not worthy of respect' and seen as *bi-shakhsiyat*, or lacking in self-respect (4:8:2); it was 'not a proper job' and taxed you both physically and mentally (4:2:3).

> 4:11:4: 'Working as a cabbie is very difficult. It's men's work. It's a male work environment. People look down on you. No matter how you look at it, it doesn't fit a woman. But we have to do it, if we want to make a living.'

This should not be interpreted to mean that all the women cabbies interviewed disliked their job. Several of the interviewees said that they 'loved driving', and at least one of them (interviewee 7) categorically stated that she had always wanted to be a cab driver. However, she also added that she liked her job because it gave her economic independence, enabled her to stand on her own feet and provide for her family. Another interviewee, who had moved to Tehran from the provinces, asked us specifically not to use her name in our study because her family did not know that she was working as a taxi driver and not all her family members would approve if they found out.

4:6:5: I need to tell you something, before we start. My family doesn't know I am working. People treat you differently if they find out that you are working. In the capital [Tehran], it is different. You are not going to use my name, are you?'

This interviewee had a university degree in Italian, but could not find a teaching position and had thus had to become a taxi driver. One of her brothers disapproved of her becoming a cabbie, but her husband supported her and signed the relevant paperwork so that she could obtain a taxi licence. The next interviewee expresses a rather different view. She starts by saying that Iranians' view of women taxi drivers appears to be rather mixed, and she goes on to add:

4:3:6: 'Some people think that it is great that women are allowed to drive taxis. But there are also those who have a different view of it, you know what I mean. [...] Some people look down on taxi driving. But I like driving a taxi.'

She had previously worked as a librarian but changed her job when her husband, who is an accountant, asked her to do so. Nonetheless, she thinks that she is treated unfairly because, at the age of 53, she has to make a living by driving a cab in the busy streets of the city. Similarly, another interviewee, with a university degree in pedagogics, who had become a cabbie, stated that she had chosen to work as a taxi driver because she likes it. The problem is that many people look down on what she does because she is working in a male-dominated occupation:

4:4:7: 'Many people think that I must be desperate to work as a taxi driver. [...] It takes time before they can accept that a woman can decide for herself and choose to become a taxi driver because she likes it.'

To give another example, one of the taxi drivers, who had studied in England and Germany and spoke several languages, said:

4:9:8: 'People who meet me for the first time are flabbergasted. They ask, "Are you sure you are a taxi driver?" Because your mannerisms and the way you speak do not fit a taxi driver's.'

This interviewee was suggesting that working as a taxi driver was not befitting an educated lady such as herself. Later she added that working as a cabbie had affected her femininity and transformed her from a respectful lady into a rude and ill-mannered person. Such discussions have a bearing on some of the points raised by other interviewees regarding the culture of driving and the class tension that characterizes how Iranian society has been organized as an economically divided and socioculturally segregated space.

One of the doctors that we interviewed argued that the use of the automobile had spread across all social classes, and as a result there were now more people belonging to 'lower' social classes driving than there were middle-class people. Consequently, driving habits had become heavily influenced by the culture and customs of the 'lower' classes. An elitist world view, which assumes that the middle classes behave 'correctly' while others belonging to the 'lower' classes behave poorly, is lurking just under the surface of these types of views. Similar ideas were expressed by a number of people, including male taxi drivers, who complained about people from rural areas who lacked culture and drove their cars like they rode their donkeys. Also, female drivers complained about migrant 'peasants':

> 4:9:9: 'I dislike Tehran; few Tehranis are left in this city. There are too many peasants here turning it into a madhouse [...]. Tehran is the only place where I have seen people driving in the traffic in reverse gear and park in forward gear. It was the same during the Shah's time.'

Another interviewee talks at some length about the differences between Tehran and rural areas, saying that 'they' (incomers from the provinces) have no discipline or culture:

> 4:10:10: 'They bring their disorder and chaos to the city when they drive their cars here. You might have heard what people ask them: "Did you sell your cows to buy a car?" They can't talk properly but drive an expensive car. [...] They drive carelessly while talking on their mobiles. They can drive like this back home, but they shouldn't be allowed to behave this way here. They cause disorder.'

This interviewee is clearly bothered by the fact that people from rural areas have the resources to buy and drive expensive cars. Incidentally, we should add that there is no factual basis to any of her concerns or her claim about 'peasants' driving expensive cars. At the same time, her attitude towards people from the provinces demonstrates the cultural divide between Tehran and other Iranian cities. Here is another example:

> 4:1:11: 'I can drive in Tehran despite all the difficulties, but not in other cities. [The interviewer asks why?] Because, when they drive a car, they think they are riding a donkey. They don't use the indicator when they want to turn and they can turn in front of you at any time without warning. They drive atrociously in cities outside Tehran, even though their traffic is not as heavy as ours.'

However, it was often in relation to the limited impact of penalties – whereby the interviewees argued that more severe fines only penalized those who earned little, but they had no effect on the rich – that issues related to wealth and income disparity were voiced. To make matters slightly more complicated, references to the 'rich' and the 'wealthy' could refer to the 'new rich', which is a different group to the traditional middle classes in Iran:

> 4:1:12: 'During the Shah's time, one could distinguish between the educated and uneducated people. The educated had proper manners. But today, a guy who looks educated and drives a decent car steps out of his car and showers you with insults. He thinks he can do that because you are a woman taxi driver.'

Again, we must reiterate that the focus of our analysis is not on the factual accuracy of the statements made by the interviewees but on how they narrate their experiences by employing various images, ideas and concepts. What is not captured in this analysis is the cultural hybridity that characterizes a metropolitan city such as Tehran, where religious beliefs, modernist and secularist views, as well as traditional Iranian values, are moulded and employed by people to create and recreate their everyday reality.

Education, Culture and Personalism

Notwithstanding social factors such as class, gender and political differences – all of which divide up Iranian society into separate, but highly fluid, camps – we find at least one belief that brings all our interviewees together, irrespective of gender or class. It is the belief in the role of education in reforming social conditions, and *farhang-sazi* as the primary method through which improvements are to be realized. This latter conviction was shared by female taxi drivers:

> 4:4:13: 'In the face of the deteriorating traffic situation and increasing number of cars, they should have carried out a proper *farhang-sazi*. They should have addressed it by tackling its root causes. I have only recently seen that they are teaching children at school about how to behave in the traffic. [...] Women got into driving very quickly, without creating a cultural basis for it so that ordinary people accept women drivers. Driving is much more than just pressing the gas pedal and changing the gears.'

The above quotation makes references to 'they' several times. This can be found in many other interviews that we conducted: 'they' should have carried out *farhang-sazi*, or 'they' do not follow the laws that 'they' introduce. In the context of the discussions, it is clear that 'they' refers to the authorities, although at the same time it is a highly ambiguous way of referring to those in charge. There are at least two related reasons for this way of referring to the State, the government, the local council, the police or other officials. One is that by not clearly mentioning those in power, one tones down the criticism – it is always unclear who, ultimately, is being criticized for the mismanagement of traffic and other problems in the country. The other is that it marks the distance that ordinary people experience in their relationship with their rulers – 'they' are a separate group who live a different life, almost on another planet.

The same belief in the force of education, which was identified in the previous interviews, is also voiced by women drivers:

> 4:10:14: 'Tehran's traffic problem is all about lack of culture (*bi-farhangi*); otherwise, there is nothing wrong with the streets. But they drive without culture. You just saw an example of it when the

car turned in front of us without first indicating. Taxis cause the traffic because they do whatever they like. They can stop where they like to pick up passengers. It is lack of culture. Pedestrians walk two metres in the road and taxis stop where they stand. [...] The culture of both passengers and those who carry them must be improved. We must have special classes to educate taxi drivers.'

We shall return to this belief in education in Chapter Eight, but for now it suffices to point out in passing that it may be attributed to the clerical regime's commitment to what Axworthy (2013: 398) calls 'education as a good in itself and a good for all, irrespective of its social or political effects'. Also, in the interviews with women drivers we find the same discursive patterns as those identified in other interviews regarding 'the culture of driving'. In the following quote, we see once again how 'the culture of driving', or lack thereof, is linked to other factors such as Iranian personalism, but also to gender:

4:12:15: 'The culture of driving hasn't found its place in our society. If drivers could learn to respect each other, we could all drive where we are going more easily. But they don't, because they are such selfish people. Especially men treat women drivers badly. They can't accept women drivers, [and so they] turn in front of them and refuse to give way [...]. Men say that women can't drive, whereas women are careful drivers. [...] When it comes to driving we are all selfish; only say me, me, me.'

Several women referred to family in their interviews, pointing out that careless driving could be traced back to drivers' 'family upbringing'. Two of the drivers explained that they respect the rights of pedestrians because the latter could be their own family members crossing the road.

4:7:16: 'I always respect pedestrians. I put myself in their shoes; they might be my mother or sister.'

The above reveals that women taxi drivers think in terms of family, but seen from a different angle it supports the idea that Iranians can care about others only in so far as they are family members. Others refer to family as the place where people learn a range of different social competencies –

from driving and respecting the law, to how to treat women. When the second female-driver interviewee was asked what came to her mind when she heard the word 'law', she said, 'family, school, pedestrian, driver [. . .]. We wouldn't have a problem if we followed the law.'

Penalties

At first glance, the women taxi drivers appear to be more positively inclined towards more severe penalties. Several women stated that the fines had had a positive effect on the traffic, although they had not necessarily improved people's driving. 'I used to drive recklessly myself,' one said laughing, 'but not since they introduced the new fines.' (4:5:17). Another argued that penalties worked better than using other measures, such as increasing the price of petrol, because 'seventy per cent of Iranians [would] not pay heed to laws unless they fear the consequences' (4:9:18). Yet another female taxi driver stated that the introduction of new fines had been an excellent idea, and that if it was up to her she would increase them tenfold. 'Fines bite, especially the stingy person's pockets', she said, adding, 'those, who although might not care for life and limb of pedestrians or other drivers, care about their money' (4:1:19). By contrast, a 52-year-old woman driver stated that the recent penalties had had no effect on the traffic or the traffic behaviour. According to her, 'the fines only hit people who don't have the money to pay them. They have no effect on wealthy drivers.'

> 4:4:20: 'In my opinion we won't be able to improve the traffic through higher fines. We must educate people from childhood to become law-abiding. [. . .] As it is now, there is traffic mayhem at busy junctions, unless the traffic police are around. It means that we have no culture of law, if we have to be threatened by the presence of the police to follow the traffic rules [. . .]. We can't correct our culture by threat of fines. We Iranians respect each other in many situations, but not in driving, because we don't have the culture of driving. [. . .] We don't understand that it is to our benefit to follow the law.'

A different point of view on penalties was presented by another female taxi driver, who said:

4:7:21: 'I am against penalties. People who break the law must acknowledge that they have done wrong. You do not restore the harm which has been inflicted on those individuals whose rights have been violated, by penalising the law-breakers.'

The emphasis placed here by the interviewee on the importance of restoring justice to individuals – or the need to do justice in respect of the parties whose rights have been violated – demonstrates a way of looking at the problem which does not prioritize its societal aspects. In the context of Iranian culture, where a 'society of strangers' is not prioritized, doing justice at the level of the individual is paramount if the law is to be experienced as legitimate.

Pedestrians

One significant difference between the male and female taxi drivers was in the way that they made use of injunctive norms when talking about pedestrians. When asked if they stop at a zebra crossing to allow pedestrians to pass, many male drivers replied by saying 'yes, we should...', while most of the women avoided the injunctive statements. Interviewee 4, for example, said that she always stopped to let pedestrians cross the road, because 'they could be members of my family crossing the road'. Another woman driver said that she would 'stop to let pedestrians pass, if it is not risky' (i.e. if another car would not crash into her from behind). At the same time, women could express themselves less generously towards pedestrians generally. Here is an example:

4:1:22: 'I always stop for pedestrians to cross the road, but if you go to the south of the city, some people throw themselves in front of cars to cause accidents and collect *diyah* [blood money]. [...] I stay away from places where there are too many pedestrians. Since they [the authorities] increased the amount of *diyah* last year, intentional accidents caused by pedestrians who want to collect *diyah* have increased.'

4:2:23: 'Sometimes I stop to let pedestrians pass. It depends where I am. Some pedestrians expect too much. They walk into the traffic and expect us to stop. What if my brakes don't work? I shouldn't

have to stop for pedestrians where there is no zebra crossing. [. . .]
The law has given them too many rights, and it is the drivers who
end up paying for it. Pedestrians have become too demanding.'

A negative view of pedestrians – the idea expressed by interviewee that
'they have been given too many rights' – is present in most interviews.
Some drivers even think that pedestrians are disrespectful towards them.

> 4:5:24: 'Not only do pedestrians have rights and the law on their
> side, they also mock transport vehicles; they treat the traffic with
> scorn. They prefer having the roads to themselves to get on with
> what they want.'

The same interviewee admits, however, that being a pedestrian in Tehran
is associated with danger, adding 'we can't say that nothing happens to
them' when they are trying to cross the road. As we argued before,
pedestrians are treated as if they belong to a different tribe, to the tribe of
the *piyadeh* (see Chapter Five). As pointed out above, this treatment of
pedestrians can also be considered as a function of Iranian personalism –
pedestrians are unknown people, and one cannot respect them unless one
can pretend that they are members of one's family crossing the road (as
interviewee 7 stated above – see 4:7:16, page 133). Another interviewee
starts by explaining the predicament of the pedestrian, before moving
back to talk about the pedestrian from the standpoint of the driver.

> 4:6:25: 'To cross the street amounts to committing suicide. You
> have to be very careful driving through the streets. Any second,
> someone may jump in front of your car unexpectedly.'

In short, although women drivers appear slightly more understanding
than men about what it means to be a pedestrian, they nevertheless view
pedestrians from the driver's standpoint. The female cabbies were also
generally critical of pedestrians, and many said that there should be fines
specifically directed at pedestrians who do not respect the red light and, by
walking across the road, cause accidents. This may be attributed to the
technology of the automobile, i.e. some aspects of driving a car (as a form
of experience) cut across gender differences. Women's negative view of
pedestrians may also be traced back to the binary opposition of *piyadeh/*

savareh, which we discussed in previous chapters. The word *piyadeh* (pedestrian), as we mentioned in Chapter Four, when contrasted to *savareh* (the rider) has a number of negative connotations in Persian (see Shahshahani 2006). At the risk of making a sweeping generalization, we can hypothesize that whenever references are made to *piyadeh*, the negative representations of the pedestrian *may* be activated at the subconscious, discursive level. Irrespective of gender, *savareh* is a person of social status and dignity, and thus worthy of respect, while *piyadeh* is a person of little means and no social status. (Incidentally, in the English language, 'pedestrian', can mean commonplace, prosaic or dull.) The technology of the automobile stimulates and strengthens not only Iranian drivers' personalism, but also their negative view of the *piyadeh*, who has traditionally been regarded as a person not worthy of respect.

Finally, pedestrians signify a 'society of strangers' unless, as one of the interviewees pointed out, one remembers they could be one's family members crossing the road. In this sense, drivers' attitudes to pedestrians can be explored as an aspect of Iranians' concept of personalism, which is partly defined against the backdrop of the larger 'society of strangers'.

Gender Conflicts

Unlike our interviews with the male taxi drivers, in which references to gender or women were rare, the interviews with female cabbies were permeated with references to gender-related concerns. These interviews show how gender conflicts, as mentioned above, go hand in hand with forms of class tension that force men and women into confrontation. One of the interviewees (4:4:26) stated, for example, that although the level of education had improved in the country, 'Iranian culture [remained] the culture of patriarchy'.[3] She went on to add that even well-educated men could be uncomfortable with the idea of women working, or having a public life of their own independently of them. That was why many of them preferred to keep their wives at home 'to make them soup'. The tension between men and women is not limited to the control of public and private spheres through access to employment, but takes many other forms ranging from *siygheh* (temporary marriages) to *diyah*, which are directly related to the denial of women's equal rights in law or to men being granted special legal rights at the expense of women. This other dimension is described by another taxi driver:

4:1:27: 'I get women passengers every day who pour out their hearts over their family problems. Iranian women invest their life and youth on their children and husband, and in return they find themselves abandoned. Most of them live in a state of personal upheaval and crisis. Their husbands leave them after a few years for a younger woman. I haven't married and have no intention of getting married. They should get rid of *siygheh* [temporary marriages]. It allows men to take several wives at the same time.'[4]

None of the male interviewees mentioned Tehran's female taxi drivers. However, many women drivers found themselves in confrontation with their male colleagues. The first interviewee stated that she was treated badly by male taxi drivers, who behaved as if she was taking their livelihood away. The other interviewees voiced similar sentiments, saying that male taxi drivers were jealous and behaved badly or disrespectfully towards them as if women had taken their place; they thought: 'my place should be in the home, theirs outside' (4:2:28). This interviewee then went on to explain that passengers generally understand her difficult situation and the fact that she had greater needs than the men, and thus chose to ride in her taxi instead.

4:5:29: 'Perhaps twenty per cent of them [male drivers] behave decently towards us. The remaining eighty per cent behave badly and make sarcastic or insulting remarks.'

4:7:30: 'You might not believe this, but I stop seeing myself as a woman when I start my car in the morning. I also tell my colleagues not to behave like women when they are driving, because they have to struggle against men. [. . .] Men drivers, both male cabbies and men drivers, think that we are their rivals.'

The female taxi drivers stated that their male counterparts see them as a threat to their livelihoods, treat them badly and, as one put it, refuse to accept them as if they were 'rivals in love' (4:8:31).[5] Another interviewee told us that when filling her tank at a petrol station a male cabbie had said to her, 'Well, you women have done very well for yourselves, haven't you? You have taken over the country and are taking all the passengers' (4:9:32). The issue of *diyah* is brought up in a different context by one of the women cabbies. When she was asked about the enforcement of the law, she said that the law must move with the times:

> 4:6:33: 'For example, the rate of *diyah* for a woman differs from that of a man. There are women surgeons and lawyers whose *diyah* is half of a male junky who has an accident crossing a road. Such a law is not just.'

Diyah (blood money) is another important concept appearing in our interviews. As we discussed in Chapter Five, the lawyers that we interviewed viewed it as a source of injustice and maintained that it should be abolished.

Shakhsiyat, Taarof and Zerangi

The way in which the female cabbies discussed other key concepts — such as *shakhsiyat*, *taarof* and *zerangi* — draws our attention once again to the way that all these concepts are related to each other through personalism. Here are a few examples, in which direct references are made to Iranians' individualistic conduct in traffic, their indifference to the rights of others and their disregard of the law:

> 4:2:34: 'It is sheer lawlessness. They disregard all the rules of traffic and the rights of everyone. Everyone drives according to his or her own taste.'

> 4:4:35: 'Laws are made for our own protection. But often we expect only others to follow them, so that we can live in comfort. We simply disregard the law if it does not serve our interest.'

> 4:5:36: 'Women are to some extent self-centred. They think that the whole world should be at their command as soon as they get behind the wheel of a car and start driving. They shouldn't drive recklessly just because they have learnt to drive. We should show the same consideration that our parents showed us and behave according to the custom they gave us.'

> 4:7:37: 'They {reckless drivers} break the traffic rules because they can see only themselves and their nearest {those they know}. They

only care about themselves and getting where they are going [...].
It doesn't matter if other people get hurt in the process or their
rights are disrespected.'

4:8:38: 'Drivers' personalities change as soon as they get behind
the wheel of a car. Talking with a pedestrian face-to-face is one
thing, meeting the same pedestrian while driving your car is
another thing. His [the driver's] *shakhsiyat* turns around 180
degrees [when he starts driving]. He thinks it is a sign of weakness
if he drives behind other cars. The car gives him power.'

When asked what came to her mind when she heard the word 'law'
(*ghanon*), the first interviewee replied 'The man of law' (*Marde-h ghanon*)
and went on to say that 'to follow the law, one shows one's self-respect'
(4:1:39). Then she asserted that owning a car did not bring *shakhsiyat*
(self-esteem or self-respect), because anyone could own a car these days.
When you did not know how to use the car properly, because you did not
have the culture (*farhang*) of using the car, owning one could not bring
you respect. Interviewee 8 used the word 'self-respect' in a completely
different context – while struggling to convey the meaning of the law.
Law for her was linked to self-respect:

4:8:40: 'We ourselves are the source of the law. [...] Those who
enforce the law try to make us understand this law. But the
problem is that we do not ourselves [follow the law]. The law is
one word, and one must respect oneself.'

As mentioned in the previous chapters in connection with other
interviews, *shakhsiyat* plays an important role in Iranian culture and in
how Iranians generally assess themselves and other people's behaviour.
This concept can be related to Iranian personalism (to their sense of
individuality), which in turn is formed, developed and supported by
their 'peer group', i.e. close circle of family and friends.

4:5:41: 'The worst drivers are those who reveal their lack of self-
respect (*shakhsyat*) by disregarding the laws. [...] If you follow
the law, you have shown your self-respect and respect for other
people.'

4:8:42: 'Reckless and dangerous driving is a sign of low self-esteem (*kam shakhsyati*) [...]. Iranians are very flexible people and are prepared to overlook a lot of things. But not when it comes to driving. [...] When they are driving they feel that they will lose their self-esteem (*shakhsiyat*) if they give way to another car. But when they are walking, or eating or trying to get in a lift, then they show excessive respect to others (she uses the word *taarof*).'

When another interviewee was asked why the driving habits of Iranians had not improved, she burst out:

4:1:43: 'But what about their *shakhsiyat*? They don't have the basic culture of talking and behaving properly, but they may drive. [...] They don't earn enough to feed themselves, but they buy a car to show that they are well-to-do. They get themselves a fancy car to mislead people and present themselves as respectable (*ba-shakhsiyat*). [...] We need to learn the appropriate culture at home. Not only the culture of speaking, but also driving needs to be learnt at home. [...] It has happened that a father with his kid sitting next to him rolls down his window while driving and throws insults at me. What is his son supposed to learn from his father's conduct? He learns how to insult a woman.'

As we saw above, *taarof*, which is Iranians' tendency to show excessive and exaggerated respect to others, is often used in the same sentence as *shakhsiyat*. This supports the idea suggested in the previous chapter that *taarof* also is linked to Iranians' personalism.

4:2:44: '*Taarof* doesn't mean a thing. It is what Iranians say to *show* deference; it is not what they *do*. [...] When the time comes they will even push you aside to get their own way. [...] You don't see anyone doing *taarof* in the traffic, because they are only concerned about getting where they are going as quickly as possible. During the 11 years I have been driving, not once has another driver stopped to give way to me in respect. [...] We get a hard time from taxis [male cabbies] and private cars.'

4:3:45: '*Taarof* in the traffic could be dangerous and cause accidents. I guess people don't *taarof* when they are driving, because they have only their destination in mind.'

4:9:46: '*Taarof* is nonsense. It's a lie. [...] I always stop to let pedestrians pass. It has happened repeatedly that I have stopped the car at a zebra crossing to let a pedestrian pass [...] and with a gesture have indicated to them, "After you." Then they don't cross the road and gesture back "No, please, after you".'

The next quotation shows a clear link between *zerangi* and personalism:

4:2:47: 'One problem we Iranians have is that we think we are *zerang* if we break traffic rules when driving our cars. What is important is that we get ahead of other drivers. [...] This *zerangi* produces lawlessness.'

These examples show that Iranians' sense of personalism operates as the backdrop against which many of the problems related to traffic, safety and reckless driving are discussed in terms of their other cultural traits, including *shakhsiyat*, *taarof* and *zerangi*.

The Law

Below we find two opposing views of the law, showing how religion and politics are invoked to express one's beliefs about the law. It should be noted that interviewee 9 (who came across as mindful of the authorities) expresses injunctive norms. She says that she respects the law, although she does not say that she follows it:

4:9:48: 'I truly believe in the validity of Islamic laws and respect them. I respect social laws, family laws, traffic laws [...]. A number of people, who are called the experts and are cleverer and more knowledgeable than us, are appointed to work out which laws are to be used. Naturally, it is to our benefit to follow the law.'

4:10:49: 'Law doesn't mean a thing. It has no meaning for our people. [...]. The law defines the duties of the father, mother, brother and sister, but we do not have a law which is enforced in a proper way. That is why it doesn't mean anything. [...] The powerful people are the source of the law. [...] Those who run this country don't care about ordinary people's welfare. [...] Our laws are no good; they don't protect women. If you complain to the court that your husband hits you and does not provide for his family or he is an addict, the first thing the judge will say is that it is the woman's duty to endure. Why? Is it what the law says? [...] The laws have no effect. The reason is that those responsible for enforcing them are unreliable. The judges are concerned only about their own business.'

Only one of the female taxi drivers, interviewee 9, defined the primary source of the law in religious terms. She said that it was 'firstly God and secondly the Quran'. This interviewee revealed a positive attitude to both laws and authorities throughout the interview (she praised the Tehran mayor for introducing a taxi culture), and she regarded Iranians as individualistic and selfish and Westerners as decent because they obeyed the law. She also stated that when she lived in Germany, she once attended the family courts in the country to finalize her divorce. According to her, the German judge had said during the court proceedings:

4:9:50: 'The laws of your country are Islamic and better than our laws, but those enforcing your laws are not good, which is why your disputes are so complicated. By contrast our laws are not good, but we enforce them well.'

This interviewee aside, most women taxi drivers referred to parliament and the government when they were asked about the sources of law and legal authority. Here, too, we came across politically cautious and intentionally vague responses:

4:4:51: 'To talk in general terms, well everyone knows [she laughs] well obviously [...] the source of law is one person alone. The rest depends on which aspect of the law you are dealing with.'

4:7:52: 'I always respect the law, even though I know it is unjust. I refrain from claiming my right by not making a fuss.'

There are exceptions, such as interviewee 8, to whom we referred above. She said that law was about self-respect, and that we ourselves are the source of law. However, when asked who the highest legal authority was, she responded:

> 4:8:53: 'I never thought about it. Every individual is responsible for upholding the law. It is the laws which are sanctioned in Shari'a and *urf.*'

This was the closest we came to defining the law in terms of Shari'a, but interestingly enough the interviewee refers to *urf* as one of the two authorities.

Several women made a similar point, in that they 'refrained' from making a claim and instead put up with various infringements of their rights. Women are expected to 'endure' hardship. However, their conception of law varies, even though they generally share a largely negative view of the law, legal processes, courts and other legal institutions. The following are typical responses:

> 4:4:54: 'You would do better to resolve your disputes yourself than turn to the courts. [...] The legal processes take too long and you see that those who have influence and money easily buy officers of the law [...]. This makes people suspicious of the law. [...] They cause women so much difficulty that women give up on their claims and rights.'

> 4:3:55: 'Iranians are not law-abiding and try to circumvent the law in certain places [she laughs and continues] — even I might avoid the law occasionally.'

The latter interviewee then went on to add:

> 4:3:56: 'The laws themselves are very good. The problem is that they are not enforced satisfactorily. You can't avoid noticing that they do not enforce the law where it is not to their benefit.'

When it comes to the relationship between driving and law, another interviewee did not think that the law could change behaviour. For

Iranians to change their driving habits, they needed education and a culture of driving:

> 4:2:57: 'The law's foundation is flawed. Had we learnt from childhood to follow the law, perhaps things would be better now and we would fasten our seatbelts. You need to know the law. {...} But those who make the law should make an example by following it. But I have seen too many times that the police break the law. They behave in a completely unacceptable way. The police should exemplify correct behaviour and not break the law in front of everyone. When I see what they do, I follow the law as long as they see me but break the law behind their back. {...} It has happened that I have been summoned to a court hearing, like when I had an accident, but otherwise I don't use the law or the courts even when I have a dispute. The courts are so busy and packed with people, you wouldn't believe it. I can't stand them. Not my sort of place. {...} In the old days, law and justice had something to do with each other, but not anymore. What is the point of the law when you can buy it with money? That isn't law. I have seen many times that the police have stopped a driver who has committed a traffic offence but let him go after he pays them off. This is important.'

Lack of trust in the authorities was evident – as were open or implied references to corrupt officers of the law and civil servants made by many interviewees:

> 4:4:58: 'Justice will be done when people become more trustworthy – when civil servants are paid decent wages {...} so that you don't have to bribe them to get things done. One of my friends was telling me that he had to bribe the council officer so that he would not misplace his file. If he didn't pay the bribe, his file would end up somewhere no one could find it.'

> 4:5:59: 'The Moral Islamic Police should not exist. They arrest girls and women and keep them for hours. {...}. This is not law.'

These discussions refer ultimately to trust, which we discussed in the previous chapters.

A Culture of Safety

A clear majority of those we interviewed (both female and male cabbies and various professionals) shared the view that the safety standards of cars manufactured in Iran were very low, and therefore were responsible for causing many accidents. With regard to the standards of roads, motorways and streets, the views varied – although many were critical of the inadequate posting of traffic signs. Perhaps more interestingly, most interviewees were quite puzzled by Iranians' disregard for safety rules – albeit that they stated that they themselves, more or less, followed these safety rules, especially with regard to wearing a seat belt. This is partly an injunctive, normative statement and partly reflects the fact that Iranians have indeed started wearing seat belts over the last five years. Teenagers and younger people were generally regarded as the worst drivers, and were said to drive too fast and recklessly: 'They will drive 80 or 90 km per hour', a taxi driver said, 'where the speed limit is 40 km per hour'. More problematically, they appear not to value their lives, with the same driver wondering 'how can you value other people's lives if you don't value your own life?' Some of the tendency to set aside basic safety rules is the result of the age of the drivers, but many accidents on the roads and streets are caused by people who do not belong to the younger generation. There is widespread disregard of safety rules amongst all generations, and dangerous driving does not limit itself to those aged under 30, even though they are overrepresented in car accidents. It is not unusual to see someone driving in reverse on the motorway in order to get back to an exit that he or she has just passed:

> 4:4:60: 'Take Tehran as an example. Everyone is in a hurry and drives like mad through the traffic to get where they are going. Here you find all sorts of driving styles and behaviour. People disregard the traffic laws, especially at the motorway entrances and exits, where you see some people driving in reverse on the motorways [...] to get back to the exit they have missed.'

This disregard for safety has many causes, one of which may be explained in reference to Iranians' personalism. However, some of the interviewees suggest other explanations:

4:1:61: 'It is difficult for taxi drivers to wear their seatbelt all the time. It can eventually cause bruises on your side. [...] Sometimes I pretend to wear a seatbelt so that the police don't stop me.'

4:2:62: 'People don't follow the law, because they don't know it. They don't wear seatbelts, because they don't understand that it is for their own safety. They have started wearing their seatbelts more often, because the police would stop them if they didn't. As you can see, I am wearing mine.'

This last point about people not knowing the rules was challenged by one of the doctors, who, referring to a previous study that he and one of his colleagues had conducted to explore Iranians' attitude to, and knowledge of, the traffic rules, stated:

Doctor 3:1:29: Besides having knowledge of the traffic rules, we generally also believe that breaking these rules is not acceptable. But in practice we behave differently in the traffic.

We can repeat here what we said in the previous chapters about the normative gap between what Iranians say in respect to how one should behave (i.e. the injunctive norms that they utter publicly) and what they actually do in practice (i.e. descriptive norms). Our interviews support the idea that the normative hiatus is a social function of Iranian personalism and how it relates itself to the individual's 'peer group', on the one hand, and to the larger 'society of strangers', on the other. The injunctive norms that are used here to express normative expectations with respect to other people's traffic behaviour concern relationships in society at large, while the descriptive norms reflect what is permitted, or tolerated, at the level of the personal community.

Concluding Discussions

Although in her interview Mrs Elahi (the 60-year-old cabbie that we referred to at the beginning of this chapter) was perhaps 'toying' with the foreign reporter, she nevertheless made two important points.

First, many women are compelled to enter the labour market for economic reasons and forced to take up certain types of work, such as taxi driving, to earn a living or in order to supplement the income of their family. Since the 1990s, Iran has been following a free-market economy model that, according to Roksana Bahramitash, has raised poverty levels among some sections of society, subsequently forcing many women to seek employment. To counteract the worsening economic situation, argues Bahramitash (2004: 165), the State began to liberalize the rules that had previously hampered women's participation in the labour market. The need for female workers proved beneficial for women and their families, as well as for the government and the economy as a whole. In this case, the government might have initially agreed to grant taxi licences to women in 2006, thus allowing them to break into the taxi service market, in order to unburden itself of the obligation to provide for them through welfare schemes.[6] A BBC report from 2008 claimed that many female cabbies were 'war widows or divorcees', who needed work and who were 'referred to the [taxi] agency by some of the big welfare foundations' (BBC News, 25 November 2008). At least one of our female drivers, interviewee 7, fits this profile. She was her family's sole breadwinner, and had been sent to the Banovan taxi agency by one of the welfare charities. Several other drivers that we interviewed stated that they had to work as a cabbie to support their families. For example:

4:11:63: 'I had to do it; otherwise, it's not the type of work I would like to do. I used to work in a car factory on the assembly line. I am doing this [working as a cabbie] because I lost my job.'

4:10:64: 'I had to do it because I was unemployed and desperate; otherwise, I was trained as a photographer and a camera operator. I couldn't start my own business because I didn't have the money [...]. There are, of course, other jobs. [...] But they don't fit my circumstances. I have to collect my daughter at 12.30 every day. Driving a taxi gives you flexibility.'

In short, economic considerations must have played as important a role in persuading the authorities to allow 'women-only taxi agencies' to operate as the Islamic regime's interest in upholding gender segregation.

Second, Mrs Elahi points out the cultural and political prejudices of the foreign reporter, when she says that after all these years Westerners are still amazed at seeing Iranian women drive cars or excel in other, traditionally male-dominated, arenas.[7] Part of the reason for this misguided amazement is that Iran has been systematically misrepresented for several decades in the Western media for political reasons. As Axworthy (2013) points out, Iran is often depicted by the Western media as a threat to the West and as a strange, alien, irrational and politically disturbing country. In a recent study by two major US magazines, *Time* and *Newsweek*, Fayyaz and Shirazi (2013: 53) show that the images of Iran and Iranians that have been spread by Western media have not aimed at describing the real Iran and its people but rather have attempted to disseminate a xenophobic stereotype of Iranians irrespective of their religiosity or political sympathies.

However, it is true that after the revolution, the Islamic regime did undermine women's equal rights by defining them as mothers whose main place was in the home (Bahramitash 2004: 165). Despite the regime's ideology of gender segregation, which translates into discriminatory laws and public policies directed against women, Iranian women have increased their participation in the public sphere and today work in all the important professions, such as the law and medicine, and in various sectors, from education to banking and trade. However, their legal rights and public standing are constantly undermined by various sections of the Islamic establishment. For example, notwithstanding the Iranian Constitution, which prohibits all forms of gender discrimination in working life, the Iranian Chief of Police issued a ban on 1 September 2014 on women working in coffee shops (*Payvand Iran News*, 1 September 2014) – women may own coffee shops, but they must employ male workers to run them in their stead. Leaving aside the fact that this law discriminates against half of the population and thus is unconstitutional even in Iranian law, the police authorities' legal power to issue labour laws remains a baffling legal oddity. The peculiar legal powers of the chief of police reveal the Islamic Republic's polycentric political make-up, and it once again draws our attention to the competing centres of power, law and authority in the country. Had the post-revolutionary political system in Iran not consisted of several competing centres of authority, the chief of police could not have enjoyed the legal competence to make labour laws – but, in addition, Iran would arguably have also long since turned into a totalitarian country. We shall return to this point in Chapter Nine.

To give another example, in September 2012, Iranian authorities restricted women's access to certain university degree courses, including English Literature, Archaeology and Business Studies, thus giving rise to renewed concerns over the rights of women to education (*BBC News*, 22 September 2012). Once again, we can interpret their discriminatory educational policy in several ways. For example, they might have decided to discriminate against women in order to balance the number of male and female university students (60 per cent of university students and university graduates are women). It could also reflect the Iranian Government's disapproval of women studying certain subjects, such as English Literature, or be an attempt to exclude them from certain areas of the labour market, where there is little demand for workers. Irrespective of the authorities' rationale, their discriminatory policy of excluding women from certain university degrees strengthens the position of male students in the labour market, but more significantly it undermines women's social and legal standing in society. When Iran is viewed against the backdrop of repeated deliberate attempts by the authorities to exclude women from the public life of the country, the foreign reporter's astonishment becomes perhaps understandable. This does not, however, justify treating Iranian women as passive victims or overlooking their agency in the ongoing battle for equal rights.

CHAPTER 8

CULTURE: REFLECTIONS ON INDIVIDUALISM AND COMMUNITY

Reza Banakar and Zara Saeidzadeh

For centuries, Iranians have had to cope with varying circumstances; sometimes they ruled supremely over vast empires, at other times foreign invaders destroyed much of their civilization. Yet whether Iranians ruled or were ruled, they displayed great finesse and resourcefulness in dealing with outsiders. Although they were often compelled to accept the conqueror's authority, they modified the new practices and integrated them into their own way of life, or they found ways of circumventing them; but they never completely relinquished their own social customs. On the other hand, the longer the invaders stayed in Iran, the more they adopted Persian customs, many of which they carried back to their native lands.

(Arasteh and Arasteh 1964: 7)

All of our interviewees referred directly to the notion of *farhang* (culture) and discussed aspects of social behaviour, traffic and driving that may be conceptualized as cultural traits. Most of them either blamed the 'lack of culture of driving' for the poor driving habits of Iranians, or referred to it when talking about their traffic experiences. We heard them repeatedly saying that 'we don't have a culture of driving' and arguing that the problem of traffic could be resolved by *farhang-sazi*. This chapter is therefore devoted to exploring Iranian culture and developing a theoretical framework that enables us to explain its social manifestations, such as driving habits.

Culture is a multidimensional and interpretive notion, which is hard to operationalize in concrete and unambiguous empirical terms.[1] Sociologists and social anthropologists often define it in terms of 'meaning' or the dynamic *processes* that make social life meaningful and help individuals and whole communities to develop their own particular world views. Expressed differently, culture refers to the process of reproducing beliefs and attitudes that people hold about the world surrounding them (Wuthnow 1987). It is, as we explained in the Introduction, '"a form of life," or a way of going about the world, seeing, making sense of and experiencing the social life' (see Geertz 1973: 89). Culture, however, is not an entirely subjective phenomenon, for its various value formations possess observable 'objective' properties (it can also refer to artefacts). Although these formations are products of human consciousness, they are by no means confined to the individual actor's subjective inner life. Values are externalized through symbolic and non-symbolic social interactions and given an objective status, which, in turn, helps to create and maintain patterns of behaviour but also thought and perception. This understanding of the subjective and objective aspects of culture are employed to the study of Iranians' driving habits, which are treated as objective representations of aspects of Iranian culture, albeit mediated through the technology of the automobile – a cultural artefact in its own right. Another objective manifestation of Iranian culture, which will be discussed below, can be found in the way in which towns, cities and neighbourhood communities have evolved over time. Embedded within the objective representations of architecture and traffic behaviour are values, world views and attitudes about how the individual's actions are related to, and influenced by, his or her 'peer group' (i.e. family and network of friends), local community, society at large, the State, the law and religion. Whereas the objective aspects of driving are empirically accessible, its subjective dimensions require an interpretation of the objective data, which in our case herein must be made in the socio-historical context of Iranian society.[2]

We shall start by briefly discussing a number of key ideas – such as Iranians' individualism, *shakhsyiat*, *zerangi* and *taarof*, which we repeatedly encountered in our interviews – in an attempt to explore their interconnectedness. Then, we move on to discuss how Iranian individualism is rooted in family and a perception of community, and therefore should not be confused with the Western idea of individualism. We conclude this chapter by identifying three basic levels of 'sociality', or the way in which social interactions take place, social relations are formed and a form of social order is maintained (see Gurvitch 1947). These three levels include 'peer group', community and society at large, each of which generates its own set of rules, norms, religiosity and ultimately its own brand of 'law' and legality. What make these three levels of sociality significant in the Iranian context is that, in them, family and community are defined in opposition to society and the State.

Iranian Personalism

Iranians often wonder why they are not a socially disciplined nation, and why they find it difficult to produce an orderly culture of teamwork. The following quote, from a speech made by the Supreme Leader on 14 October 2012, expresses a political concern with the implications of a weak sense of teamwork for manufacturing, business, trade and even, interestingly enough, driving habits and obedience to law:

> Why is the culture of teamwork not strong enough in our society? This is a problem. Westerners have claimed [the virtue of] teamwork for themselves [...]. Why is our driving not disciplined enough? This is a problem. The way we drive in the streets is one of our problems. And this is not a small problem: it is a major problem. [...] To what extent do we respect the rights of other people? [...] To what extent do we observe the law? Why do some people break the law? The tendency to break the law is a dangerous malady. To what extent do our people have a sense of responsibility? To what extent are we committed to social discipline?
>
> (Supreme Leader Ali Hosseini Khamenei)[3]

According to Chehabi (2002: 401), 'team sports', such as football and basketball, which require a number of players working jointly towards achieving a shared objective, were initially promoted in Iran deliberately 'to foster a spirit of cooperation among Iranians'. As it transpired, one required much more than football and basketball to establish the spirit of teamwork across a nation that has learnt throughout its history that all the socio-economic, as well as the political, relationships that constitute Iranian society at any given time are best understood and treated as short-term projects (Katouzian 2009). Not surprisingly, Iranians' difficulty in working together as a team is regularly brought up and discussed in connection with their poor performance in team sports. Despite the huge popularity of football in Iran, and although during certain periods the country has invested heavily in training its national football team, it has nevertheless, as a rule, performed poorly in international competitions. In contrast, Iran has always done well in sports such as wrestling and weightlifting, which require individual performance. The poor performance of the Iranian national football team has many interrelated causes, including corruption, nepotism and personal rivalries, all of which have hampered the effective management of the game in the country (Chehabi 2002: 400). However, many other countries in Africa and South America with similar managerial failings have succeeded considerably better than Iran in international competitions. This is why Iranians' sense of individualism, which undermines their collaborative efforts, has been treated as one of the main causes of their poor performance in team sports. To borrow from Chehabi again:

> A sports team is ideally more than the sum of its parts, but in Iran one has the uncanny impression that the team is at times less than the sum of its parts. In the 1930s, an English observer wrote about football players in Kerman that while the idea of team-spirit was growing, 'on less important occasions [...] some men will not pass the ball'. Three decades later, in 1967, the American basketball coach of the national Iranian team noted that he had to work with individuals who related atomistically. The key relationships, he reported, were not cooperative patterns of teamwork but rather competitive interpersonal relationships that extended well beyond the basketball court.
>
> (Chehabi 2002: 401)

The above quote, being based on an Englishman's and an American's accounts of Iranian's behaviour, reveals perhaps more about their 'gaze' than about Iranian culture. Nevertheless, their accounts are in line with the numerous empirical studies demonstrating a strong sense of individualism amongst Iranians (this was, incidentally, supported by our own interviews). These studies often blame Iranians' individualism for their inability to cooperate in a disciplined, orderly and effective – that is rationalized – fashion (see, for example, Namazie 2003; Tayeb 1979). Against this background, one might expect Iranian society to be categorized as individualistic. Paradoxically, in Geert Hofstede's world-wide studies of national cultures (Hofstede 1984, 1991), Iran scored only 41 points on the scale of individualism, while Sweden scored 71, Denmark 74 and the UK 89 points. Thus, according to Hofstede:

> Iran, with a score of 41, is considered a collectivistic society. This is manifested in a close long-term commitment to the member 'group', be that a family, extended family, or extended relationships. Loyalty in a collectivist culture is paramount, and it overrides most other societal rules and regulations. The society fosters strong relationships where everyone takes responsibility for fellow members of their group. In collectivist societies offence leads to shame and loss of face, employer/employee relationships are perceived in moral terms (like a family link), hiring and promotion decisions take account of the employee's in-group, management is the management of groups.
>
> (Hofstede Centre 2014)

Hofstede's studies do not capture how Iranians distinguish between two levels of sociality, i.e. one representing their 'peer group' and the other consisting of the larger 'society of strangers'. Thus, they do not explain how this distinction influences attitudes, perceptions and actions in different social situations. While Iranians show collectivist tendencies as far as their loyalty to, and trust in, their 'peer group' is concerned, they act 'individualistically' towards the larger 'society of strangers'. Hofstede's methodology uses Western individualism as its yardstick, and thus it fails to reflect the differences in Iranian and western Europeans' concepts of individualism. At the risk of making a sweeping generalization, the Western individualist entertains a public self-image and propensity to rational action, which are defined in terms of 'I' rather than 'we'. This individualist is never free of social forces, but neither are his or her actions a function of family ties. Due to the historical separation of state and society, the Iranian individualist (a person with a *zerang* mentality) does not act in a collectivist spirit either, but instead he or she distinguishes between 'I' and 'they' and acts accordingly. 'I' is a product of the 'peer group' and 'they' is understood, in the first instance, in terms of the 'system' or authorities (historically speaking, the rulers of Iran) and, in the second instance, in terms of the larger 'society of strangers'.

The local community or neighbourhoods – which were previously called *mahalleh*, i.e. the more or less discrete urban quarters that still exist in Iranian cities and towns – also play a role in the distinction made between 'I' and 'they'. The traditional *mahalleh* was a local network – organized along the lines of ethnicity, clan or religion – creating a social space distinct from the public and political centres of Iranian cities (Mirgholami and Sintusigha 2012; also see Madanipour 1998). The extended families, the elders and local mullahs were joined through the *bazaar*, or the local traders, and the local mosque(s) in the socially cohesive and supportive environment of the *mahalleh*. With the reign of Reza Shah, which started in 1925, Iranian cities were redesigned and divided into residential quarters representing different social classes rather than clan and ethnicity (see Bayat 2010). From the 1960s onwards, the *mahallehs'* cultural homogeneity and social cohesion were further undermined by the growing social and physical mobility among the population, and by migration from rural areas as well as from other cities, towns and even other *mahallehs*. These new residential areas redefined the duality of public and private spaces that existed in the *mahalleh*; the traditional clan has, indeed, disappeared from the face of cities and the extended family has been dispersed across the city. Nevertheless, as Morteza Mirgholami's and Sidha Sintusigha's study of Narmak, a modern neighbourhood in Tehran, shows, the cultural norms that regulated public behaviour in the *mahalleh* have to some extent survived the modernization of the city. The residents of Narmak continue to perform traditional rituals in the neighbourhood, while women reproduce a sense of community through close, daily interactions and collective activities such as 'eating and supervising children in the semi-public squares across the neighbourhood'. The neighbourhood also upholds the patriarchal norms and relationships of the family as well as performing surveillance functions. By carrying out these social and normative functions, it continues to integrate and assimilate its residents into a modern form of built environment (see Mirgholami and

Sintusigha 2012: 238–9). These neighbourhoods are thus modern versions of *mahalleh* communities, which are closely linked to the modern family and generate their own forms of social order and law.

There are at least two interrelated reasons for the social and cultural role that neighbourhoods continue to play in the life of Iranian cites: first, they support the family as a provider of security and identity for the individual and, second, they protect the family against society at large and the State. As long as the State and civil society are separated and pitted against each other, the *mahalleh*, or its modern version of residential neighbourhood, will continue to mediate between the different public spheres of the city, providing a feeling of community belonging and also a sociopolitical buffer zone protecting the 'I' from 'them'.[4]

Since Iranians' sense of 'individualism' is not the same as the Western concept that informed Hofstede's studies, following Katouzian (2009: 16–8) we called this cultural trait personalism. This chapter hopes to show that other cultural norms, values and practices specific to Iranians, as well as the cultural patterns of behaviour that embody them – ranging from *zerangi* and *taarof* to their driving habits – are dependent ultimately on their personalism. Before we discuss these cultural traits further, we must however highlight Shi'i Islam as an integral part of the cultural history of Iran and exemplify how it has influenced the way in which modern Iran has developed into a defiant, revolutionary state. Any discussion of Iranian personalism remains necessarily incomplete without considering the influence of Shi'ism on the country's culture, society and politics. Many of the dualities that we mentioned above were historically constructed as integral parts of the Iranian cultural characteristic as Persians adapted themselves to the rule of Islam, while developing their own version thereof. Shi'ism was first developed in Iraq, and, thus, was originally an Arab, rather than a Persian, construction.[5] Although it spread to Iran during the eighth century, it was first transformed into a political force in the sixteenth century when Iran was subjected to a 'systematic policy of Shi'ization by the Safavid dynasty' (Halm 2007: ix and 110).

Shi'ism: 'Every day is Ashura[6] and Everywhere is Karbala'

In Chapter Seven, we argued that the Islamic Republic revolutionized the country on a daily basis by placing various social groups up against each other. Here we suggest that this revolutionary ethos may be explained in reference to Shi'ism, which has shaped the formations of a politics of opposition (or resistance) at the level of the State and a defiant attitude to social order at the level of the individual. As part of his populist strategy to uphold a revolutionary sprit, Ayatollah Ruhollah Khomeini used the dual image of *mostakberin*, which refers to the arrogant oppressive powers that are, by definition, the enemies of Muslims and other exploited and disinherited people, and *mostazafin*, which refers to the downtrodden and the oppressed groups (see endnote 5, Chapter One). The notion of *mostakberin* is derived from the historical events of the Battle of Karbala (commemorated on the holy day of Ashura, described in endnote 6, Chapter Eight) revealing its Shi'i connotations, and was employed before and after the 1979 revolution to formulate a populist agenda capable of mobilizing the discontented masses (Taremi 2014: 7). According to Abrahamian (1993: 47):

> By the eve of the revolution, Khomeini was portraying society as divided into two warring classes, each with economic attributes. On one side was the upper class (*tabaqeh-e bala*), which he identified, in his own terminology, as formed of the oppressors, the rich, the exploiters, the powerful, the feudalists, the capitalists, the palace dwellers, the corrupt, the high and mighty, the opulent, the enjoyers of luxury, the gluttonous, the lazy timeservers, and the wealthy elite. On the other side was the lower class (*tabaqeh-e payin*): the oppressed, the exploited, the powerless, the slum dwellers, the barefooted, the street folk, the hardworking poor, the hungry, the unemployed, the disinherited masses, and those deprived of education, work, housing, and medical facilities.

The distinction between *mostazafin* and *mostakberin*, writes Afrachteh (2014: 114), 'is closely akin to the differentiation between Marxist proletariat and bourgeoisie' and reminiscent of Frantz Fanon's *The Wretched of the Earth* (Abrahamian 2014). The Islamic Republic was not, however, a Marxist but a 'middle class movement that mobilized the masses with radical sounding rhetoric' against the internal and external enemies (Abrahamian 2014: 37–8). It was the propagation not of Marxism, but of a populist agenda that promised the redistribution of the country's wealth without questioning private property. Instead of discussing class conflicts or the objective characteristics of class domination, it used 'notions of virtue and justice' to rally mass support for its policies (see Keshavarzian 2007: 150). Domestically, this antagonistic image of the oppressed and oppressor was employed to mobilize the traditionalist sections of society to wage class war on its secular section, suppressing freedom of speech and women's rights. As part of this war, the *Basij-e Mostazafin*, which means Mobilisation of the Oppressed – a paramilitary organization that recruits predominantly from the traditionalist and religious sections of society – was created after the revolution and allowed to operate outside the law.[7] Regionally and internationally, this dual image served as a platform from which to launch Iran's foreign policy against the 'neocolonial powers'.

According to Halm (2007: 135), 'Shi'ism is not revolutionary per se', and was transformed from a religion of 'the quietly enduring martyr' into an insurgent revolutionary movement partly as a reaction to Iran's more recent experiences of neocolonial domination. Nevertheless, it could be turned into a forceful rebellious social movement, because it had institutionalized at its core what Fischer (1980) calls 'the Karbala Paradigm', the injustice done to Imam Hossein and the sense of guilt of all Shi'a who were not there to help him. The ideologues of the Islamic Republic tapped into this paradigm, using the imagery of the *mostakberin*, in order to unleash class war on their opponents. In contrast to Halm (2007: 135), who sees the pre-revolutionary Shi'ism as 'quietistic', Hamid Dabashi describes it doctrinally and historically as a religion of perpetual protest:

> Shi'ism is a religion of protest, born and bred on the backbone of a combative history – a history gone (for Shi'is) awry. [...] Vindictive, Shi'ism is revolt: from Imam Hussein in Karbala to Ayatollah Khomeini in Iran, to Muqtada al-Sadr in Iraq, to Hassan Nasrallah in Lebanon. Shi'ism is to say 'No'. Where it thrives, Shi'ism is a majority with a minority complex. It is not just that Shi'ism is political; politics is Shi'i in its quintessence.
>
> (Dabashi 2011: xii–xiii)

Shi'ism flourishes, Dabashi (2011: xiv) goes on to say, 'when it is combative and wages an uphill battle; it loses its moral authority and defiant voice the instant it succeeds and is in power'. It is, thus, not a religion of governance, and in order to maintain its political vigour and moral authority it has to preserve a rebellious attitude and oppositional approach to those in power. This was amply demonstrated when Shi'ism triumphed over the Shah and established itself in Iran during the 1979 revolution. Once in power, 'it began to rule with vengeance', eliminating all opposition and suppressing all minorities (Dabashi 2011: 314). When all the opposition was removed, its proponents had no alternative but to search for new causes of defiance and protest. Externally, what Iran's leaders saw as the neocolonial powers and their puppet regimes in the Middle East served as the ideal targets. Internally, socio-economic disparities and class differences emerged as a manifestation of injustice and discontent, against which one could articulate a new sense of dissatisfaction and mobilize both men and women. At the same time, gender (or sexuality) was presented as an unruly threat to the authority of the patriarchy, and was employed in order to mobilize men against women.

Another related factor, which influences Shi'as' attitude to the State, is the belief that Mahdy, the 12th Imam, is in occultation. Consequently, all forms of government are temporal and no earthly authority can be legitimate during Imam Mahdy's absence. Out of this belief emerge two approaches or schools of thought – one parallel to Halm's 'quietism', the other in line with Dabashi's 'religion of protest'. The so-called quietists, although opposed to the temporary rulers, await the *Zuhur*, or insurrection of the 12th Imam, before they seek justice. The militants, on the other hand, 'argue that waiting for Mahdy should be accompanied by struggling against the tyranny and creation of a just society' (Amjad 1984: 39). Thus, neither the 'quietists' nor the militant Shi'a recognize the legitimacy or authority of any government. In the meantime, while awaiting the Second Coming of Mahdy, the *mujtahids*[8] become responsible for leading the community of believers – which scenario, by implication, identifies the Mosque as morally superior to the State (Afrachteh 2014: 101). This is, however, according to Shi'i doctrine, and in practice is not valid across the whole of society in Iran. The role of the mosque varies depending on whether we are in a traditional *mahalleh* in the rural areas (or south Tehran) or in a modern middle-class neighbourhood of a large city (for example, in north Tehran).

At the level of the individual, this restless, discontented, rebellious, anti-state philosophy of life, which is formulated against the perennial injustices inflicted upon the Shi'as, constitutes an aspect of Iranian personalism. To liberally borrow from Dabashi, an Iranian Shi'a is an individual who suffers from (or perhaps 'enjoys') a minority complex even when he or she is in the majority and in power. This perception of being the constant underdog and the object of the injustices of the majority (as epitomized by Imam Hossein's martyrdom at Karbala) is compatible with, and constitutes an aspect of, Iranian personalism. In everyday exchanges, it is defiant in the face of the arbitrary power of the State, while continuously searching for ways of transgressing the norms of society at large and beating the system, whose legitimacy and secular authority it cannot recognize.

Beating the System

In Iran, we have *zerangi*, a concept that loosely means 'cleverness'. *Zerangi* can be both ethical and unethical. Coming to America and starting a successful business? That's *zerangi*. Finding a way to avoid paying taxes? Also *zerangi*. Cutting in line? *Zerangi* at its finest. François likes to remind me that people from all cultures cut in line, including his own [from Mexico]. True, but I like to think that my people have turned it into an art form.

The above quotation is from an online blog by an Iranian woman living in the USA (see Dumas 2010). Interestingly, the blogger defines *zerangi* individualistically as 'coming to America and starting a successful business' and socially in terms of transgressing (1) the norms of the State, exemplified by avoiding taxes, and (2) the norms of society at large and the rights of strangers, exemplified by queue-jumping.

As we discussed in the previous chapters, *zerangi* may be translated as 'cleverness' or 'being smart', and to be *zerang* is a positive attribute suggesting that one is clever, quick, innovative, independent and capable of achieving difficult goals with little effort. However, the consequences of *zerangi*, depending on the social context in which the act is performed, can easily transcend its positive applications and turn into a negative form of action, i.e. to be quick and innovative (starting a business) can easily turn into deceitfulness (cheating the tax authorities and violating other people's rights). Although *zerangi* has a dark side, which involves manipulating people or situations to one's own benefit, it is nevertheless admired by Iranians and is culturally endorsed as long as it concerns 'beating the system' and society at large (involving people who do not belong to one's 'peer group'). In short, *zerangi* is deeply individualistic in the sense of requiring social action at the level of the individual. Moreover, it is a subversive manifestation of personalism, in that it aims at defying the system and transgressing the rules of the 'society of strangers'. At the same time it is rooted in the community of one's peers, i.e. the network of family and friends from which the individual receives his or her normative cues as well as endorsements. Without the close community of peers, which endorses one's *zerangi*, the larger 'society of strangers' cannot be identified as a meaningful social entity and a well-defined target for transgression.

Children who do very well at school are said to be *zerang* – one could be the *zerang* of his or her class, but also the envy of his or her peers at the same time. Thus, the positive connotation of the word *zerang* is implanted into the minds of children at an early age, setting the ideal image of a successful person. If *zerangi* is about beating the system, how does it manifest itself in the context of education?

The Importance of Education (*Amoozesh*)

One of the ideas voiced by almost all those that we interviewed concerned the role of education in counteracting the traffic problem. Here is an example from our interviews with the male taxi drivers:

> 1:10:13: 'Laws are not enforced properly. However, I think one should not start with the law but instead try to educate the people, because they don't know about the rules. [...] Not only do we need good laws, but we need to train and educate our drivers from day one'.

During the nineteenth century, the Iranian elite had already identified the central role of education in resolving the country's economic and technical backwardness. In retrospect, this might have been based on a rather simplistic understanding of the reason for the technological advances made by the European powers. The modernization process initiated later by the Pahlavi regime (1925–79) also placed education at the top of the agenda of policies to be implemented. Educated Iranians, who often belonged to the upper middle classes, were among those who benefited greatly from the central role that education came to play in the new Iranian society (Moghissi 2008: 544).

Concealed behind Iranians' positive attitude to education, generally, and to educational attainments, in particular, we find the force of their personalism and the support of their community. Education elevates individuals' social standing, enabling them to advance and better themselves, and to gain *shakhsiyat* (respect as well as self-respect). This positive attitude to education cuts across gender and class differences (even though parts of the Iranian middle classes are almost obsessed with the educational success of their children). Higher education is valued culturally, and having a university education ensures a degree of respect and the possibility of attaining high social status (as we shall see below, *shakhsiyat* is, in the first instance, a function of one's upbringing and family).

After the revolution of 1979, and the Islamization of the Iranian state and society, university became the only legitimate safe space for women to socialize publically. University education for girls was valued, because it increased their social status and brought respect to their family (Hegland 2009: 71). However, it would be a mistake to suggest that Iranian universities became a free, public, political forum because although they provided political space from which to voice dissent, they were nevertheless controlled and monitored by the State and used instrumentally for promoting specific political agendas and realizing an Islamic cultural revolution. As Golnar Mehran (1991) has pointed out, the State used education generally for the politicization, Islamization and socialization of men and women, and ultimately for creating a new moral order in the country.

Many traditionally minded families, especially those living in rural and remote areas of the country, were against the idea of their daughters attending public institutions such as a university or taking up employment in public or private institutions and businesses. Compulsory veiling (*hijab*) and the Islamization of education, generally, and higher education, in particular, were amongst the factors that helped to remove any objections and encouraged them to allow their daughters to attend universities, many of which were situated in large cities that they themselves might never have visited. We should hasten to add that forcing women to wear the veil in public did not in itself put the minds of these families at rest – they were persuaded that it was safe for their daughters to study and work in public institutions when they realized that this was an integral part of a complete Islamization of society based on strict gender segregation. In the name of Shari‘a, and through law and policy measures, the State stepped in to establish the rights of men to control women's sexuality. This point underlines two significant aspects of Iranian society. First, the control of sexuality, generally, and gender segregation, in particular, plays a decisive role in the organization of culture and society, and is one of the key points in understanding Iranian politics (this point is directly linked to the most basic duality of veiling/unveiling in Persian culture). This was demonstrated by our interviews with female taxi drivers and is discussed at length in Chapter Nine.[9] Second, the sociocultural values of gender segregation were not initially introduced from above by the State, but were the embodiment of patriarchal family structures (as we shall argue in the next chapter, these gender values lay the basis of a form of 'living law', which is embedded in Iranian culture).[10] The Islamic government's commitment to enforcing strict gender segregation and controlling women's sexuality has enabled it to forge a cultural alliance with the traditionalist sections of society. This alliance is formed directly between the Islamic state and large sections of the male population – beyond the usual political divisions and ideological disagreement – by upholding the values of patriarchy that are embedded in the deep cultural structures of the Iranian family and articulated in the rules and norms of the neighbourhood communities.

Policies of gender segregation aimed at controlling women ironically enabled some girls belonging to the traditionalist sections of society to attend institutions of higher education, obtain university degrees and enter the labour market. This gave them a level of economic independence, and helped them to establish new social identities for themselves and to negotiate the culturally constructed gender obstacles that have been designed to hinder their participation in the public sphere. Furthermore, attending educational establishments has enabled many girls to leave home and create their own future – one that is not governed by marriage. In this sense, the widespread belief in education, paradoxically combined with policies of gender segregation, has had a positive impact on the social conditions of many young Iranian women by allowing them to realize their potential, and thus their personalism.

To be successful in education, to be the *zerang* of your class, can indeed help you to beat the system — especially if you are a girl from the more traditional sections of society.

Collective Unconsciousness

If the Iranian psyche is formed by personalism, how can Iranians act collectively? In fact, they are quite capable of mobilizing themselves and acting jointly — as was demonstrated by the 1979 revolution and, more recently, the widespread protests against the 2009 presidential election results, when the incumbent President Ahmadinejad was accused of vote rigging. One explanation is provided by Bayat (2013), who argues that Iranian people maintain their capability under the constraints of arbitrary rulers through what he calls 'non-movement', which refers to the collective action of non-collective actors. According to Bayat, the street as an urban public space becomes an arena for expressing one's discontent, which in turn creates public disorder. Bayat argues (2013: 11) that 'street politics' achieves more than the mere expression of people's conflict with the authorities, in that it also shapes their identities and sense of being in society. Street politics, as a medium of political action, enables people to interact, find similar interests and exhibit temporary solidarity. The will of the people — as in the 1979 revolution, the 2009 protests and the women's protest in Tehran and Isfahan in October 2014 'after a string of acid attacks on women in the city' (*Guardian* 28 August 2014)[11] — is the result of collective action by non-collective actors. Another example is youths' discontent and their unconscious, collective, defiant actions against social and political controls imposed by the State. These youths non-collectively share the same habitus — including lifestyle, appearance and interests — and act to reclaim their youthfulness by transgressing the strict norms of Islamic morality that are imposed on them by the State and policed in public spaces by the *Basij-e Mostazafin*.

Culture-Building (*Farhang-sazi*), Intelligence (*Sho'ur*) and Awareness (*Agahi*)

The frequent use of the term *farhang-sazi* by our interviewees suggests a belief in social engineering, top-down interventions and the ability of the authorities to carry out campaigns aimed at bringing about social reform and progress (*pish-raft*). Those interviewed also showed that *farhang-sazi* was linked to Iranians' faith in the power of education (*amoozesh*, which also means 'learning')[12] and the conviction that if people were informed (were given *agahi*) about laws and rules of driving and the dangers of disregarding them, they would change their ways. In fact, *farhang-sazi* is but a form of education – some might say an indoctrination – with a set of clear public-policy objectives. It has been used as a method in the Islamization of Iranian society, but occasionally also employed to tackle socio-economic problems such as population growth. (The Iranian authorities succeeded in reducing the country's rate of population growth by 1.5 per cent between 1986 and 1999, through a well-orchestrated campaign that informed families of the advantages of having fewer children.) Looking back at our interviews, we find many quotes that bring together *farhang-sazi* and education as a vehicle for informing people. For example, one of the male taxi drivers (see interview 1:1:12, page 68, in Chapter Four) explained that the traffic problem was a function of 'insufficient training and education', which could be addressed only if the authorities invested in *farhang-sazi* (for a similar quote, see 1:3:14 – also in Chapter Four).

On the one hand, *farhang-sazi* is used to refer to public-policy measures that have to be carried out by the authorities. For such measures to be successful, Iranians need to trust the authorities who are expected to implement policies that are aimed at *farhang-sazi*. On the other hand, our interviewees generally did not trust the authorities, and to various degrees argued that the laws were poorly enforced. Thus, those that we interviewed readily placed their trust in *farhang-sazi* although they did not trust those who were charged with implementing it. One explanation is that Iranians distinguish between education and legal or political regulation. They see education 'as a good in itself and a good for all' (Axworthy 2013: 398) and thus put their trust in it, whereas they view the legal system or the state administration in a negative light. They also see education as a medium for passing on *agahi* – that is awareness, information and knowledge – to ordinary people. *Agahi* was treated as a positive and politically neutral attribute of *farahang-sazi* that empowers people. This was, however, only in the context of our interviews, and should not be generalized to the whole of the population. There are also other reasons for the apparent contradiction that we found with respect to *farahang-sazi*. Some of the female taxi drivers argued that it had to start from childhood through family socialization, which endowed children with *sho'ur* (intelligence) and *agahi* (information):

4:4:65: '*Farhang-sazi* must start from childhood [...]. A person must learn from an early age not to jump in the middle of the street [...]. There is chaos wherever there are no police in the street, which shows you the lack of the culture of driving, and [how ineffective it is when] obeying the rules [is] based on fear.'

Another interviewee expressed a similar idea:

4:1:66: 'The culture of driving should start with the family. Some families can't even teach their children to talk properly, but they can buy cars. But, you know, they don't have the *sho'ur* to use it.'

The role of the authorities (as in the aforementioned campaign to reduce the rate of population growth) is to empower families by educating them, which means providing them with *agahi* and letting them to implement it according to their *sho'ur*, i.e. intelligence and common sense. *Sho'ur* is related to, but is not a function of, formal education. One of the female taxi drivers clarified this point by pointing out that one did not improve one's social conduct by attending university but by way of the knowledge and training that one received in the course of socialization from an early age. Another woman taxi driver stated that well-educated men still wanted their women to stay at home and remain housewives. This suggests that in the context of Iranian culture, *sho'ur* and *agahi* are not functions of *formal* schooling but of primary socialization, which is produced within the family. Several interviewees argued that driving agencies provide training and technical instructions on how to drive a car in accordance with the rules of the traffic, which normally lead to passing a driving test. They are not, however, responsible for ensuring that drivers obtain the type of *sho'ur* and *agahi* that is required for respecting the rights of people. Women interviewees in particular insisted that one had to learn *sho'ur* at home. Once again, the individual is defined in terms of his or her 'peer group', thereby suggesting that the key cultural concepts generate meaning by linking the actions of the individual to the family, which in turn gains social significance once contrasted with the norms of the 'society of strangers'. Finally, raising people from childhood with *sho'ur* and *agahi* produces people with prestige (or *ba-shakhsiyat*) who, besides being well mannered, are law-abiding.

The point made here is that *farhang-sazi*, which started with a revolutionary cultural ethos and a belief in controlling social change, must be brought down to earth and turned into factually based ideas to be implemented at the discretion of the family. More significantly, it suggests that the family sets the limits for the efficacy of social policy measures in Iran. While *farhang-sazi* was successful, say in controlling the population growth because families could see the socio-economic advantages of it, it has arguably been unsuccessful in Islamizing Iranian society in the way that the ideologues of the Islamic Republic had hoped. That is why the *Basij-e Mostazafin* has to police the behaviour of ordinary Iranians in public (and, when they can, also in private) spaces and to *impose* their Islamic codes of conduct by force and through violence. Clearly, Islamization does not work by disseminating *agahi*, because at the level of family many Iranians do not share the need for the strict codes of Islamic conduct that are propagated by conservative clergy.

Shakhsiyat (šæxsiæt)

The concept of *shakhsiyat* refers to 'self-respect' and connotes a range of other words such as 'character', 'personality' and 'honour'. According to Koutlaki (2002: 1742), Irving Goffman's interrelated concepts of 'pride' and 'honour' correspond with *shakhsiyat* and *ehteram* (respect). We argue, however, if we reduce *shakhsiyat* to 'pride' and 'honour', we overlook a complex array of relational mechanisms which link the individual's actions and social standing to his or her family, on the one hand, and to the larger society, on the other.

Shakhsiyat is understood here as the effect of various factors, including family background, upbringing, social class and education (Koutlaki 2002: 1756). Koutlaki (2002: 1755) regards it as a 'public face' which reveals the individual's standing among his or her cohesive circle of friends and 'the nuclear and the extended family'. The conduct of a person who is *bi-shakhsiyat* (without *shakhsiyat* or ill-mannered) brings disgrace upon his or her family. To show the centrality of family in relation to *shakhsiyat*, we can refer to the notion of *bi-khanevadeh* – literally 'a person without family' – which, when used in a British context, could mean a person who is not married and has no children, but in a Farsi context it refers to a vulgar and disreputable person who behaves disgracefully. In contrast, a person who behaves gracefully in public is called *khanevadeh-dar* (with family). The way in which *khanevadeh* is employed in everyday Farsi to make moralizing and judgemental statements on people's public conduct demonstrates the extent to which Iranians view the individual person, and his or her public behaviour, as a social function of his or her family. In a way, we could say that Iranian culture is embedded in the family, where the initial cultural socialization (*tarbiyat-e-khanevadegi*) takes place and where a person learns the cultural codes and values which determine how he or she reacts in different situations and interacts with different people and groups.

Shakhsiyat is a subtle status-seeking characteristic, which is why it is easily linked to social class conduct and family background, while it rests uneasily with *zerangi* which *could be* a socially subversive. The former is norm-establishing and norm-following behaviour, while the latter can involve circumventing rules and manipulating situations to one's benefit. To refer to the interviews with women drivers again, '[...] disrespecting the law reveals a person's [lack of] *shakhsiyat*', and 'someone who doesn't respect the traffic rules is *bi-shakhsiyat*'. The interviewees here are expressing injunctive norms which do not refer to how Iranians actually behave but to how they should ideally behave in traffic. But we have also seen that breaking the law, and getting away with it, can be admired as *zerangi*. Concepts such as *shakhsiyat* and *zerangi*, which at first glance appear incompatible, are nevertheless brought together in the same cultural framework because, contradictory as they potentially may be, they constitute aspects of Iranian personalism, which is in turn rooted in, and dependent on, the individual's close-knit community whose final judgement and view of a person's conduct is decisive for that person's standing and *shakhsiyat*. None of these contradictory cultural ideas and traits could work harmoniously, albeit in a highly puzzling manner, had it not been for the separation of Iranian society into two opposing spheres, i.e. the tight network of family and friends, regulated by interpersonal trust, as opposed to the larger society of strangers, regulated by the arbitrary exercise of power.

To sum up, a person's *shakhsiyat* can be preserved through self-respect, but to maintain one's respect, the person has to acknowledge the *shakhsiyat* of people with whom he or she is interacting (Koutlaki 2002:

1756). *Shakhsiyat* may also throw light on other cultural traits such as *taarof*. A person with *sho'ur* and *agahi* treats people with due respect – engaging, amongst other things, in *taarof* – and thus is considered as a person with *shakhsiyat*.

Taarof

Taarof is a ritual through which Iranians offer gifts, make compliments and show courtesy to each other. It may also be described as a 'language game' that they employ in face-to-face interactions in order to demonstrate excessive politeness to each other (Taleghani-Nikazm 1998: 4). In that sense, it is an indispensable cultural property of the way in which Iranians interact with each other in everyday life and a subtle method that they use to negotiate their social relations (Koutlaki 2002: 1741). Paying respect to other people through *taarof* can be viewed as a method of engaging them in a reciprocal relationship, wherein the individual who initiated the process is indirectly establishing his *sho'ur*, *agahi* and, subsequently, *shakhsiyat* while at the same time making a discreet (at a socioculturally unconscious level) claim to be recognized as a respectable person. The logic is simple: courtesy can be taken seriously and received as a compliment, but only if the person who is extending it is worthy of respect. In that sense, *taarof* is as much about paying respect to the other as it is about establishing one's own *shakhsiyat*, social standing and upbringing, which by implication relates the individual to his or her family.

Although it is normally used positively, to show civility towards others, it can also be used ritually as an 'empty formality' or without goodwill (Koutlaki 2002). There is a Persian expression that denotes making an offer without genuinely meaning it (*taarof-e shah abdul azimi*) or offering something worthless (*taarof-e aabe hamam*), which literally means offering someone the 'bathwater'. The complexity of the way in which *taarof* is used in everyday exchanges can, in certain situations, bring so much ambiguity into exchanges as to make the most competent Farsi-speaker baffled as to the meaning of what is being implied between the lines, or what exactly is offered and what is expected in return. Those who fail to perform the ritual of *taarof* (to make offers and compliments) and those who take an offer made through *taarof* immediately, and do not reject it at least once, are perceived as uncultivated and bad-mannered.

As we pointed out in Chapter Four, in connection with the interviews with the male taxi drivers, Iranians' cultural need for self-respect does not work in a traffic situation, because their interactions with other drivers are not mediated face-to-face (interpersonal) or through the use of language.[13] They are instead mediated through the use of the automobile – they might not even see the other driver eye-to-eye – and therefore doing *taarof* would not amount to establishing one's self-respect in traffic. One of the medical doctors that we interviewed in Chapter Six also linked *taarof* and eye contact:

> Doctor 3:1:30: 'What is viewed as generosity and good manners, such as *taarof*, has not been extended to, for example, driving. My colleague, who also does research on traffic injuries, always says that Iranians avoid eye contact when they are driving [...] in case they recognise each other.'

Attempts to engage in *taarof* while driving can, as one of the female taxi drivers pointed out, cause unexpected problems:

> 4:7:67: 'There is saying that "one can never predict what comes out of *taarof*". Once it happened to me that the right of way was mine [but I stopped to let the other car pass]. The other car stopped to give way. So I told the other driver, "Go", but he replied, "No, please you go first." The result was that the traffic built up behind us.'

This is an example of what might happen when two drivers make eye contact and try to enter into *taarof*. More often, however, such eye contact does not take place, and the driver's attention remains on the movements of other cars rather than on who is driving them. The meeting of the eyes has a social function, which was first discussed by Georg Simmel (1903/1971a and 1903/1971b) and later adopted in the studies of 'mobilities':

> Of the special sense organs, the eye has a uniquely sociological function. The union and interaction of individuals is based on mutual glances [...]. This mutual glance between persons, in distinction from the simple sight or observation of the other,

signifies a wholly new and unique union between them. The limits of this relation are to be determined by the significant fact that the glance by which one seeks to perceive the other is itself expressive. By the glance which reveals the other, one discloses himself [. . .]. What occurs in this direct mutual glance represents the most perfect reciprocity in the entire field of human relationships.

Drivers of automobiles do not, and cannot, orient themselves towards each others' movements through eye contact, and therefore they cannot be expected to abide by such customary rules as *taarof*. This, however, is a generally valid point across cultures, in that drivers cannot interact socially with each other while driving, which is why they need to trust strangers, pedestrians and other drivers to follow certain rules and respect each others' rights in specific spaces (such as motorways, roads, streets and pavements) where mobility is played out. According to John Urry, 'automobility' prevents the realization of the social significance of the eye in interactions between drivers and others such as pedestrians:

Especially for the non-car-user, roads are simply full of moving, dangerous iron cages. There is no reciprocity of the eye, and no look is returned from the 'ghost in the machine'. Communities of people become anonymized flows of faceless ghostly machines. The iron cages conceal the expressiveness of the face, and a road full of vehicles can never be possessed. There is no distance and mastery over the iron cage; rather, those living on the street are bombarded by hustle and bustle and especially by the noise, fumes and relentless movement of the car that cannot be mastered or possessed.

(Urry 2004: 30)

The automobile as a *technological* artefact impacts upon social behaviour irrespective of the culture of the driver.[14] It would be misleading to treat the 'car driver' as an individual with ordinary social psychological properties. According to Nigel Thrift (1996: 282–4), the notion of the car driver is 'a hybrid assemblage of specific human activities, machines, roads, buildings, signs and cultures of mobility' (see, also, Urry, 2014: 26). In addition, the automobile has a symbolic social value and can stimulate drivers' senses in various ways. As most of our interviewees pointed out, the automobile had been transformed into a symbol of wealth. Subsequently, interactions in traffic can even signify economic and power relationships.

Coping with Uncertainties

On Hofstede's scale, Iranians score 59 points on 'uncertainty avoidance' while the British score 35, the Swedes 29 and the Danes 23 (Hofstede Centre 2014), which shows that Iranians experience a relatively high degree of anxiety with respect to the future, which they feel they cannot control. Anxiety caused by the perceived instability of sociopolitical institutions is, however, nothing new in the Iranian context, and has been one of the historical forces that have shaped Iranian culture and society. It has promoted short-term projects at the expense of long-term planning, which would require reliance on the greater society and existing political structures. Under such conditions, Iranians have devised a tradition and a form of social organization that they have preserved together with their language (Farsi), in order to ensure some degree of social continuity, economic certitude and political security. The family, the extended family and the small community of friends constitute the basic units of this form of social organization and Iranians' personalism its primary socio-historical manifestation. Reza and Joséphine Arasteh unfold this point in the following way:

> The tenacity with which Iranian people have held on to their traditional way of life results from a system of value which encourages the individual to overtly accept adversity without forsaking his integrity. Throughout Iran's long history barbaric invaders and oppressive rulers, along with unfavourable geographic conditions, have compelled the inhabitants to submit to fate or to find ways to circumvent the imposition. While outwardly bowing to circumstances, Iranians have devised artful ways of avoiding submission, either by manipulation of the environment or by detachment from the material world as best expressed in Sufi mysticism.
>
> By its very nature, the Iranian value system in providing for diverse circumstances permits the individual considerable flexibility in his behaviour. Iranian culture does not condemn a

man for resorting to trickery to deceive the government or others who have traditionally robbed him of his possessions and security. On the other hand, the individual's relations to his family and friends call for honesty and sincerity.

(Arasteh and Arasteh 1964: 40)

The social and historical aspects of personalism are intertwined with its political dimension, i.e. it exists on the one hand through the support of the individual's 'peer group', while on the other it also shapes the relationship between the individual and the government or authorities. Therein we also find a tentative link between personalism and Shi'ism's belief that no 'temporal' government is legitimate during Imam Mahdy's absence. Moreover, as we explained in Chapter Three, Iranian rulers have traditionally exerted their power in an arbitrary fashion, as a result of which their relationship with their subjects has become permeated by mutual distrust and tension. Outwardly, Iranians submit to authority and demonstrate respect for those in power, without genuinely entertaining loyalty towards them (rulers can come and go at the drop of a hat). However, inwardly, they subvert the rulers' domination and their top-down attempts to regulate society. To refer to Hofstede's scale again, on 'power distance', which reflects the individual's cultural attitude towards inequality, Iran scores 58, the UK 35, Sweden 31 and Denmark 18. According to Hofstede, this means that Iranian society is a hierarchical one, where 'people accept a hierarchical order in which everybody has a place and which needs no further justification' (Hofstede Centre 2014). At the other end of the scale, the Danes' score of 18 indicates their egalitarian mindset and their belief in autonomy, equal rights and superiors who are accessible. It might be that Iranians generally accept the political hierarchy as a reality, but this does not mean that they submit to its arbitrary exercise of power. The tension between Iranians and their authorities was demonstrated in many of our interviews, wherein the interviewees voiced their distrust of the political apparatus and stated that it existed to preserve the interests of those in power. Since the authorities also make and enforce the law, Iranians' negative perceptions and experiences of their authorities' arbitrary exercise of power also define their attitude to the law and the legal system. Iranians are therefore constantly seeking ways of 'circumventing' the constraints that are imposed upon them by their rulers. That is why 'beating the system' is highly admired among Iranians, and a person who succeeds in doing so is regarded as *zerang*.

Concluding Remarks

If family constitutes the most basic social unit of Iranian society, then personalism is its most basic cultural manifestation. The socio-political importance of family and the cultural significance of personalism have evolved together as aspects of the same reaction to the unstable nature of Iranian society, and as a strategy for managing the volatile nature of its political order. Thus, personalism has emerged as a short-term micro strategy for coping with macro uncertainties generated by living in an unstable society incapable of ensuring long-term social, economic and political stability and security. The key ideas that were identified in our interviews, such as *zerangi*, *sho'ur*, *agahi*, *taarof* and *shakhsiyat*, as well as belief in education and *farhang-sazi*, are linked together through family and constitute aspects of personalism. These, separately and jointly, describe how the individual's identity, actions and relationships are formed through his or her 'peer group', but against the backdrop of society at large. The *Gemeinschaft* ('community' in sociologist Ferdinand Tönnies's terminology) that we find at the level of family is reproduced by contrasting itself with the norms and authority of society at large (see Tönnies 1955). The concept of *zerangi* throws light on the degree to which the individual's conduct is pitched against the 'society of strangers', and *shakhsiyat* reveals the extent to which the public and private persona of the individual is a function of his or her family background.

As we shall explain in the next chapter, the Iranian family is undergoing a transformation in large cities and urban areas of the country. Notwithstanding the changes that the family is subjected to, it continues to play a central role in the context of Iranian society, suggesting that Iran has maintained a traditional social structure. Needless to say, it is also within the family that the individual forms his or her class identity, internalizes gender roles and learns to treat the oppressiveness of the patriarchy as socially normal. It is also within the family that one learns to distinguish between neighbourhood community, society at large and the State. All this takes place against the backdrop of the Perso-Islamic culture of Iran, i.e. a culture that is partly pre-Islamic (still celebrating Norooz and Yalda) and partly Shi'i Muslim (mourning the martyrdom of Hossein ibn Ali and his family and friends). How the changing constitution of the family will affect the formation of Iranian personalism is among the topics that we shall discuss in the next chapter.

We have argued that culture had subjective dimensions produced by shared values, perceptions and norms and objective manifestations such as driving habits. We have also referred to the way in which towns, cities and neighbourhoods have evolved over time as cultural objectifications of how Iranians relate themselves to each other and to society. The very structure of Iranian cities and the architecture of traditional and more modern Iranian houses suggest a world view that perceives social life in terms of oppositional dualities such as private/public spaces, inside/outside, inner/outer personas, religiously related/unrelated and veiled/unveiled (see Naficy 2000; Mirgholami and Sintusigha 2012). Our understanding of the duality of the 'veiled' and the 'unveiled' does not limit itself to the *hijab*, or the *chador* (cloak), but to ideas, images, perceptions and, ultimately, the forms of life that are caught up in an incessant opposition between what is concealed and suppressed and what is disclosed and brought into light. These dualities introduce tension and cause conflict in every walk of life, give birth to false dichotomies such as *mostakberin* and *mostazafin*, and, through their oppositional interplay, invoke transgression, defiance and rebellion but also produce and reproduce Iranian personalism over time. Expressed differently, personalism is the behavioural materialization of the dialectical interplay of the dualities incorporated historically in Iranian culture and society. However, neither Iranian culture nor personalism is only about defiance and rebellion. They are equally about upholding mutual respect in relationships, and involve consensus-seeking rituals such as *taarof* and deeply rooted beliefs in the force of education as a public and private good. According to Manoukian (2012), for example, Iranians relate to society not through conflict but through their poetry, which in turn partly deals with dualities – albeit in an aesthetically refined manner. These more consensus-oriented properties of Iranian culture have been put out of action in the context of traffic, partly due to the technology of the automobile.

Iranian motorists find it difficult to respect the rights of other drivers and pedestrians, who are strangers with whom one does not even see eye to eye and whose rights are a function of state law. However, one of our interviewees explained that she would respect the rights of pedestrians and stop to let them cross the street once she viewed them as members of her family.[15] This point is significant not only in making sense of Iranian society and culture, but also in understanding Iranians' driving habits and, by extension, Iranian *legal* culture. It also explains the excessive discrepancy that we find between descriptive and injunctive norms among Iranians. Descriptive norms, which reflect the norms of behaviour that people actually follow, often belong to the sociality of immediate community, to the 'private' sphere wherein individuals are related-through kinship, to the 'insiders', the 'inner self' and the 'unveiled' part of the dichotomies constituting the Iranian culture. These norms often reflect practices that are based on interpersonal trust and mutual dependency, and represent the sociality of the extended family and the *Gemeinschaft* of the neighbourhood and the traditional *mahalleh*. Its form of law is that of the customary *urf*, which several interviewees referred to. By contrast, injunctive norms, which refer to what people *ought* to do in specific social situations (for example, a driver *ought* to stop at a pedestrian crossing to let people cross the street), are norms of the larger 'society of strangers' and are the rules dictated by the authorities. These signify the 'public' sphere, people who are '*un*related', the 'outsiders', 'the outer self', and to 'the veiled' part of the dichotomies. The sociality of the public arena is that of the *Gesellschaft* (the 'society' of Tönnies's dichotomy), and its form of law is state law. How *urf* and state law interact with each other within the framework of Shari'a to produce the Iranian legal culture forms the subject matter of Chapter Nine.

CHAPTER 9

IRANIAN LEGAL CULTURE: LAW, GENDER AND CLASS DIVISIONS

Reza Banakar

As a matter of sociological and historical – even psychological – fact, an Iranian is a product of centuries of Islamic social and cultural experience, even though he or she may not be a believer; and likewise he or she cannot rid himself or herself of ancient Persia if only because it is the historical background to Islamic Iran and has considerably influenced it in cultural terms, so that, historically, Islam in Iran has been distinct from Islam elsewhere, in other Muslim countries.

(Homa Katouzian 2009: 12)

This chapter concludes our study of driving behaviour by bringing to bear cultural insights gained in the previous chapter on our interviewees' experiences of law and legality. Their conceptions and experiences of the law are then placed in the broader context of the country's social history and politics to produce a theoretical starting point for understanding Iranian legal culture as an opposition between its dual manifestations: state law (Shari'a) and custom (*urf*). We shall argue that the tension between *urf* and state law resonates with a number of other forms of opposition, such as descriptive and injunctive norms, private and public conduct, inner religiosity and outer religious ideology,

Figure 9.1 Mullah in Shiraz © Jeppe Schilder.

related and unrelated people, and ultimately the 'unveiled' (disclosed) and the 'veiled' (concealed and suppressed). The chapter starts by describing how *urf* (or customary practices) has been gradually recognized and incorporated into Islamic law, before it moves on to recount how it has been employed in Iranian law and state administration since the beginning of the sixteenth century. The chapter will then go on to develop a sociolegal model for how Iranian society is held together through three levels of sociality, each with its own form of normativity or law.

Urf

One way to understand a legal system in its socio-historical context is by exploring how it has reacted and adapted to its environment, and the extent to which it has incorporated changing social, cultural, economic and other practices. *Urf* (spelled alternatively *orf*) has been used traditionally as one of Islamic law's mechanisms of adapting to its shifting environment (see Chapter Eleven for a presentation of how *urf* is used in Iranian law today). It originated etymologically from the Arabic word *arafa*, which literally means 'to know' or 'that which is known' (Lambak and Tahir 2013: 265). It refers to verbal and practical customs that are known and acceptable – i.e. regarded as 'right', 'good' and 'reasonable' – to a community, and are followed by its members to such an extent as to appear binding upon them (Salisu 2013: 134). As a source of law, *urf* is secondary to the Qur'an, *sunna* (tradition), *qiyas* (analogy) and *ijma* (consensus), which means that it cannot exert legal force on its own and must be employed in legal decision making in combination with one of the four main sources of law. Islamic law, being a divine legal system, did not recognize from the outset earthly customs based on ordinary people's conduct as a formal source of law. It was later, between the end of the ninth and the beginning of the sixteenth century, that, according to Libson (1997: 137), jurists incorporated 'practical custom in the law without granting it formal recognition'. This was often achieved indirectly by identifying it with *sunna* or *ijma*.[1] It was at the end of this period, in 1501, that *urf* courts made their first appearance on the legal scene in Iran. As *urf* was formalized and brought under political control in Iran, it lost much of its ability to mitigate the tension between state law and customary practices at the grass-roots level.

Against this backdrop, it is hardly surprising that several of our interviewees referred to *urf* and the customary practices that continue to exist beyond the formal scope of the laws of the Islamic government. The first interviewee in the pilot study (see pilot: 1) explained that *urf* was more powerful than laws promulgated by parliament. One of the lawyers argued that ordinary people held in much higher regard laws that were formed in accordance with their religious beliefs (which are not necessarily the same as the government's Islamic ideology), and they normally followed them. He also added that Iranians had a nonchalant attitude to traffic laws because traffic rules were not seen as moral or religious obligations, and had no basis in their belief system (see interview 2:11:36, page 101). Another lawyer stated that Iranian merchants and traders may well evade paying taxes to the State, but they did not avoid paying their *khoms* and *zakat* (religious dues amounting to one-fifth of their net profit), because Iranians believed in the value of these dues and considered it a lawful duty to pay them. The case of *bazaari* merchants paying their religious dues, we argued, was also a reflection of their standing within the socially conservative merchant community, which constituted not only a political force with ties to the *ulama*, but also their role in their local community. The same lawyer went on to add that Iranians behaved according to *urf* but nevertheless defied the State and tried to circumvent its laws (see interview 2:2:39, page 103). References to *urf* also appeared in a number of interviews with non-lawyers, suggesting its significance as a legal guideline within Iranian culture. In Chapter Seven, to give another example, one of the female taxi drivers explained that 'every individual [was] responsible for upholding the law' which, according to her, consisted of 'the laws which [were] sanctioned in Shari'a and *urf*' (see interview 4:8:53, page 144). We are once again confronted with a paradox: *our* interviewees express a secular understanding of the law, but at the same time they reflect the widespread religiosity embedded in Iranian culture.

The way in which *urf* is used in the interviews – to refer to the unwritten customary norms and practices invoked by ordinary people to regulate their everyday transactions and maintain the social order – is in keeping with traditional Islamic jurisprudence's conceptualization thereof. It is, however, not consistent with how *urf* was employed in Iran prior to the Constitutional Revolution of 1905–11, because until the Constitutional Revolution, the principles of Shari'a, as interpreted by the clergy, constituted the source of law in Iran, although Shari'a courts operated in parallel to the *urf* (or *orfi*) courts. Furthermore, they regulated interpersonal relationships and resolved disputes, while the *urf* courts were used to deal with administrative issues, to decide on matters concerning the State and to deal with the 'four crimes' (murder, assault, rape and theft). According to Arasteh and Arasteh (1964: 159):

> In traditional Islamic times, *shari'a* courts generally had jurisdiction over religious and family matters, whereas the *urf* courts dealt with criminal and political offences. The *shari'a* law of the Shi'ites grow out of four religious sources [. . .]. In contrast, *urf* was based, not on an established series of precedents or regulations, but on the prevailing outlook of the monarch in power. As a result, decrees were arbitrary and hastily made. On the local level, *urf* courts were administered by the village headman or the city governor and his officials, at the upper level by the provincial governors, and ultimately by the shah and his ministers. The establishment of the constitution in 1906 replaced much of the *urf* system with a civil code, which at the time was largely based on the *shari'a*.

Urf courts existed during the sixteenth century and throughout the Safavid period (1501–1736), and they continued to operate during the Qajar dynasty (1785–1925). They were 'supervised by a secular minister of justice' (Mir-Hosseini 2010a: 324) and were ultimately controlled by the shah, who appointed senior judges and personally resided 'over the *mazalem* [injustices] tribunals that were intended to deal with the abuse [of power] by governmental officials' (Enayat 2013: 33). The jurisdiction of *urf* included administrative and public matters as well as matters concerning 'either the security of the realm (such as military uprising, rebellions or treason), public order, or the "four crimes"' (Enayat 2013: 33). *Urf* courts operated on the basis of the customary laws of the State and not the customary practices of the people, they were often highly informal, were not based 'on an established series of precedents or regulations', reflected 'the prevailing outlook of the monarch in power' and produced arbitrary and hasty judgements (Arasteh and Arasteh 1964: 159). Since their sources for decision making included the whim of the Iranian rulers, and they could not ensure a degree of predictability and uniformity in decision making, strictly speaking they cannot be regarded as *legal* tribunals. Nevertheless, they infringed upon, and undermined, the jurisdiction of the Shari'a courts, which were headed by the clergy and which employed Islamic jurisprudence.

Qajar Iran, Enayat (2013) maintains, did not develop a codified *urf* law similar to that which existed in the Ottoman Empire, and continued to enforce unwritten rules rather than a set of established legal principles. As a result, *urf* came to lend itself easily to arbitrary decision making, as the use of unwritten rules freed Iranian rulers from both the substantive and procedural rules of Shari'a and allowed them to justify their arbitrary administration of justice in the name of customary practices. This dual administration of justice continued in various forms until the first volume of Iran's civil code was introduced and a modern legal system was established by Reza Shah in 1925. The Iranian Civil Code was composed of two parts, the first of which was 'a secularised version of Shari'a and the second [a] translation of *Code civil des Français*' (Shahidian 2000: 53). However, with the establishment of a modern legal system and the increased significance of civil courts, the role of the clergy was gradually undermined and, finally, in 1932, they were officially banned from performing notary acts.

The legal history of *urf* supports the idea that a secular form of law, administered by secular judges, has existed in Iran for a long time, and that this law has largely expressed the arbitrary rule of the State, which has existed independently of the customary practices of ordinary people. Moreover, *urf*, as the customary law of the state administration, has encroached upon the jurisdiction of Shari'a and prevented it from developing into an all-encompassing legal system capable of regulating both public and private affairs (see Katouzian 2009: 6). Parallel to the secular law of the State, Shari'a existed and operated as a separate legal system during the rules of the Safavids and the Qajars, but not the Pahlavis, under whom a modern, secular legal system was introduced. Moreover, as Shahidian (2000: 53) has pointed out, in times of political instability and upheavals, when the State could not perform its normal functions, judicial authority would be transferred to Shari'a courts. Although Shari'a provided a more stable legal system from 1501 onwards, it was only after the 1979 Islamic Revolution that it was elevated to the level of state law. This demonstrates that there is a long history of secular law, albeit a law which was largely practised by Iranian rulers in an arbitrary fashion, from 1501 to 1979, when the Islamic Republic re-established Shari'a as the law of the land.

With the elevation of Shari'a to state law, the clergy became the 'high priests' of the judicial order and held the authority to interpret and enforce the law, while the distance between people's religiosity and the Islamic law of the State started to grow. The legal system was reconstructed by introducing a strict version of Shari'a and by bringing the judiciary under the control of the clergy. As part of this Islamization process, the new clerical state 'redefined' *urf* – which had been traditionally distinguished by Islamic jurists as a customary entity distinct from, but related to, Shari'a – as 'what is in the interest of the regime'. As Mohammadi (2008: 127) explains:

> The religious establishment replaced the 'orf with *maslahat-e nezam* (the expediency of the regime) after the Islamic Revolution of 1979. The 'orf and the necessities of governing of the ruling caste, i.e. *maslahat-e nezam*, substituted [for] the dynamic custom of the society. [...] A general or specific 'orf could not supersede a general or specific rule of Shari'ah as presented by a jurist, but it is the power of government vested in the Expediency Council that can supersede the Islamic rules and beliefs.

This may be viewed as a return to the pre-Pahlavi understanding of *urf*, with the exception that this time around Shari'a is the sole basis of state law and *urf* is incorporated into it as 'the expediency of the regime'. Expressed differently, the regime recognizes custom as a source of law in as far as it deems it politically expedient. Thus, to refer to Mohammadi (2008) again, the redefinition of *urf* allowed the ruling clergy to ignore the idea that changing local customs should be recognized and incorporated into Shari'a. It must be emphasized that the idea of *urf* that we have come across in our interviews is not the ideologized version of the clerical state but organically generated customary norms and practices. At the level of spontaneous practices in everyday life, *urf* is embodied in the culture of ordinary people and survives as their 'living law', distinct from the norms that express the State's political expediency.

In this context, we should mention the role of *fatwa*, which in the West is associated with death sentences against individuals such as

British author Salman Rushdie. A *fatwa* is issued by an Islamic jurist (a *mufti*, a Grand Ayatollah or a so-called *Maraj'e-Taghlid*) and normally consists of a verdict on a question or a response to a specific circumstance that has not been previously subjected to legal scrutiny. Expressed differently, the jurist will, often at the behest of an individual or a group, resolve or clarify the question of law, in a case in which Islamic law has been unclear or silent. It can be in relation to international law (see a recent pronouncement against the use of nuclear weapons[2]), the use of technology such as the internet,[3] the permissibility of sex changes[4] or the everyday practices of ordinary people concerning family law or contract. A *fatwa* may be compared to the legal ruling of a supreme court, albeit a ruling which is made outside the institutional settings of the legal system, and, as Kamali (2012: 162) explains, it is not binding 'on the person or persons to whom [it is] addressed, unless it is issued by a court in a case under its consideration, in which case the decision would carry a binding force'. The *fatwa*, therefore, can be a potential source of law – according to the Constitution of the Islamic Republic, courts may refer to the sources of Islamic law, including *fatwa* and the advisory opinions of the *ulama*, 'only in cases of absence of codified regulations' (Moschtaghi 2010: 3) when passing judgements – and can reflect how Islamic jurisprudence evolves with respect to contemporary social developments and problems over time. Nevertheless, it is neither the same as legislation issued by parliament nor comparable with *urf*, which emerges spontaneously out of everyday exchanges as sociocultural practices.

The Separation of *Urf* from State Law

Let us return to *urf* in its original sense of custom and usage (also *adat*, which refers to habits) at the grass-roots level, which is how it was employed in our interviews. As a secondary source of Islamic law, *urf* operates *bottom-up* through cultural and customary practices, or, to be more accurate, it articulates the long-standing practices and usages of the community in terms of rules and norms, which are then endowed with a sense of legality, i.e. a binding force, with or without the endorsement of the State. In contrast, state law operates *top-down* through legislation, official interpretation and the enforcement of legal rules or by making legal decisions, often upheld by the implicit or explicit threat of violence against non-compliance. This means that *urf* often reflects descriptive norms that have legal significance, in that they play a crucial role in how ordinary people de facto organize their exchanges and activities. State law, on the other hand, includes a large number of injunctive rules, which communicate to the wider society how things *ought* to be. This is not a clear-cut distinction, though, since there are overlaps between these two types of law, i.e. *urf* can contain injunctive norms (it includes not only customary 'doings', but also 'sayings', which can include what ought to be done) and aspects of state law can mirror descriptive rules, which are often embedded in cultural practices. Nevertheless, the descriptive/injunctive distinction helps to identify the sociological characteristic of *urf* as a form of 'living law', embedded in cultural practices, in contrast to the body of positive rules, which the State might have devised for ideological or administrative reasons and imposed from above (for discussions on bottom-up and top-down legal regulation, see Banakar 2015: 162). Moreover, *urf* as a source of law is employed by Islamic jurists to institutionalize some norms and values embodied in everyday cultural practices at the level of the legal system of the Islamic Republic. However, the relationship between *urf* and Shari'a is obfuscated by the separation of cultural values and the sense of religiosity existing at grass-roots level (at the level of the extended 'peer group' and community) from the ideological imperatives and the economic realities of the macro institutions of politics and administration.

To unpack the sociolegal significance of this point, we shall use Jürgen Habermas's distinction between the *lifeworld* and system, which was originally developed to describe the crisis of modernity in Western democracies with well-developed social welfare states. *Lifeworld* is created through the everyday interactions of ordinary people and constitutes the bedrock of social life, out of which grow norms and values as well as perceptions of solidarity, morality, religiosity and identity (see Habermas 1975, 1984). It is at this level of face-to-face interaction/communication that the ground for an intersubjectively shared world view is laid. 'System', as adopted by Habermas, refers on the other hand to subsystems constituting the economic and political/administrative superstructures of modern societies.[5] Although Habermas's descriptions and analysis of the legitimation crisis of secular welfare democracies are not directly applicable to Iran's theocracy, they can nevertheless be used to tease out some of the specificities of the relationship between Iranian law, society and the State, which operate in a modern global context. The multiple centres of religious, military, political and legal authority that together constitute the Iranian state do not operate under the constitution and are not accountable under the law in the sense that we find in Western democracies – and yet they, too, are dependent on legitimation for their political survival.

Tapping into the *Lifeworld*

In the context of modernity, in which the system and the *lifeworld* are differentiated, certain parts of the legal system, such as public and private law, become media through which the independent functioning of administrative and economic systems is institutionalized. At this level, the law needs to operate independently of the *lifeworld* by freeing itself from the burden of morally justifying its decisions on an individual basis, if it is to support the macro organization of society in an effective manner (Habermas, 1975, 1984). This does not, however, mean that law is permanently divorced from moral consideration or can operate effectively without legitimation for its general policies. Above and beyond legality, modern liberal law continues to require a degree of legitimacy and moral justification for the way in which it administers society – a form of legitimacy that it can obtain only by maintaining a link with the *lifeworld*. Therefore, some areas of the law – such as family and criminal law, as well as social welfare legislation – maintain links with the *lifeworld*, transforming cultural values into legal norms and practices.

Unlike modern, secular legal systems, Iranian law is based on Shari'a and thus is dependent on religious doctrine and divine sources of legitimacy that are not available to Western legal systems. Nevertheless, it also has to steer a modern economy and administration in an effective fashion, and its failure to do so would create economic crisis and political mayhem, which in turn would undermine its legitimacy and authority – and the Iranian regime came very close to political or economic collapse several times between the student riots in 2003 and the general election in 2014.[6] Thus, the religious law of Iran also has to free itself from the normative demands of the *lifeworld* in order to steer the economy and administration of the country. The decision to allow women to break into the male-dominated taxi profession was not, for example, in accordance with *urf*, and, as our interviews showed, mainstream culture disapproved of women taxi drivers. Instead, the decision to grant women taxi drivers' licences was based on economic expediency and aimed at creating employment opportunities for certain groups of women. Either these women, many of whom were war widows, were allowed to work and support their families or the government had to step in and provide for them. The government chose the latter option. Our interviews show that many families, whether traditionally minded or secular middle class, felt that taxi driving was not suitable for their daughters or wives. At the same time, many men saw the presence of women taxi drivers as a challenge to the patriarchy or (in the case of male taxi drivers) a threat to their livelihood.[7] To legitimize it, the government had to dress up its decision in terms of enhancing gender segregation, and, admittedly, creating women-only taxi services had a segregating dimension. By emphasizing gender segregation, the government could nevertheless obtain some support from the mainstream. This exemplifies how even the non-secular regime of the Islamic Republic has to steer the economic system by making decisions that are in breach of the cultural norms and values prevalent across society. At the same time, it shows how the regime can make use of values embedded at the level of the *lifeworld* – in this context, values related to gender and the control of sexuality – to obtain support for its economically driven policies.[8]

Thus, state law ensures a degree of popular legitimacy for the political system by recognizing *urf* as a secondary source of law, as long it serves its purpose and in so far as it does not conflict with the principles of Shari'a. Expressed differently, the Islamic state taps into the *lifeworld*, adopting social norms that are used to regulate, for example, private agreements, marriage and divorce, or women's sexuality. These are transformed into laws of contract, inheritance, family and *zina* (prohibited sexual acts; see Mir-Hosseini 2010b). The State, being a Shi'i theocracy, 'ideologises' these norms, as it institutionalizes them at the level of macro administration, articulating them in terms of politico-religious doctrines. The Council of Guardians, which can veto bills passed by the Iranian Parliament (the *Majlis*) for being non-Islamic, acts as an ideological checkpoint, exemplifying the way in which all laws of the land are ideologized beyond the restrictions imposed by the constitution.

The independent reasoning of *ulama* (called *ijtihad*, which constitutes the second important source of Shari'a after the Qur'an and *sunna*) and their legal opinions (*fatwa*) also provide important links between society and the state administration. These are as much concerned with maintaining continuity in legal thought and reasoning (thus maintaining the integrity and identity of Islamic law) as with adapting Shari'a in view of new circumstances and social change. These legal opinions, however, are tinged by the jurists' own cognitive (interpretive) interests and mediated through the internal legal and theological discourses of the community of *ulama*.[9] Using established methods of reasoning, such as 'analogy', 'considerations of public interest' and 'juristic preference' (Kamali 2012: 11), they provide a vital channel through which contemporary concerns with new social developments and the daily problems of ordinary people can be explored legally and brought to the attention of the legislature, courts and policy makers. They can also amount to political interference with the operation of the legal system, which is why in some Islamic countries procedures have been put into place to restrict the widespread use of *fatwas*. Since within the community of *ulama*, we find great diversity of views and opinions on various legal matters, one jurist's pronouncement cannot become binding and will not necessarily translate into the law of the land. In some countries, such as Saudi Arabia and Malaysia, *fatwas* automatically become laws of the land; however, such automaticity does not appear to exist in Iran, although the *fatwas* of Ayatollah Khomeini proved to have the force of law even on matters such as the permissibility of sex changes, where there was no consensus among Islamic jurists. As Najmabadi (2014: 174) explains, it was the political authority of Ayatollah Khomeini, and 'his unique position as the leader of the most massive revolution in the late twentieth century', which bestowed indisputable legality on his *fatwas*. Otherwise, as we explained above, according to the Iranian Constitution, *fatwas* and opinions of the *ulama* gain legal force when, in the absence of codified legal rules, courts employ them in order to pass judgements (Moschtaghi 2010: 3).

The State's Islamic ideology, dysfunctional as it might be in a modern global economy, is nevertheless the imperative of the theocratic system, and therefore it is employed in macro administration. This ideology, however, must be distinguished from the sense of religiosity existing at the level of the *lifeworld*. There are, as illustrated above, instances in which Islamic ideology breaches the religious values of mainstream Iranian culture. To make matters more complicated, it would be misleading to suggest that there is one centralized political apparatus in operation that is capable of generating a coherent Islamic ideology and exercising uniform administrative control at the level of the government. Instead of a government that operates under the constitution, we find several centres of authority, normativity and legality, which compete with each other – often in breach of or beyond the constitution – for political stakes at the macro level of state and society.

Legal and Political Polycentricity[10]

When passing and implementing laws, when assigning individuals different tasks and discharging them from their service and during all tasks that follow this political-civil system, Islamic Shari'a should be observed. All tasks in this system revolve around democracy. [...] Commitment to Islamic Shari'a is the soul and truth of the Islamic government. [...] If Islamic Shari'a is completely observed in society, this will ensure both civil and individual freedom [...]. If Islamic Shari'a is observed, it will ensure both justice and spirituality in society.

(The Supreme Leader's [Ali Hosseini Khamenei's]
Speech on 6 June 2014)

According to Hunter (2014), the Islamic regime from its inception was divided into a 'left' faction, consisting of social reformists who advocated a liberal interpretation of Islamic laws and traditions, and a 'right' faction, made up of conservatives favouring the strict interpretation of Islamic jurisprudence and the strict application of Islamic moral principles. These two rival blocs consisted internally of 'extreme' and 'moderate' groups, each generating their own political discourse and brand of Islam. From the 1980s up to the presidency of Khatami, the left was in the ascendency, while the right struggled to establish itself until it finally succeeded in seizing power in 2005. These so-called 'factions' have not existed one at a time or consecutively but *co-existed* simultaneously as rival centres of political control and power:

During the 1980s, the left dominated the discourse, politics and policies of the Islamic republic, but the right was not without influence on many aspects of policy through elements of [the] clerical establishment and the merchant community, and by controlling some important institutions. For example, figures identified with the right obtained positions in the Guardian Council (*Shoray e Negahban*), charged to ensure the compatibility of laws passed by the Parliament with Islamic injunctions. Additional figures identified with the right occupied significant positions in the government [...]. This uneasy balance was maintained by Ayatollah Khomeini in order to avoid an open rift within the Islamist elite ranks. He even at times tried to bridge their differences

(Hunter 2014: 136).

The Islamic regime is a polycentric system with a number of political and legal centres of power, influence and authority, such as the Supreme Leader and his circle (including the Assembly of Experts, the Council of Guardians and the Expediency Council), the Ministry of Justice, parliament, and the Revolutionary Guards Corps (the *Sepah*) and the *Basij*,[11] not to mention the *ulama* and a few powerful seminaries in Qom, which control 'enormous economic resources, including the sizable portion of the government's budget and government-owned "charitable" foundations' (Sadri 2004: 118). The *ulama* are in turn linked to the *bazaar*, which, as mentioned above, remains one of the centres of socio-economic and political influence in every Iranian city. The elected government – currently that of the moderate Hassan Rouhani – might have the support of the majority of the electorate in the country and might at times even appear to be in charge of the administration, but in order to introduce and implement new national and foreign policies it has to negotiate with, and obtain the approval of, a powerful coalition of the conservative right, which de facto dominates sociopolitical developments in present-day Iran (see Sadri, 2004).

Similar centres of power and political interest exist in all modern countries. Whereas in Western democracies they have to work within the 'the rule of law' (or by following due process of law), as defined ultimately by a constitution, and are accountable for their actions under the law, in Iran they operate above the law, albeit under a contested

Islamic ideology, which, in turn, is incapable of ensuring predictability and uniformity in decision making or safeguarding the rights and duties of citizens. Although a clear basis for due process is incorporated within the Iranian Constitution, the principle of the rule of law (*hakemiyat-e quanon*) remains, as Moschtaghi (2010: 1) demonstrated, 'largely absent from Iranian constitutional doctrine'. The Iranian judicial system consists of a hierarchy of courts that operate under the constitution and allow for the possibility of appeal. However, it also has 'special' courts, which either do not operate within the legal system (such as the special courts of the clergy) or, as the revolutionary courts, are not accountable to any higher authority within the judicial order for their decisions. Both these courts have been subjected to intensive critique by human-rights organizations for their proceedings (see Künkler 2009: 20 and Moschtaghi, 2010: 6). We shall discuss the court system in more detail in Chapter Eleven.

There are also organizations that are created by law but which operate with impunity and outside the law. The *Basij-e Mostazafin* (Mobilisation of the Oppressed), which was created by an act of parliament and was put in charge of policing the populace and punishing deviations from the countless moral laws of the Islamic Republic, is a case in point. As Golkar (2011: 217) explains:

> As royal militia groups, the Basijis serve as the regime's arm in confronting citizens. Although according to the law the Basij is allowed to do so only when a crime is observed, there are many reports of Basijis disrupting private gatherings and parties under the pretence of 'countering immoral behaviour'. Moreover, reports have also recounted incidents of the Basij attacking international organisations in big cities to check whether employees are following Islamic codes.

The *Basijis* are often called out onto the streets in order to suppress civil unrest and anti-government demonstrations. In the anti-government protests following the 2009 presidential elections, the *Basij* militia was accused of killing seven people after they opened fire on the protesters (*BBC News*, 18 June 2009). In a novel entitled *Death to the Dictator!*, Moghadam (2010), who participated in the demonstrations, tells the story of a young man who was arrested during the anti-government protests in Tehran in June 2009. In her novel, Moghadam describes how the *Basij*, the police, the secret service and the courts operate independently of each other, exemplified by the allegation that the young man in question was arrested, detained, questioned and tortured by the *Basij* without the knowledge of the police authorities or the courts.

Thus, the polycentric make-up of Iran's political system, instead of enhancing democracy brings uncertainty to the administration of public life and generates contradictory policies that may be implemented simultaneously by different groups. In Chapter Seven, we referred to a ban issued on 1 September 2014 by the Iranian chief of police prohibiting women from working in coffee shops (*Payvand Iran News*, 1 September 2014). According to this order, women may own coffee shops but they may not serve customers themselves. This new order discriminates against half of the population and is unconstitutional even in the Iranian context, where women do not enjoy the same rights as men. Moreover, it openly challenges the new government's hesitant attempts to liberalize gender policies and shows how different sources of power and authority can compete with each other, undercut each other's authority and produce simultaneous, contradictory policies. Another interesting development concerns a *fatwa* issued by the conservative Grand Ayatollah Nasser Makarem-Shirazi against the use of G3 mobile services, which, according to him, violate Shari'a law and the norms of morality (*Washington Post*, 30 August 2014). We could interpret this *fatwa* as a reaction to technology and the fear of the internet, but it may also be seen as a response to the Iranian President's campaign to improve access to the internet, which opens the gates of the world to the younger generation but also requires contracts with multinational companies in the West.

Had the political system in Iran not consisted of several competing centres of authority, the chief of police could not have enjoyed the legal competence to make labour laws. However, this form of polycentricity is not all negative, and does bring with it unintended advantages for ordinary Iranians. What appears as a form of political disorder manifests the Iranian version of democracy and republicanism within the framework of Shi'i Islam, on the one hand, and a long-standing tradition of *estebdād*, on the other. The simultaneous existence of multiple centres of authority does not allow the total domination of one single political group, and prevents the establishment of a totalitarian regime in Iran. I must hasten to add that the price paid for this unconstitutional polycentricity is high, for since these centres do not operate under the law they perpetuate the arbitrary exercise of power by public authorities.

This polycentric state of affairs in law and politics is mirrored in the three ongoing, competing normative discourses that constitute the intellectual life of Iran, affecting both public and private spheres of action. According to Kamrava (2008), these consist, first, of a conservative religious discourse that aims at justifying the continued dominance of the traditionalist clergy within the state apparatus. This discourse should not be confused with the State itself, argues Kamrava, but runs parallel to, and independently of, it. Although the conservative discourse is promoted by the dominant section of the State, i.e. the traditionalist clergy, it does not permeate all sections of society and is, arguably, quite limited in its sphere of influence among the general population. The excerpt above, taken from the Supreme Leader's speech, in which he emphasizes the central role of Shari'a in law and law enforcement, is a case in point. Second, Kamrava describes an Islamic reformist discourse that competes (at times successfully) with the traditionalist discourse by expressing the disenchantment of many intellectuals and former supporters of the Islamic Republic, as well as the middle classes, with the increasingly authoritarian tendencies of the Islamic regime. The reformist discourse tries to 'strike a balance between Islam and modernity' (Kamrava 2008: 11). This voice is clearly captured in our interviews with the professionals. Many lawyers and other professionals that we interviewed were critical of the state of affairs in Iran, though they remained committed nonetheless to a democratic form of Islam. Finally, Kamrava identifies a secular, modernist discourse that wishes to depoliticize religion by restricting it to the private realm and, instead, promote a secular form of politics. This secular discourse exists in embryonic form, i.e. its contours are not yet fully shaped, in response to the State's theocratic excesses. What was described in the Introduction as the 'medicalisation' of the road traffic accidents (RTAs) (but also the way in which, for example, transsexuals have been treated in Iran, which we shall discuss briefly below) exemplifies aspects of this secular discourse that have found legitimate outlets for their expression through claims to scientism.

A Society in Transition: Changing Community and Personalism

Iranian society is in transition, and undergoing fundamental changes precipitated by a number of developments – including its demography (more than 60 per cent of the country's 73 million people are under the age of 30);[12] its high rate of youth unemployment; the strict control of the activities of young people and repressive sexual policies; changing family structures, including a growing rate of divorce; the intensification of urbanization and mobility; improved access to university education, which has had a significant impact on women's entry into higher education; the widespread use of digital technology (including social media); and, subsequently, the changing lifestyles of the majority of people (see Khosravi 2008). To take just one of these developments as an example, improvements in women's education have allowed many of them to enter the labour market, thus changing the employment structure of the country's economy while at the same time giving them greater socio-economic autonomy (Shadi-Talab 2001). This has in turn precipitated a notable rise in women's marriage age, as many of them now postpone marriage in anticipation of building a career outside the home (Torabi et al. 2013).[13] This also means that women have different (or greater) social and economic expectations in life, which, in turn, brings about a different attitude towards, and even the rejection of, traditional family values and roles (Edalati and Redzuan 2010). For example, write Daniel and Mahdi (2006: 174), 'although Islamic law allows divorce, social norms neither encourage nor easily accept it'. Notwithstanding the social and legal obstacles that prevent women from initiating divorce proceedings, and the cultural stigma attached to female divorcees, the rate of divorce has nevertheless rocketed in urban areas generally, but in Tehran in particular (Mahdi 2006: 175). Despite this unprecedented rise in divorce rates, many researchers continue to see the Iranian family as a 'very strong institution' capable of fostering 'a strong tradition of family morality rooted in social contracts between large extended families' (Aghajanian and Thompson 2013: 112). Nevertheless, upholding the continued centrality of family is becoming increasingly difficult in the face of the changing landscape of Iranian society.

Admittedly, similar demographic changes are influencing a number of developing countries in the world and are not specific to Iran. What makes Iranian development distinct is, first, the central role of personalism in culture and society and, second, the way in which a combination of gender and class conflicts is played out by the authorities in order to uphold the political status quo. Changing family values and traditional family structures will inevitably impact on Iranian personalism, which is largely dependent on the individual's family and 'peer group'. As regards gender and class conflicts, which are perpetuated by the Iranian Government as a strategy for neutralizing opposing political forces, they are unfolded against the backdrop of an ongoing societal process of merging 'tradition' and 'modernity'.[14] A gradual change of family structure, which is already under way in urban areas, will slowly challenge and destabilize the traditional values that are reproduced at the level of the family. This point was highlighted by the psychologist that we interviewed in Chapter Six, who stated (on the basis of her professional experience) that Iranians were becoming increasingly 'individualistic' and independent of their families. She also said that in times of economic crisis they were becoming selfish and avoiding sharing their material goods, which in turn caused many family conflicts (see Chapter Six, interview 3:6:4, page 110). The 'individualism' that she referred to marks a move away from personalism, which is rooted in the family network, towards a more Western notion of individualism.

Similarly, the comparison between our pilot study and the later interviews suggests a possible transformation of the Iranian community. Many of those who were interviewed in the pilot study referred to the role of elders in resolving disputes whereby, instead of turning to the legal system, the *older* interviewees stated that they would turn originally to the community elders. Although in the subsequent, larger study in Tehran a few references were also made to the role of elders and community-based mediation, the *younger* interviewees stated that they would use the legal system, and they did not make a point that community elders play a central role in resolving disputes. This may have a couple of possible, overlapping explanations. First, the younger interviewees have not experienced legal disputes which require the intervention of a third party, and their replies are not based on experience. Second, Iranian personalism is undergoing a change in large cities, where it is increasingly difficult to maintain a traditional form of extended family and a community of peers based on interpersonal trust. Neighbourhood communities are disintegrating and community elders are giving way to mediation centres, which have been introduced by the government to unburden the legal system by resolving minor disputes out of court.

The local community of elders, although not the same as state officials, should nevertheless not be confused with the individual's 'peer group'. The local community represents a medium-range social order, which plays a greater role in the more traditional parts of south Tehran than in the more secular north of the city. It is also more central to the life of small towns and rural areas of the country than to the life of large cities.

The 'Unholy Union' of Patriarchy and *Estebdād*

In the previous chapters, we interpreted the results of the interviews that we conducted in a historical context in order to argue that Iranians were generally distrustful of the State, and distinguished between their 'peer group' and the larger 'society of strangers' upon whom they could not rely. Many of those that we interviewed stated that Iranians were not a law-abiding people as far as state law was concerned, although they respected the customary rules of *urf*. Somewhat oversimplified, official law represents the values and demands of the State, which imposes obligations without granting them corresponding rights and thus is, at best, applicable to a 'society of strangers'. Iranians' disregard for traffic laws exemplified their troubled relationship with the State and officials, while their negative attitudes towards pedestrians illustrated their view of society at large. We explained these points with reference to Iranians' personalism and the historical separation of state and society, on the one hand, and the distinction made between one's 'peer group' and the larger 'society of strangers', on the other. Disregard for the rights of strangers, our lawyer interviewees argued, should be understood in the context of how many Iranians experienced their rights as citizens in relation to the State. According to the lawyers, the State had failed in fulfilling its social contract to its citizens. The distrust of authorities, coupled with disregard for state laws and the rights of others, lay the social foundations upon which Iranian legal culture rests.

In contrast, *urf* – understood as commonly accepted sayings and 'doings' – is the living law of the community and is embedded in the *lifeworld*. It represents Iranian's cultural practices, some of which are pre-Islamic, and a sense of religiosity that is deeply rooted in Shi'ism. Moreover, the relationship between *urf* and state Islamic laws and policies is sociologically complex and paradoxical in that, on the one hand, state law taps into *urf* for legitimacy and to ensure some form of social and legal continuity, while on the other hand it recognizes it only in as far as it serves the Islamic regime's purpose. This does not foster trust among ordinary Iranians, who continue to be wary of state law and its strict interpretation and selective enforcement of the principles of Shari'a. The tension between ordinary Iranians and the State, however, has another source – one which is related to Shi'i Islam, according to which Shi'as do not recognize the authority and legitimacy of temporal rulers and governments. Following Dabashi (2011), we argued that Shi'ism was a religion of protest that fostered a type of collective personality in line with Iranian personalism. This animosity, arguably, is extended to the Islamic state, which ideologizes Shi'ism and employs its images and legends as a source of legitimacy in order to run a modern administration and economy. Even the *bazaaris*, who have traditionally supported the *ulama* and share the government's conservative values, cannot avoid coming into conflict with the Islamic state (Keshavarzian 2007). Thus, one of the arguments of this book has been that the historical rift between state and society, and subsequently between cultural practices of the people and state law, continues to define Iranian society.

When discussing the modern transformation of Iranian society, the debates tend to focus on historical events, political development and ideological discourses at the societal level. Kamrava's (2008) study, to which we referred above, engaging and important as it is, provides a case in point. As a result, much of the research on Iran explores the macro level of politics, or immerses itself in historical examinations, at the expense of studying the micro levels of the everyday experiences of ordinary people, the role of the family and smaller communities. As mentioned above, family remains one of the most important sources of normativity in Iranian society, whereby not only Shi'i religiosity but also the basic grammar of the patriarchy are generated – both of which, as we shall argue below, feed into the personalism of ordinary Iranians (see Daniel and Mahdi 2006: 157).

Within the Iranian family network, social control takes on interpersonal, emotional, hierarchical and, above all, patriarchal forms, supported by deeply embedded religious values, while within the larger neighbourhood community social order is generated informally by the custom-based rules of *urf*, which itself is used spontaneously to ensure a form of social order. It is within family and community that we find religion as an entrenched value system that informs and regulates many aspects of the individual's private and public conduct. Religious belief, which exists within everyday reality and informs the social organization of the family, local communities and even businesses, is not ideological but an integral part of the *lifeworld*, and thus forms an important aspect of Iranian culture. The *bazaar* – with its network of traditional wholesale merchants, traders and shopkeepers – exemplifies the idea of a community that, although religious and socially conservative with close ties to local mosques, nevertheless follows *urf* rather than state law. As mentioned in Chapter Five, *bazaaris* support local religious schools and pay *khoms* and *zakat* to the local clergy rather than to the taxman who represents the state. It is arguable whether all *bazaaris* are sincere in their religiosity or are devout Shi'as, but there is no doubt that they wish to maintain close ties with the local and national clergy. That is why they publicly express their religiosity by organizing, celebrating and actively participating in Shi'i ceremonies. Their religiosity is not ideological but is part of their cultural capital as a community-based, rather than state-based, economic and political agent (see Keshavarzian 2007). Their alliance with the clergy and the mosque keeps them rooted in the local community; it is 'good for business' and it also 'protects them against the oppressive state' (Khosravi 2008). This is why the *bazaar* has retained a degree of independence from the State and played a significant role in political events and developments in Iran. Within the socio-economic life of the *bazaar*, interpersonal trust and cultural capital play an important role in facilitating a large part of everyday activities and exchanges – including business transactions – which are otherwise mediated informally and through customary practices. In contrast, in the larger society, state law and Islamic ideology are employed jointly to regulate behaviour and to administer societal activities. This ensures neither legal legitimacy nor efficacy of the law and policies introduced from above by the State. Policies dictated by the government, even when they are legitimized through *fatwa*, might indeed lack support among Iranians. As mentioned above, authorities can even introduce Islamic policies that are not compatible with, or that even violate, religious norms of everyday life.[15]

Policies that enshrine ideologized Islamic values aimed at imposing a state Islamic culture (what our interviewees referred to as *farhang-sazi*), for example criminalizing everyday behaviour that deviates from a strict conception of Islamic morality, often aggravate the sense of frustration felt by non-traditionalist sections of society and breed resistance rather than conformity. As Khosravi (2008: 3) showed in his study of youth in Tehran, this does not necessarily take the form of political confrontation but can express itself as 'defiance', which he defines as 'a spontaneous, uncoordinated everyday challenging of the social order'. The covert political defiance expressed by middle-class youths is, to large extent, a manifestation of their personalism. We find here a tentative link to the risky and dangerous driving habits of the younger section of society, which cause many deaths in the streets and on the motorways. Even these risky driving habits may be linked to the urge to defy the social order that is imposed from above by the State.

One single discourse, dominant as it might be at the level of macro politics, cannot capture the nature of the Islamic state, which is internally 'fractured and factionalised' (Kamrava 2008: 11). It is horizontally divided into social classes, a division that is mirrored in the spatial division of cities into south and north. At the same time, it is vertically differentiated into opposing forms of power and 'sociality', with state administrations, the military organs of the Revolutionary Guards, officialdom, and the *ulama* and their economic foundations on the top, and civil-society organizations, the *bazaar*, local community networks, extended family systems and individual Iranians at the bottom of society. In addition to the three normative discourses mentioned by Kamrava, which operate at the macro level of state and society, we have the micro organizations of personal networks, which also generate their own forms of normativity and religiosity distinct from, but nevertheless related to, the Islamic ideology of the State. Even at this level, we cannot find a set of social, cultural and religious values or norms that dominate society in a uniform and totalizing fashion. Society is horizontally divided and different social classes hold somewhat different cultural values with respect to, for example, education, religious practices or the rights of women. Nevertheless, general respect for patriarchy comes very close to providing a common form of micro organization for Iranian culture across social classes and between the urban and rural populations. The patriarchy, being inherently conservative and repressive, manifests the macro *estebdād* of Iranian rulers at the micro level of social organization. By tapping in to the *lifeworld* and supporting the repressive patriarchal values and practices of the family, the Iranian legal system links the micro and macro forms of *estebdād*, thus ensuring a degree of legitimacy for itself.

The union of state–*estebdād* and family–patriarchy is hardly a marriage made in heaven, but is rather an expedient agreement temporarily and balanced on a knife-edge, as Iranian personalism is distrustful of the State and wary of the authorities' arbitrary use of force and violence. Furthermore, the union of *estebdād* and patriarchy legitimizes state law and administration as long as Iranian men feel threatened by women's desire to break free from the constraints of tradition (Afary 2009: 198). To keep men's perception of the looming threat from female sexuality alive, traditionalist conservative groups employ distorted versions of modernity and Westernization in order to create sources of personal fear into which the regime can tap.[16] They use the somewhat one-sided image of the decadent and over-sexualized Western woman as one of the symbols of Westernization and, by extension, as a basis for discrediting secular, democratic ideals. By tapping in to the fear of Westernization, the government tries to achieve two objectives at the same time: it keeps alive the male population's fear of women getting out of control, while it legitimizes the political repression of its critics and opponents, who are often dismissed as anti-Islamic or *gharbzadeh* ('intoxicated by the West'). However, as long as Iranian society is experienced as a short-term project and the State is seen as a hostile force, none of these strategies provides the State with an enduring source of legitimacy.

A Tentative Framework for the Study of Iranian Legal Culture

Those that we interviewed in Shiraz and Tehran, as part of our pilot study, defined the sources of the law in secular terms of parliament (the *Majlis*) and various authorities responsible for enforcing the law, rather than in terms of the divine sources of Islamic law. A secularized conception of the law and legality also emerged out of the subsequent interviews with taxi drivers, lawyers and other professionals. Surprisingly, most of our lawyers also defined sources of law without reference to the authority of Shari'a, the Qur'an, or in terms of the *sunna*, *qiyas* or *ijma*. Even when the interviewees were asked about justice, they often described it in terms of how 'positive laws' were enforced. A typical lawyer's response was that 'law and law enforcement have nothing to do with justice' (interview 2:1:34, page 99), for the courts could not know the absolute truth and made their decisions on the basis of the evidence brought before them. In that sense, not even their notion of justice was related to a higher form of natural law, although in Shi'i Islam justice (*adle* or *edalat*) is among the properties attributed to God (Dabashi 2011: xii–xiii). It should be added that two of the lawyers that we interviewed explained that justice involved 'placing things in their right place', which, as we noted in Chapter Five, is the definition of justice in Islamic law (see Kamali 2012: 30).

The second set of interviews provided a much more complex view of the relationships between law, culture, religion and society in Iran. Although many of our interviewees saw law and the legal system as instruments in the hands of the authorities and experienced it as an arbitrary exercise of power, law was nevertheless understood as something more than the operations of the legal system or an expression of *estebdād*. A female taxi driver stated that 'to follow the law, one [shows] one's self-respect' (see 4:1:39, page 140), while another explained that 'we ourselves are the source of the law' (see 4:8:40, page 140) and went on to add that law meant 'respecting oneself'. Similarly, one of the lawyers said that 'Iranians regard themselves as the primary source of the law – they consider themselves as a source of unwritten law' (2:10:40, page 104). The interviewees also linked self-respect (*shakhsiyat*) through driving with the law: 'The way you drive and behave in traffic is an indicator of your *shakhsiyat*' (2:7:13, page 90), and to quote another interviewee: 'The worst drivers are those who reveal their lack of self-respect [*shakhsiyat*] by disregarding the law. [. . .] If you follow the law, you have shown your self-respect and respect for other people' (4:5:41, page 140). Yet another interviewee, who viewed the same question from a different angle, stated that 'reckless and dangerous driving is a sign of low self-esteem [*kam-shakhsiyati*]' (4:8:42, page 140). With *shakhsiyat* being an aspect of personalism, our interviewees related the law to personalism, and by extension understood it as an expression of values, norms and practices that exist at the level of the family and community networks such as local neighbourhoods, which, as we discussed in the previous chapter, also continue to generate norms and monitor the behaviour of their residents. Thus, according to our interviewees, Iranians are not law-abiding in so far as they do not readily follow the laws of the State, but they do regard themselves as the source of law and follow a 'personal' set of norms and rules. These personal rules, however, are not the figment of the individual's imagination but one which is shared intersubjectively at the level of the 'peer group' and supported by the local community. This personalized law is constantly contrasted against state law, causing apparent confusion. Looking back at the interviews, it is often difficult to say to which type of law the interviewee is referring. For example, one of the female taxi drivers (4:10:49, pages 142–3) stated that the law does not mean anything to Iranians, because 'the powerful people', who according to her do not care about ordinary people, 'are the source of law'. In the same breath, she added that 'the law defines the duties of the father, mother, brother and sister'. However, the law that defines such duties is not the law of powerful people or the 'positive law' of the State but customary law (*urf*), which is embedded at the level of the family and the local community.

It is understandable if our interviewees, who have largely not had cause to distinguish between sources of law and forms of legality, experience the law as a chaotic flow of normativities emanating from various institutions, ranging from the family to parliament. For our purposes here, we must nevertheless distinguish between at least three levels of normativity – namely, the 'peer group', the local community (or modern *mahallehs*) and the state administration. The notion of 'sociality' is borrowed from Gurvitch (1947) to capture the social–psychological mechanisms determining the intensity of interactions, the types of communications and the forms of relationships that reproduce various levels of social reality over time. According to Gurvitch, the study of the 'forms of sociality' is inseparable from the study of 'kinds of law', or, expressed differently, every level of sociality generates its own form of law and legality, through which social integration is realized (Gurvitch 1947: 156).[17] Following Gurvitch, we argue that Iranian legal culture is a product of the interplay between three levels of sociality, defined by:

(1) The 'peer group' – or family kinship, extended family and a network of friends – which captures the most basic form of sociality, religiosity and spontaneous normativity. This level of sociality generates the basic norms of *urf* and is socially integrated through interpersonal trust and the authority of patriarchy.

(2) The local community, dominated by everyday mundane practices, exchanges and expressions of religiosity. This level is dominated traditionally by the mosque and its elders and varies from one area of a city to the other. In its modern manifestations in large cities such as Tehran, women and youths can play a central role in the reproduction of neighbourhood sociality (Khosravi 2008; Mirgholami and Sintusigha 2012). The law that maintains this level is a combination of *urf* and state law.

(3) The political system and state administration. At this level, various centres of normativity operate and compete with each other for authority, and they exert influence within a broadly defined Islamic ideology. The sociality of this level is maintained through state law, which combines a politicized interpretation of Shari'a, the application of *urf* as long as it is politically expedient, and the brute force of *estebdād*.

These three levels are socially linked in various ways. Politically, the State recruits from the traditionalist and conservative classes in order to uphold Islamic order in society. This in turn creates a communication channel and a relational dependence between the Islamic state and certain strata of society, while alienating the other sections. More importantly, this strategy creates an ongoing and unresolvable class and gender conflict across society, thereby minimizing the likelihood of a popular social uprising, which would include all sections of Iranian society, against the Islamic regime. Legally, we argue, these three levels are interrelated through *urf*, albeit in a temporary and socially dysfunctional fashion, and also as an integral part of ongoing class and gender conflicts. Finally, we maintain that both the family and local community levels, which continue to be linked together socially, are in transition. The concept of family is being redefined as socio-economic conditions change and a new lifestyle prevails across urban and rural regions of the country, precipitating the transition of *mahallehs* into modern neighbourhoods marked by growing mobility and cultural and ethnic diversity. Even that bastion of local tradition, social continuity and political conservatism, the *bazaar*, with its long-standing links to the *ulama*, has been undergoing fundamental changes. As Keshavarzian (2007) has shown, the *bazaar's* internal solidarity has been partly undermined, not only through the selective value-oriented patronage of the Islamic regime but also because their trading relationships cannot stand outside the ongoing globalization of commerce. How can Iranian society maintain a traditional social structure notwithstanding these ongoing changes? The answer to this question is found in the 'unholy union' of *estebdād* and patriarchy.

Concluding Remarks

Patriarchy is embedded deeply in Iranian culture, and determines the way in which many aspects of family and community relationships are defined over time. The government's segregation policies find resonance, as well as an important source of legitimacy, at this level. Expressed differently, upholding the repressive values of the patriarchy becomes a medium through which the state administration and family can act jointly to realize a common project aimed at maintaining a form of social order. At the same time, the State's policy of class confrontation divides up Iranian society into opposing classes, sections, factions and groups along economic as well as religious/secular lines – pitting the disadvantaged against the wealthy, and the religious and the traditionalist against the secular modernists – thus eliminating the possibility of collective, political and social action against the State. One of the reasons for the political failure of the anti-government demonstrations, which followed the 2009 elections in Iran, was that they were not all-inclusive and did not include all sections of Iranian society. Instead, they mostly represented the dissatisfaction of the modernist sections of the middle classes living in Tehran. Looking back at the last two revolutions that Iran experienced during the twentieth century, we see that only when people unite across class divides and act jointly can they bring about fundamental political change. Moreover, both revolutions involved a movement of people who rose up against the arbitrary power of the Iranian state, rather than just one class such as workers or the landless peasantry rising up against capitalists or landlords (see Homa Katouzian 2011: 764). The former scenario was true with respect to the Iranian Constitutional Revolution of 1905–11 and the popular uprising against the Shah. The 1979 revolution did not happen as a result of class conflicts; instead, it was an uprising by the whole of society against the State. Large sections of the population that supported the revolution did not do so for ideological reasons but because they wished to overthrow the Shah and his regime.[18] Similarly, the Constitutional Revolution of 1905–11 was made possible by a political alliance between civil-society forces, including the *ulama*, *bazaaris* and even sections of the royals, with different social roots and divergent political interests, against the Qajar state. These forces were brought together by their conviction that the rule of *estebdād* had to be replaced by a culture of *qānon* (see below).

In *A Treatise on One Word*, an essay on constitutional government written in 1871, Yusef Khan Mustashar od-Dawleh argued that all Iran needed, in order to transform itself into a modern nation, could be summed up in one word.[19] This magical word was *qānon* (from the Greek *kanon*), which he went on to describe as a French-style body of written legal codes uniformly applicable to all. Mustashar od-Dawleh was not alone in wondering why Iran had stagnated economically, and was in a state of social disarray while European countries were prospering through technological progress. He was, however, amongst the first few to identify the main cause of the country's economic backwardness and social malaise as its failure to develop a modern, constitutional government.

Echoing Mustashar od-Dawleh, we can only repeat that all Iran needs today to transform itself from a modern theocracy into a democracy is still summed up in one word: *qānon*. We also know that this law is much more than a set of legal codes and principles cohering logically in a larger legal system based on some abstract notion of Western democracy or Perso-Islamic justice. To realize the law that Mustashar od-Dawleh had in mind, we also need a form of institutionalized culture and practice adhering to values and principles enshrined in a constitution. Such fidelity to the values of law and legality requires rule by law (if not the rule of law), and will remain incompatible with the rule of *estebdād*. In the years to come, the driving behaviour of Iranians and the rate of RTAs will be measures of the extent to which Iranian society has come to terms with its internal contradictions and moved away from the ancient culture of *estebdād* towards a culture of *qānon*. Until that day, Iranians will individually and collectively project the duality of their inner and outer self and the antinomy of the veiled and unveiled that lies at the heart of their world view in their driving habits, by showing their disregard for outsiders and those who are not 'related'.

This is hardly the final word on the relationship between Iranian law or culture and the driving habits of Iranians. At best, this book has only touched on the surface of the Iranian legal culture, and by uncovering its empirical complexity has draw attention to the sociopolitical significance of the ordinary, everyday cultural practices of Iranians. Moreover, It has tried to show the the need for mapping the transformation of family and middle-range communities such as the local neighbourhoods. Research concerning Iranians, their society and politics must leave behind the ideological obsession with macro political discourses, the political elite, *fatwas* and Shari'a doctrine, in favour of learning more about the empirical reality of the social practices of ordinary people and how they view and experience the law, authority, politics, technology and religion in their daily lives.

PART II

SUPPLEMENTARY CHAPTERS

CHAPTER 10

THE REPRODUCTION OF MEANING AND WOMEN'S AUTONOMY

Behnoosh Payvar

This chapter draws attention to one specific aspect of female taxi drivers' experiences by focusing on how gender-related values and perceptions are generated through the production and reproduction of meaning. This will be done by re-examining the same 12 interviews at the Banovan Taxi Service in Tehran that we discussed in Chapter Seven.

In relation to meanings that flow through and in the course of interactions, the study considers attributes related to the position and potential of/for women in the private and public spheres. Also, legal and social frameworks, regulations and norms in relation to women are considered to be engaged in the flow of meanings. Moreover, the interviews indicate that ideas in the area related to feminism, as well as religious and secular world views, in addition to international and domestic discourse, are considered as contributing to meanings.

The chapter starts by presenting the profession of taxi driving in relation to women and the Banovan (Women's) Taxi Service (BTS). It then goes on to explore the experience of working as a taxi driver against the backdrop of the various sociocultural forces that constitute the public and private spheres in Iran. Furthermore, taking as its point of departure the idea of working as a woman taxi driver, the chapter discusses the values and the dominant perceptions in Iranian culture that determine what is 'appropriate' for women. In addition, the chapter – in the context of reproduced meanings around the idea of 'women taxi drivers' – explores the course of change for *the appropriate*. Finally, the chapter presents reflections in relation to the case of 'women taxi drivers' and the systematic reproduction of meanings.

The Banovan Taxi Service

The idea of starting the BTS was initiated and supported by the government. In its inauguration speech, it was emphasized that women who were taking a large number of taxi trips every day conveyed their desire for a safe service, and the city, with half of its population being female, needed to respect the various aspects of their rights. Meanwhile, gender-segregation policies were applied in the public and private spheres. The BTS sets regulations for women drivers that provide a service using its taxis. Based on these regulations, the BTS drivers are required to carry only female passengers and are expected to observe the formal *hijab* (compulsory veiling) as officially described and regulated. In the meantime, *private taxi service agencies* complemented their service by employing women drivers. However, according to the observations that we have made, the limitations and regulations that the BTS employs for regulating its service providers do not apply to private agencies – i.e. their women drivers may carry both men and women passengers and their choice of *hijab* is left to the discretion of the driver,[1] and is, therefore, more relaxed[2] compared to the official regulations imposed by the government-initiated BTS. However, having the choice of 'not the strictest form' means that women drivers working for private agencies follow the general rules and observe norms in relation to patterns of behaviour and ways of being in public. Besides the BTS and private agencies, there are *private taxis* organized by women drivers in Tehran. In this case, since the woman driver works independently, she may choose the passengers as well as deciding the conditions of the fare.

The fact that the service provided by the BTS generates gender-segregation meanings and policies invites critical reflection. However, the interviews and observations indicate that the meanings are reproduced along with the values in the 'conservation higher-order type' of values discussed by S.H. Schwartz's value theory,[3] which, apart from *conformity* and *tradition*, also promotes *security*. The values, in this higher-order type, deal with the 'conservation' and encourage individuals 'to preserve the status quo and the certainty it provides' (Schwartz and Boehnke 2004). Hence, the service offered by the BTS is perceived as 'security' and 'privilege' for some women. 'Some women' here refers to women whose value system and beliefs require them to undertake a conservative path in their actions and everyday life, and also those who take advantage of the service not particularly to follow the value system but due to the socially generated conception of 'security' and being safe in Tehran. Girls' and women's use of the service provided by a woman driver can also be encouraged and recommended by male partners, husbands and family members.

The BTS created job opportunities for women, and can be seen as a means of empowerment and change in the public sphere. All 12 interviewees started to work as taxi drivers for economic reasons, i.e. in order to earn a living. The BTS job opportunity is seen as beneficial and as an advantage for women who are in search of an income and are mostly the main providers for their families, although it may be seen as a challenge to male taxi drivers. Hence, compared to the situation of having no, or very little, economic means and support, becoming a BTS driver can create economic benefits and stability as well as autonomy for some women – although it might not be their first choice of occupation. The highly competitive job market and the flood of unemployed university graduates into the workforce explain the challenge facing the most vulnerable and least skilled people in Iran's cities. However, as we explained in Chapter Seven, we also found a number of university graduates among the women taxi drivers, who, due to various labour-market-related reasons, had chosen to become taxi drivers in order to gain an income, and we would point out that their choices should be recognized and respected.

Extra Facility for Women

The idea that *women taxi drivers carry only women passengers*, with emphasis on the meaning 'carrying only women' initiated by the BTS, delimits their fares and work conditions. At the same time, another meaning arises out of this idea/rule conveying *women drivers carry women passengers*, and this time the meaning stresses 'women driving women'. In the latter meaning, the *delimitation* of 'allowed to carry only women' is replaced by the *option* of 'female drivers for female passengers' that did not exist before in practice. This new option not only implies but also practically promotes *choice* for women, even though the choice can be viewed as being enforced in the framework of a segregation policy. Hence, the idea of a woman taxi driver can be perceived as providing job opportunities for women and also as a service sought by women. This aspect of women's taxis generates social forces with varying potentials to produce sociocultural meanings, which in turn affect the way in which public spaces are constructed and reproduced in the city. The reflections made by the interviewee in the following quote were also made by other women taxi drivers:

> 4:4:68: 'Women are very happy and satisfied with the Banovan Taxi Service. They think taking a ride with a woman taxi driver is a different experience. They trust us to drive the kids and are more comfortable while they are in the car.'

It is worth taking into account the fact that this service, provided by women for women, regenerates some of the values in Iranian culture that are influenced by religious beliefs and norms, which form, and are formed by, perceptions and attitudes towards the gender aspect of how individuals are/supposed to be in relation to one another in the public and private spaces.

> 4:4:69: 'I prefer my daughter to ride in a taxi with a female driver. Driving needs talent! I do not like to be colleagues with men drivers because of their attitude and way of speaking [...] I prefer working with women drivers and having women passengers, and except for the traffic problem, we have a good work environment.'

The gender-segregation policy, in the case of women taxi drivers in the context of Tehran, is reproduced among drivers and passengers in such a way that, apart from being the constant carrier of 'segregation' meaning and experiences, promotes counter forces with regard to women experiencing *security* values in the city. This is while the experience of *being a woman* in Tehran leads the woman taxi driver to say in the above-mentioned interview, 'I prefer my daughter to ride in a taxi with a female driver'. In fact, she is referring to security values in the sense of *safety*, reaching for *freedom from risk of danger*. However, her expression is influenced by, and is framed within, the setting of conservative actions and beliefs that facilitate the reach of security by inviting tradition and conformity values. Meanwhile, this example of *preserving the status quo and the certainty it provides* is a response to the systematic threats posed upon security in the sense of *freedom from doubt, anxiety and fear* in society.

In the meantime, experiencing the same setting – not just as a woman, but this time as *a woman taxi driver* – she refers to working only with women drivers and carrying women passengers as her preferred work environment, avoiding male drivers as colleagues because of their 'attitude'. In this case, going back to the *option* and *choice* created for women in the profession of taxi driving, we observe a kind of autonomy and independence experienced by women drivers as a result of driving their taxis. However, this experience of autonomy is relative and contextual, as it reflects attitudes and, perhaps existing, discriminatory patterns of behaviour towards women in general.

The context that offers the kind of *security* and *autonomy* experienced by women taxi drivers provides women with an advantaged position in a conservative way, i.e. the 'circle' of meanings in the provided space favour traditional views and values. Yet, although the core purpose of this flow of meaning tends to oppose change, the dynamics of the flow are inevitably influenced by the characteristics of institutions in the post-modern era. These force the flow to unavoidably contribute to alteration in society, as the relevant sociocultural meanings are being reproduced among people. Meanwhile, if the existing conditions promote security, in the sense of *preserving the status quo and the certainty it provides*, the flow deviates from security in the sense of *freedom from doubt, anxiety and fear* among individuals. Hence, the existing context promotes doubt, anxiety and fear in the relationship between women and society, which leads to insecurity and lack of trust between the genders.

In this way, the construction and reproduction of public spaces, in as much as they take place in the private sphere, are dependent on the flow of meanings that are engaged in an interactive interchange pattern with people through culture and society on a daily basis. These meanings include the input of interactions supported by the law, legal institutions, and 'family values'. In this context, one of the interviewees, who is a

46-year-old woman working for a private taxi agency providing services by women and only for women, said:

> 4:5:70: 'My family wanted me to be in a safe place. It was difficult for my husband in the beginning. But when I came here and he knew that it was an all-women taxi agency, he felt more at ease about it. It was difficult for us because of what people think. Some of our neighbours took up taxi driving, but they were men. When a person is retired or in any other situation, people should be able to provide their needs and not be forced into this job.'

Job Opportunity

The women taxi drivers; service provides opportunities for women to financially support themselves and even their families. Interviewees noted that economic problems and social vulnerability were among the prime criteria for women to seek licenses for taxis.

> 4:2:71: 'I was married and had a family. I am now divorced. He [her husband] never asked me how I was doing and how I got the money. He never cared. He was also working himself [driving]. When I earned more than him, he used to tell me that they give me money for nothing. No, people do not pay me money for not doing anything. They feel sympathy for me. When they see a Pride taxi is standing there and I am waiting for passengers, they choose to ride in my taxi because they realize my need is greater, they understand [...] I started working in 2001 with a Peykan [an Iran-manufactured car]. Then I heard that there was a possibility of getting a taxi. First, it was just to earn a little more money, [but] before long I found myself driving a taxi full-time.'

Responding to the question, 'What is it like being a woman and being a taxi driver?' the same woman taxi driver said:

> 4:2:72: 'You see how difficult life has become? In a day's work, a civil servant might deal with four people like himself who work in the same area, but I have to deal with all sorts of people of different ages and from different classes. Do you know how patient I have to

be to get through my work? I am not satisfied with my work and do it only because I have to. Backache, foot ache [...]. I am in a state when I finish my work at the end of the day. I chose this job because I lost one of my daughters, and it was difficult for me to stay inside and do other jobs. I like this one better because I meet people and I forget about myself.'

Also, another BTS driver stated:

4:1:73: 'I have been driving for 20 years. It was not planned when I started driving, I had to. Men drive their cars and make money when they need money, but it is not the same for women. I started with the private agencies and then I heard about the Banovan Taxi Service and I managed to get one [a BTS taxi], although it was difficult.'

Among our women taxi drivers, there were several people with a university education and relative social and economic stability in the family, according to their own statements.

4:3:74: 'I started driving a taxi for economic reasons [...]. I was working as a librarian before, but left my job.'

Those were the remarks of the 53-year-old woman taxi driver with a bachelor's degree in philosophy, who, due to her husband's illness, recently started working for a private taxi service where only women work.
Another interviewee reflects:

4:4:75: 'I have a bachelor's degree in education and I love driving. But when it is rush hour in Tehran, I reconsider my interest in driving; I would like to drive in a quieter environment. From 6 to 8 in the afternoon are the worst hours of traffic.'

This means that taxi driving has become a job opportunity, even for women who are not among the most vulnerable. In response to the question 'How did you choose this job?', the interviewee with a degree in the Italian language responded:

4:6:76: 'My children were too young, and I was not able to work outside the home. They (schools) did not need a language teacher. I knew mathematics and would have liked to teach that, but they [the school] said no you should have an academic degree [in mathematics] to be able to teach math.'

The interviews indicate that the gender-related definitions of 'man' and 'woman' regarding their position and role in society are being reproduced via interactions.

These predefined definitions, or rather perceptions, of gender roles retain their influence on how a woman taxi driver perceives herself and how other people see and treat her, even though taxi driving as a job for women *per se* is a source of new meanings and consequently alterations in perceptions. In fact, the job opportunity of *taxi driving* for women was the entrance point for the creation of a space for a new form of women's presence and participation in Tehran. The *space* that is created and maintained in relation to the woman-taxi-driver phenomenon in the city of Tehran involves people in the city and engages their interpretations. People, as the participants of this space in the city of Tehran, interpret and reinterpret the new meanings relevant to the possibilities of the new job opportunity 'woman taxi driver'. As people interact, they participate in the exchange of ideas and meanings and, in this way, contribute to the process in which meanings flow and move around from person to person and place to place. These meanings can be related, for example, to *future prospects* and *women's potential* in everyday life. This entire setting would be a field for the re-creation and flow of related meanings, in which women taxi drivers work every day and earn their living. Hence, the entire interaction of women drivers with passengers and their presence in the city as taxi drivers contribute to the process of redefining gender roles and women's potential. Meanwhile, as we see in the following quotation, pre-established perceptions towards women maintain their impact on the field (engaging city, people and drivers) and space (involving rules, norms, perceptions and interactions) for the flow of meanings (space in which meanings flow), and influence the way in which women taxi drivers experience their job in Tehran. One BTS woman taxi driver asserted:

4:2:77: 'Men don't treat women well at all! Male taxi drivers treat us badly, as if we were taking their livelihood away, like if I were not there (working as a driver) they would have earned more. Male drivers are jealous; it has always been like this for the two years that I have been driving. But, men are good passengers, they have always been good. They know that if this 50-year-old woman is working as a taxi driver {it is} because she has to. This is not a good job. Nobody sees driving as a job, especially for a woman. I am the woman of the house and a man out of the house.'

Empowerment

The nature of the female taxi drivers' job promotes independence with respect to women's economic and social life. Consequently, the relative social and economic independence gained through the 'safe' and 'legal' service empowers women taxi drivers in their life context.

4:2:78: 'This is not a safe job [...]. I had to buy the taxi so people wouldn't look down on me.[4] It is even better for my children. I am more comfortable like this [...]. It doesn't bring more income than other jobs [...]. I tried to work in the hospital after my daughter died, but it didn't work out. I found her empty place everywhere. I felt I was more comfortable with this job. At least I am my own master and lady. It is like my house – when you don't have a proper place or have family problems, whenever you are rejected or feel low, you can go to your car and sleep there.'

In the above quotation, the woman driver describes the fact that a car means much more than a vehicle for transportation: 'It is like my house'. Meanwhile, 'At least I am my own master and lady' has the potential to represent the desire for autonomy, freedom, power, control, status and identity. The project's pilot study refers to the sense of *control over the physical environment* that can be generated via automobiles, and also a relationship between the car and a sense of individualism, freedom, certain cultural values and the experience of time and space.

The interviews reflect the efforts made by women to prove that they are equal citizens and to regain some of the rights that they believe are denied them in the public and private spheres. The prevailing norms, both in the legal and social spheres, encourage and reproduce counter forces that make women's paths even more challenging. Although, even in the most patriarchal cultures, women have the responsibility of bringing up and teaching children, in this significant space made (for women), many times women might be the source and medium of reproducing the patriarchal culture and ways of doing things. In other words, patriarchy-related meanings can be a fundamental part of people's perceptions to the extent that some women might inevitably re-create and strengthen these meanings[5] in their interactions with their children – and hence, the patriarchal culture is handed even more opportunities to dominate the flow of meanings. The meanings that are reproduced by mothers and transferred to the family can be persistent due to their interactions. However, the patriarchal way has itself been through transformations, and with the emergence and advancement of communication technologies, these meanings are no longer restricted to one space. Therefore, the dynamic life and the re-creation of meanings offer implications that force interactions to undergo new ways of encountering the worlds of our minds. Therefore, as information technology is the *everyday* for many today, the reproduction and circulation of knowledge is pervasive compared to the situation even ten years ago. In the meantime, the dynamics of knowledge influence the motivating or driving forces in the circulation of meanings, which would be engaged not just to influence the system and conditions (Hydén 2008) but to actually require them in the first place. Hence, the chances for the flow of recreated meanings increase. Women, and specifically women taxi drivers in this case, would, either directly or indirectly, encounter the pervasive flow of meanings, and re-create their own understanding of new ideas. Consequently, women would also take part in conveying the meanings that they encounter through interactions, and actively face the long-lasting patterns of thought and action, as the content of re-created meanings differs from that of older structures. The woman taxi driver working for a private taxi agency who has a bachelor's degree in education sciences asserted:

4:4:79: 'Iranian culture is the culture of patriarchy. Even though the majority of people are better educated than before, still men – even the well-educated ones – want to keep women at home to do housework. The idea of women working outside has not yet been accepted [. . .]. Not even educated men would allow their wives to work outside if women did not show resolve [. . .]. They will force women to stay at home and make soup for them.'

The fact that women taxi drivers went beyond just speaking about the limitations and discrimination that they experience – conveying meanings by words – and actually took action by acquiring the driving job created, under their own specific circumstances, is an outstanding record. The interviews reflect the fact that women's empowerment – meanings of 'security' and 'privilege' gained via the profession of taxi driving – and also meanings derived from the rule that the BTS women taxi drivers should only drive women are linked for some women. The woman taxi driver with a secondary-school education, said:

4:5:80: 'When women prove themselves, there will be no difference between them and men. If one obeys the law and respects everyone, there will be no problem. When women drive, they want to show everyone that they have learnt to do it. They are very proud of what they do [...]. Women passengers are more comfortable riding with women drivers [...]. Men drivers don't like women taxi drivers.'

Even though taxi driving has been a source of independence and empowerment for women drivers, the pre-existing meanings still concern and engage women drivers regarding the description of this profession and its gender-specific reputation. Therefore, part of the circulation of meanings engages 'empowerment' versus the perception of *taxi driving* among women taxi drivers. In response to the question 'Why did you chose this job?', one woman taxi driver said, 'I love driving. I like to choose the jobs that are for men and "masculine" [...] the hard jobs.' Q. 'Why?'; 'I do not know why. I like it that way. I do not like delicate jobs.' Q. 'Why did you choose this job among the male-dominated jobs?'; 'Because I love driving, I love nature, and I love variety! You meet more people, you are more in the society, and see more different people' (4:5:81).

Transforming the Public Sphere

The service of 'women driving women' requires and facilitates the presence of women in the public sphere. Women drivers are active participants in economic and social life in the everyday context of the city, and this fact adds to the character and relations of the public sphere with regard to gender roles, perceptions and interactions. Considering the fact that the history of religious, political and social grounds, as well as culture and law (Afshar 1998; Kar and Hoodfar 1996; Paidar 1995), generate symbolic meaning in relation to women – and, specifically, women in the public sphere – the service of 'women driving women', supported by the gender-segregation policy, contributed to a significant change in relation to the norms around women and the public sphere – a process that is evident today in the case of women taxi drivers. More than a decade ago, Shaditalab (2002), in her book on development and Iranian women's challenges, discussed the results of her study indicating fundamental changes in the segregation of gender roles, even in the private and public sphere, of rural society. Shaditalab (2002) argues that rural women play an active role in providing the family's financial resources, and significantly contribute to the economy of the family. The results of her study show that since rural women are familiar with the banking system, they are present in the public sphere – either to work in the system or to pursue their right to financial and credit services from the banks.

The counter forces negotiating gender relations and the position of women in society and the law suggest *conservation* versus *change*. The values and relevant meanings on either side contribute to the perceptions, motives and core driving force of the interactions. The social norms that are interwoven with religious ideas and rulings reproduce conservative actions and beliefs, which would define specific *ways of being* for women in the public sphere and underline what is considered 'appropriate' in women's choices. The consequences of this relationship go further than norms and social sanctions, as the law introduces and necessitates the responsibilities suggested by those norms that have a religious origin. According to Article 1117 of the Civil Code of Justice, a husband is entitled to prevent his spouse from having certain jobs. The article states that the husband can prohibit his wife from employment that harms the reputation of the family or is against family values.

The legal and social definitions in women taxi derivers' life environment reproduce assumptions and theories that propagate 'subordination' and 'conservation'. Meanwhile, the law sustains and protects the relevant cycles of meanings and values, as in Article 28 of the constitution, which states that everyone is entitled to choose and select his or her desired employment, as long as it is not against Islamic principles, public interest and does not interfere with the rights of others'. This, while women are seen as valuable and protected within the framework of beliefs – 'Article 75 of the labour laws: 'Hard, laborious and dangerous jobs are forbidden for women'.

Negotiating the Public and the Private

Social spaces, including the legal field, retain the circulation of meanings through interactions; these meanings, irrespective of their content, follow the course of, and are influenced by the underlying meanings induced by dominant forces. The law and society reproduce the meanings that maintain the track of actions and attitudes, and in this way the direction of the flow of meaning is sustained according to the direction of those underlying meanings that exercise the most influence and control. The discourse created through conversations with the interviewees helps us to move away from abstract terms and see how these meanings are led by, and interacted with, in actual conversations. Mehrsa, the 50-year-old woman taxi driver with a bachelor's degree in humanities who graduated from Tehran University 23 years ago, said, 'None of our relatives know that I have a taxi' and described her experience of being a taxi driver as:

4:6:82: 'There has been patriarchy in our country. When the man comes home, he expects the woman to serve him tea and food. But when a woman like me works outside, besides doing my job, when I get home I just take off my coat and directly go to the kitchen to prepare food. And there is no one to offer me even a cup of tea.'

As Mehrsa describes the situation and the way of being in her life environment, she indicates the gender roles and implies her unrealized expectations. However, at the same time, she is hesitant and makes sure she is keeping the conversation socially and politically 'correct' as she points out the priority and significance of home and family:

4:6:83: 'But, I have to continue for the sake of my life. I, of course, don't have that much financial need. I am not working because I need money and my husband always tells me "come back home

when you are tired". My home and family is first and then comes
my job, it [this job] isn't like being an employee of an office.'

The private domain is perceived by law and society to be the priority for
women, and deviations from this course will result in social and legal
sanctions. Perhaps taxi driving is a way of reclaiming a desired *way
of being* for Mehrsa – rephrasing her *self* in the city and consuming
public space by adopting a more participatory and active approach.
However, she has to meet the required social and legal requirements in
order to achieve her goal. If we assume that Mehrsa's will is to attain a
more independent and active life in the city, as is evident from her
utterances, we also know that she has the knowledge regarding the
possibilities and risks on the way to realizing her wish; she also shows
competence in taking actions and managing circumstances. However,
she needs to find her way through the 'system conditions'[6] (Hydén
2008) that exist in her life environment – as the possibilities and
conditions for the true fulfilment of her *will* are not directly present in
her everyday life.

At this point, the interactions undergo a negotiation of public
and private with regard to Mehrsa's desire and choices. The private has
the possibility of applying more influence due to the fact that, apart
from social sanctions, the law provides support for the norms around
marriage, family and the concept of 'the appropriate' job and ways of
being for women (in both the public and private spheres). On the
other hand, the public offers potentialities and variety in the course of
which the *self* enjoys possibilities other than those offered by the
private. Meanwhile, inevitably, there has been a discord of ideas and
opinions due to the pre-established norms and values. However,
the practice of *taxi driving* by women has influenced the course of
meanings and the content of norms around this concept in the city.
In this regard, Mehrsa continued, 'People treat us good and they
tell me [why] do you do this difficult job and hide it from your
relatives!?' The more popularity that women taxi drivers gain, the
more systematically the meanings supporting this practice will be
reproduced. The reproduction of meanings takes place through the
interactions of individuals – in this case, people in the city of Tehran
– with each other and with other factors, e.g. the city environment in
general, the law, the media and religion.

Values and Resistance

In the course of negotiations between public and private, women make their way with effort. A woman taxi driver, due to the established order of life in Iran and the existing social norms and values, may (if not *ought to*) need to be engaged in negotiations in relation to dealing with, for example, family and relatives in order to convince them about *her* choice of job. In other words, women taxi drivers, in their circles of interactions, cope with, and may need to convince, individuals to recognize their choices by using arguments and evidence in order to make a firm impression and create trust about their course of action. Existing definitions (social norms and values) can hinder the way by not completely supporting the independent woman taking up a male-dominated profession and assuming extensive presence in the public. Meanwhile, social norms in Tehran, amongst other factors, are influenced by traditional interpretations and religious values. The importance of the choice of job – 'the appropriate' – ways of appearing in the public and private spheres, religious and social values, and the sort of responsibilities suggested and defined for women (both at the legal and normative levels) form part of the circles of meanings around the woman and her choices in life. However, women taxi drivers still insist on their 'choice', negotiating their way – despite all definitions and social/legal sanctions – as if resisting against the defined 'appropriate'.

Mehrsa started driving seven years ago, and has been working as a taxi driver for five years. Yet, her experience of facing the 'appropriate' choice considering her life context, including education and the level of economic stability in her family, has been relatively peaceful albeit challenging. Mehrsa mentioned that her relatives were not informed that she had a taxi, reasoning:

4:6:84: 'Because their thinking is different. That is why I don't want to say anything about myself. One of my brothers was against it. He was saying that this job does not suit me because I had a bachelor's degree. He didn't want me to start this job. But my other brother and sister were saying "no it doesn't matter". But I was very much depressed because of my sister's death; I wanted to come out of the house. I was always home and sleeping. To get rid of the depression, my husband said: "The income isn't as important as [the fact] that you go out and not be depressed all the time. The important thing for me is that you are happy." It is important for me that my husband has a good job. Until the last moment that I got the taxi, he asked if I really wanted to go and do this job and I told him yes, didn't you sign to agree with this yourself? And he said: "Yes, I did, but I was thinking maybe you wouldn't go yourself in the end." He had to agree and sign [a document] to show his consent for me to be able to start the job. He is an accountant and finance manager.'[7]

Yet, the opportunity granted by the BTS for women to participate in the public sphere as authorized taxi drivers, although it has limitations and has been compromised by religious norms and rulings, provided the grounds and conditions for the possibility and growth of this option as a choice of job.

The Course of Change for 'the Appropriate'

The norms around the concept of 'the appropriate' or 'the proper' are changing as new meanings are produced around the idea of being a woman taxi driver. The social circles of meanings concerning *how a woman would be and act* are reproduced in the course of interactions, and can change through time. Updates on the motivational continuum, which holds underlying meanings, sustain the rhythm of the flow of those meanings.

According to the interviews, *being a woman taxi driver* was previously not recognized as being an acceptable, 'proper' or 'appropriate' job for women. The main reason for the rejection of this occupation, according to the interviews, was that taxi driving was seen as a male-dominated profession that required extensive and unexpected interactions. Another was the constant presence of the woman in the public sphere that the job would entail, which restrains her responsibilities at home and puts the woman driver at risk. It worth taking into account the fact that the policies and norms around the idea of a woman taxi driver have been part of a larger context. One of the events, regarding policies on segregation of men and women in public and private spaces, that led to particularly extensive comments was the gender segregation in Iranian higher education. Official news agencies in Iran publish commentaries condemning the use of the phrase 'gender segregation', arguing that the aim of the policy and law was promoting 'respect' for women and not 'segregation'. In this context, the *Fars News Agency* (28 January 2014) published a text approved by the Supreme Council of the Cultural Revolution that was made public on 7 August 1987, emphasizing the rules in relation to the workplace and the boundaries of Islamic ethics in interactions and social life.

The Banovan Taxi Service, which was established with government support in order to provide the service of women driving women, and partly in line with the general policies on gender segregation of public spaces, was supported by social and legal norms. Hence, *being a woman taxi driver* was introduced as a profession in society. Following the establishment of the BTS, changes occurred in perceptions regarding the profession, and *being a woman taxi driver* was then recognized and became relatively acceptable. In the meantime, private taxi agencies welcomed the idea and hired women as taxi drivers. Amongst women, those in search of income opportunities, following the newly recognized norm of the profession 'women driving as taxi drivers', took up the job, both at the BTS service and also at private agencies. However, observations show that private agencies do not often require women to follow the segregation policy, and mostly focus on the business *per se*. Although, at private agencies, women drivers can drive both men and women, and perhaps sit in the same room as male colleagues do in order to wait for their turn, the private agencies' focus on the 'business' is valid in the context of social and legal norms. The agency, drivers' life context and valid ways of being in their environment, as well as values, set parts of the frame of interactions, which create and maintain working conditions for women. Hence, a considerable step is taken in relation to women's participation in the public sphere.

The women taxi drivers record the interplay between social ways of being, and individual and collective perceptions – concerning the choice of appropriate job and actions for women in the public, in this case – and also the relationship with the social and religious norms and attendant interpretations. Women's contribution in a public field has been determined, taking into consideration gender roles and the interpretations of religious sources that influence social norms and perceptions.

Conclusions

In all interviews, the individual's family life and economic condition was mentioned as the main reason for the interviewees to participate in the job market as women taxi drivers. This along with other incentives – for instance, gaining independence – were mentioned by the women respondents as reasons for their choice of taking jobs as taxi drivers.

Meanings continue to emerge out of dominant values and policies in the context of women taxi drivers' lives. The government establishes women's taxi agencies, and hence, women taxi drivers drive only women to protect the values and security of other women. These meanings are re-created by individual social actors through interactions. Meanwhile, as the re-created meanings spread in the city, conveying the message of the possibility of having a woman taxi driver – 'a woman taxi driver is possible', 'a woman taxi driver is needed' – more private taxi agencies hire women as taxi drivers, but they implement other conditions and their women drivers can drive both men and women. This time, the meanings are re-created, indicating that *women have the possibility of working as taxi drivers in the city,* even though it had been a male-dominated profession. Interactions proceed as women drivers drive people throughout the city, working for both private and public agencies. As a result, meanings are recreated, conveying the fact that *women can work as drivers and taxi driving is not a profession specific to men.*

The *space* that is created and maintained in relation to the woman-taxi-driver phenomenon in Tehran contributes to the quality and extent of space for women in public and private life, as well as their presence and participation in the city. Meanwhile, the space for the circulation and development of the primary cluster of meanings – including gender segregation, security and family values – gained the possibility to grow in line with dominant underlying meanings at the level of policy and law, as well as among people in society. The characteristics of this space lead mostly in the direction of 'conservation higher order type of values' (Schwartz and Boehnke 2004), stressing security and traditional values, and promoting gender segregation as well as religious values. Yet, in this context, women taxi drivers driving through the city play a specific role, and have a particular significance in relation to the generation of new meanings and perceptions regarding women in/and society and law; hence, new directions of meanings find the space in order to grow.

Women taxi drivers indicate a greater presence of women in public spaces, which distinguishes women's position and potential, both in character and in the extent of their effectiveness and participation, compared to the period between 1979 and 2014. Consequently, women are seen as effectively 'allowed' to be *in* social life and the public sphere, even in male-dominated professions that were perceived to be specific to men. A higher presence of women on the streets, actively participating in organizing daily life, brings change to perceptions regarding the role and potential of women *and* society. Meanwhile, the possibility of working as a woman taxi driver has increased women's chances for participation, even if we assume that this possibility arose as a result of a gender-segregation-based thinking or policy.

The everyday experience of women taxi drivers, despite the limitations, implies economic and social empowerment and autonomy for women. The woman taxi driver's role proves women's potential as independent and productive citizens, and not subordinate and supported family members portrayed in the legal discourse. Moreover, while women – and married women in particular – have been potentially and practically responsible for maintaining family values and fulfilling not only raised social expectations but also legal requirements (See Iranian Civil Code, Chapter 8, Articles 1105; 1106; 1108; and 1117), the woman taxi driver functions despite the legal setting and backdrop to women *and* law.

The transformations and alternative practical examples in the case of *the appropriate choices*, the presence of women in the public space and their participation as taxi drivers in the job market indicate the function/traces of legal and social norms in relation to the position of women and interpretations made by traditional Islamic doctrine. Considering the principles of Islamic values, which define the boundaries for participation, there can be a question as to whether granting this possibility to women taxi drivers would have required new interpretations of religious norms concerning women and the public sphere, and whether new directions/possibilities have appeared in this regard. The possible conflicting perspectives regarding Islamic norms and women might have appeared in relation to the extent and quality of women's presence in the public sphere – and specifically to 'the appropriate' choice of job stressed by the interpretations made about responsibilities, in relation to family and children, and values suggested by the religion of Islam in Iran after 1979.

The re-creation and reproduction of meanings in relation to women taxi drivers' everyday experience take place in a space that is situated in a local, yet also global, context of meanings. Criticism raised by women taxi drivers about, for example, general patterns of patriarchy and their noted experiences reveal their knowledge of alternative value systems in other societies and their claim to being citizens of modern society. Hence, gender-related meanings are reproduced, in the course of the flow of meaning, through the perception and knowledge of women taxi drivers, their passengers and observers.

CHAPTER 11

THE IRANIAN LEGAL SYSTEM

Shahrad Nasrolahi Fard and Reza Banakar

All civil, penal, financial, economic, administrative, cultural, military, political laws and other laws or regulations must be based on Islamic criteria. This principle applies absolutely and generally to all articles of the Constitution as well as to all other laws and regulations, and the fuqaha [*Islamic jurists*] of the Council of Guardians are judges in this matter.

(Article 4 of the Iranian Constitution of 1979)

Introduction

The legal system of the Islamic Republic is frequently criticized for its lack of autonomy and, as we repeatedly heard in the course of our interviews, for failing to uphold ordinary people's rights, generally, and women's and minority rights, in particular. Its judiciary is described as 'politicized' and its legal profession as feeble and ineffective (see Arjomand 2013; Mohammadi 2008; Rezaei 2008). These criticisms, which highlight the discrete shortcomings of the Iranian legal system, ultimately concern the way in which 'the rule of law' – i.e. the principles of legality and due process that ensure continuity, predictability and certainty in legal decision making – has been incorporated into the constitution and is implemented by courts and other legal authorities. As Moschtaghi (2010: 7) maintains:

Rather than adhering to the rule of law, Iranian constitutional doctrine gives absolute preference to the rule of *Sharia* and its specific Shiite component, the principle of *velāyat-e faqhih*. Hence, beside a formal separation of powers and the adoption of the principle of *nulla poena sine lege*[1] hardly any aspects regularly associated with the rule of law have been incorporated into the Iranian legal system.

Nevertheless, as Mir-Hosseini points out (2010a: 334), Iran's return to Shariʿa was not a return to the 'classical *feqh* notion of plural and uncodified laws', and the Iranian judiciary 'has retained not only many of the legal concepts and laws of the Pahlavi era, but also the notion of a centralized and unified legal system'. Although the Iranian legal system does not live up to the rule of law as defined in western European constitutions, it nevertheless appears to function as a unified juridical order. This chapter will present the laws, law-making processes, procedures and institutions that constitute the Iranian legal system, in order to explore how these are unified – in theory and in practice. We shall start by considering how the Iranian Constitution allocates responsibilities, rights and powers to various legal institutions in accordance with 'Islamic criteria', before we move on to discuss its court structure and the sources of law. The chapter concludes by reflecting on the fragmentation of the court system, which has undermined the jurisdiction of public courts over political matters, and the rift between a politicized judiciary and a legal profession fighting an uphill battle for its independence.

The Authoritative Structure of the Islamic Constitution

Iran is a constitutional Islamic republic wherein the distinctive powers, characteristics, objectives, activities, rights and responsibilities of its institutions are outlined in the constitution, which was adopted in 1979.[2] According to this constitution, the legal system comprises a network of institutions operating on the basis of Shariʿa laws and principles, which, in turn, are employed to generate an Islamic legal order. Moreover, the Leader, as the highest authority of the State, is appointed by the Assembly of Experts (*Majles-e-Khobregan*).[3] The constitution defines and establishes the powers, functions and duties of, and relationships between, the main public authorities. Moreover, it classifies these authorities into three categories – namely legislative (with the power to create laws); executive (with the power to execute public policies and decisions, and implement laws); and judiciary (with the power to adjudicate disputes, decide cases and pronounce appropriate sentences). However, these authoritative powers must operate 'under the supervision of the absolute religious Leader and the leadership of the *ummah*' (the Iranian Constitution, Article 57). The working relationships between legislative, executive and judiciary powers are described in such a way as to govern the State through constitutional arrangements whilst maintaining a balance of power. The constitution also establishes the separation of powers (Article 57), recognizing that the independence of the power of each authority, in line with the execution of their powers, is a constitutional requirement.

Legislative Authority

The Islamic Consultative Assembly (Parliament, or *Majlis*) is empowered to legislate laws 'within the limits of its competence laid down in the Constitution' (Article 71), but this empowerment requires parliament to ensure that the implementation of different laws is consistent and in full compliance with the constitution as well as the laws, criteria and principles of Shari'a (Article 72).[4] In the legislative process, an important question is whether parliament is the sole and supreme law-making authority of the State. This question gains importance once we realize that parliament's legislative power is limited by a number of factors; for instance, the constitution restricts a bill from becoming law without the Guardian Council's approval (Article 93).[5] In the absence of the Guardian Council's endorsement, any proposed legislation is returned to parliament in order to address the required amendment(s) (Article 94). In the case of any conflict between parliament and the Guardian Council over a controversial bill, the Expediency Council (*Majma-e-Tashkhis-e-Maslehat-e-Nezam*) will step in to mediate and resolve these differences (Article 112).[6] The Expediency Council is convened at the order of the Leader, and it can also serve in the capacity of an expert advisory role for said Leader. Any decision taken by the Expediency Council in its mediatory role is final and affects the sovereignty and constitutional position of parliament, which is indicative of how these centres of normativity, which exist within the legal system, interact and compete with each other within the law-making process whilst struggling to establish valid law.

Looking at these institutional interactions from another angle, the Guardian Council (*Shora-ye-Negahban*) is empowered to safeguard Islamic ordinances and the constitution in accordance with Article 91. It is made up of 12 members, six of whom are 'Islamic *Faqihs*', i.e. experts and jurisconsults in Islamic law, appointed by the Leader and who possess legally overriding powers, while the remaining six are appointed by parliament, albeit recommended by the Head of the Judiciary.[7] The Head of the Judiciary, in turn, is appointed by the Leader – which is politically significant, since it does not require the approval of parliament or the government – and the Guardian Council is made responsible for supervising the election of members of parliament.[8] Whilst 'the majority vote of the religious men' is essentially required to determine the compatibility of legislation with the 'laws of Islam', 'the majority vote of all the members of the Guardian Council' is required for establishing the compatibility of the legislation with the constitution (Article 96).

Executive Authority

The government is based on the constitution, and the power and authority of the executive branch (government) lies with the president. Under the constitution, to achieve the objectives stated in its Article 2, and for the purpose of achieving justice and other stated objectives, the government 'has the duty of directing all its resources to attain these goals' (Article 3). According to Articles 133 and 134 of the constitution, the president has the right and responsibility to appoint and supervise the operation of the Council of Ministers (the cabinet), as well as to coordinate and implement governmental policies that will be presented to parliament for a vote of confidence. A presidential candidate is required to pass through three stages: the candidate must first be approved by the Guardian Council; second, he will need to be elected by the public, through a majority vote; and then, finally, he must be appointed by the Leader.[9] The constitution positions the president as the highest authority after the Leader, and makes him responsible for implementing the constitution in all matters but those which fall under the authoritative power of the Leader. Furthermore, the president is elected through the vote of the people for a term of four years, with the possibility of one further term.[10]

Judicial Authority

The head of the judiciary is appointed by the Leader for a period of five years, in accordance with Articles 110 and 157 of the constitution, whereas the minister of justice – who is responsible for all matters relating to the relationship between the judiciary and the executive and legislative institutions (Article 160) – is appointed by the president as a result of nominations made by the head of the judiciary. The head of the supreme court and the prosecutor-general are appointed by the head of the judiciary following a deliberation with the supreme court judges, as described in Article 162. Similarly to other institutions, the ultimate authority over the judiciary lies with the Leader, and may be exercised directly or indirectly. The Leader appoints the head of the judiciary, who in turn appoints high-ranking people in the judicial system as well as the judges. Although the president appoints the minister of justice, the president himself is required to be endorsed and approved by the Leader, as mentioned above.

Shari'a laws and principles act as the foundations for the judiciary, and these are predominantly evident in Articles 61 and 156 of the constitution. The former article states that the function of the judiciary, as performed by the courts, must be in accordance with the criteria of Islam, and that the courts are authorized to examine and settle lawsuits, protect the rights of the public, deliver and maintain justice and implement the 'Divine limits' (Article 61). The latter article empowers the judiciary to settle disputes; restore and promote justice; supervise the enforcement of laws, prosecutions and punishments under the Islamic penal code; and take steps to prevent the recurrence of crimes (Article 156). Additionally, the constitution demonstrates how, in the absence of any applicable law, judges are obliged to deliver their judgement according to 'authoritative Islamic sources and authentic fatwa' (Article 167). According to Tellenbach (2009: 692), this '[A]rticle seems to allow the judge to directly deduce new unwritten law from Islamic sources and fatwas if no relevant codifies laws exists' without referring to *urf*.[11] Moreover, although many have tried to interpret this article in a way that is compatible with the principle of legality – for example, by confining it to civil cases – Tellenbach claims that it can also cover criminal cases. Article 167 can therefore allow punishment for an act that is deemed criminal in religious law but has not been criminalized in 'positive law'. In general, the courts are charged with resolving conflicts through the process of legal interpretation, but the purpose of their intervention is to ensure that a constitutional arrangement and the significance of Shari'a have been satisfied through applying and interpreting laws in accordance with the constitution. Essentially, if any ambiguity arises, the courts must ensure that their decisions are consistent (and compatible) with Shari'a. The interpretation of laws is therefore an important part of the operation of the courts, in that judges interpret laws throughout the course of their judgements. Notwithstanding their interpretation of laws, judges' authority to interpret laws is divided into two categories, whereby the onus for ordinary laws lies with parliament (Article 73)[12] whilst constitutional matters are bestowed upon the Guardian Council, although any decisions require the consensus of 75 per cent or more of its members (Article 98).

The constitution sets out the structure of the courts and their jurisdiction as determined by law (Article 159). As such, they must follow established procedures and mechanisms when examining cases and making rulings on the procedural aspects of laws. Therefore, in this section, the following interlinked factors relating to the judicial system will be studied concisely: (1) the structure of the courts and (2) the specific jurisdiction of the courts. The analysis also encompasses the study of different types of judgements applicable within the civil and criminal procedural codes.

The Structure and Operation of the Court System

The Iranian court system is hierarchically constructed and composed of numerous layers of public and specialized courts with different jurisdictions and competencies, headed by the supreme court, which is the highest judicial authority in Iran.

The Supreme Court

According to the Article 161 of the constitution, the supreme court must supervise 'the correct implementation of the laws by the courts, ensuring uniformity of judicial procedure, and fulfilling any other responsibilities assigned to it by law'. In Article 366 of the Civil Code of Procedure for public and revolutionary courts,[13] it is provided that the appellate procedure consists of reviewing whether or not a judgement that has been appealed has complied with legitimacy and legal criteria – which, in turn, are based on the principles of Islam, referred to as 'the Islamic criteria'. The importance of these 'Islamic criteria' for the judiciary goes further than just processing appealable judgements. Under the New Islamic Penal Procedure Code, in cases where the head of the judiciary has observed inconsistency between final rulings (delivered by any court) and the legitimacy/Islamic criteria, he will transfer the case/s to the allocated supreme court for re-examination and judgement (the New Islamic Penal Procedure Code, Article 477).[14] From the appellate jurisdictional perspective, the supreme court is the last judicial resort for re-examining these appealable civil and criminal cases in its designated criminal and civil appeal branches. According to the New Islamic Penal Procedure Code, criminal appellate branches have the authority to hear the appeals of judgements delivered by public and revolutionary courts. Criminal appeal authority resides with the appellate court of the same province except in cases for which the supreme court is the only appellate authority allowed to hear crimes carrying the following legal punishments: execution (*Salb-e-hayat*), amputation (*Naghs-e-uzv*) and life imprisonment, as well as press and political crimes (the New Islamic Penal Procedure Code, Articles 427 and 428). Under the Civil Code of Procedure, civil branches have the jurisdiction to re-examine appeals originating from judgements where those of the public courts have become final, since none of the parties has appealed to the provincial appellate courts within the set timeline. Essentially, it must be noted that once the judgement of the public courts has become final, any appeal is restricted only to specific cases, instances of which include cases in which the value of the claim is over 20 million Rials or cases concerning marriage, the annulment of a marriage (*Faskh*), divorce, paternity or incapacity (*hajr*).[15] In cases in which normal appeals to the provincial appellate courts have been followed, the supreme court can hear appeals on these judgements – albeit only in restricted areas, such as cases concerning marriage and annulment (*Faskh*), divorce, paternity or incapacity (*hajr*).[16]

Appellate Courts

Provincial appellate courts were established to hear appeals against the judgements of the public and revolutionary courts in both civil and criminal cases, whereby in civil cases they have jurisdiction to hear a range of appealable judgements – namely in financial disputes over a value of 3 million Rials, and all judgements relating to non-financial disputes.[17] In relation to criminal cases, the provincial appellate courts have jurisdictional authority to examine all appealable criminal sentences except where the judgements fall within the jurisdiction of the supreme court (the New Islamic Penal Procedure Code, Article 426 and 427). If applicable, appellate court rulings can be referred to the supreme court. In relation to certain serious crimes, provincial appeal courts are in fact preliminary courts and have jurisdiction to examine such grave offences. In this respect these courts do not operate in the capacity of an appeal court but rather as a preliminary court, a status which will be discussed further in the following section.

Public Courts

Public courts are divided into civil and criminal entities, with respective jurisdictions to examine civil and criminal cases (Hashemi 2013). Some of these courts, known as specialist courts, possess only specific jurisdiction to hear cases relating to defined areas of speciality and responsibility – for example, family courts, military courts, Islamic revolutionary courts, the Court of Administrative Justice and the Special Court for the Clergy[18] – which will be studied further below. Apart from the jurisdiction of the following specialist courts – the criminal court of provinces, clerical courts, revolutionary courts, military courts and criminal branches of dispute settlement councils – the criminal courts have authority to investigate all criminal cases.

The provincial appeal courts are authorized to hear 'serious crimes', which we listed above and which can lead to execution. Hence, in this regard, the provincial appeal courts are considered the first designated judicial authority to hear and prosecute the aforementioned crimes, and their role is not in the capacity of an appellate court but rather of a preliminary public court, known as the criminal courts of the province. This is to say that although the provincial appeal courts are classified as higher courts within the judicial system, they are the first authority to carry out preliminary prosecutions and any investigations of these crimes.

However, under the New Islamic Penal Procedure Code, which compiles all general and specific provisions, criminal courts are reclassified as first-class and second-class 'penal courts' (*Dadgah-haye-Keyfari*), revolutionary courts, or children and juvenile courts.[19] As a consequence, investigations, prosecutions and criminal proceedings in relation to press and political crimes, which require the attendance of jury members, will fall within the scope of the jurisdiction of the first-class criminal courts and will be heard in the presence of a jury.[20] The selection of the jury and its powers, and the definition of 'political offences', however, will be determined in accordance with Islamic criteria, in order to meet the requirements of Article 10 of the press law.[21]

This New Islamic Penal Procedure Code, nonetheless, has faced some obstacles in its implementation despite going through all required legislative processes, such as the necessity for parliament to pass the law, followed by the approval of the Guardian Council, then publication in an official gazette and the formal endorsement of the president. Having followed this required procedure, the president also forwards the law to the judiciary for implementation, which is also a requirement if any bill is finally to become binding in law. Although the New Islamic Penal Procedure Code has become binding legally, nonetheless it has not yet been implemented due to a number of practical issues – including the head of the judiciary requesting an extension until the summer of 2015.

Military Courts

These courts investigate and judge an individual who has been accused of an offence in relation to military or security duties; hence, they have authority to examine crimes committed by members of the army, the Islamic Revolution Guards Corps, the police and other military-related personnel (the Iranian Constitution, Article 172; Armed Forces Procedure Code, Article 1). The Armed Forces Procedure Code (*Ghanoon-e-Aeen-e-Dadresi-Nirouhaye-Mosallah*) has classified these courts into first- and second-class military courts, in accordance with certain crimes and punishments.[22]

Islamic Revolutionary Courts

These courts examine crimes ranging from violating national and/or international security, 'waging war against God and sowing the seeds of corruption on earth' (*Mofsed-e-felarz*), insulting the founder of the Islamic Republic and the Leader, conspiracy and treason against the Islamic Republic, armed violence and crimes, assassination and the destruction of institutions for the purpose of opposing the Islamic Republic, to all forms of smuggling, including guns; drug-related crimes; public-order offences; acts of terrorism; and all other crimes that fall within the scope of these courts (the New Islamic Penal Code, Articles 297 and 303). When the revolutionary courts were established, their decisions were set as final and not open to appeal, but in 1989 a law was passed to grant the supreme court the appellate jurisdiction to hear revolutionary courts' judgements (Hashemi 2013).

Court of Administrative Justice

According to the constitution, under the supervision of the head of the judiciary, these courts were established in order to rule on administrative cases concerning people lodging complaints against government officials and organs such as ministries, organizations, institutes, revolutionary institutes and statutes (the Iranian Constitution, Article 173; and the Administrative Procedure Code, Article 1). The constitution further provides that 'Everyone has the right to demand the annulment of any such regulation from the Court of Administrative Justice' (Article 170). Under the Administrative Procedure Code (*Ghanoon-e-Tashkilat va Aeen-e-Dadresi-Diyvan-e-Edallat-e-Edari*), subsequent to recent amendments, these courts changed from one-stage trials to a hierarchical framework consisting of higher and lower courts; the former include court of appeal branches, which are then subdivided into public and specialized appellate branches.[23]

Special Court for the Clergy (Dadgah-e-Vizh-e-Ruhaniyyat)

According to the Procedural Code for the Special Courts for the Clergy (*Aeennameh-Dadsaraha va Dadgah-haye-Vizheh-Ruhaniyyat*), the Leader supervises these courts and appoints their chief judges and prosecutors.[24] These courts therefore operate independently of other courts, and are answerable solely to the Leader. Furthermore, they have exclusive authority to deal with transgressions and crimes involving the clergy and/or those which may potentially have been committed by the clergy.[25] However, civil cases against the clergy are examined by the public courts – except in specific cases, which are heard by the Special Court for the Clergy following the prosecutor's decision to refer such cases accordingly.[26] The decisions of the special clerical courts are not appealable through the normal appellate courts, and thus they require an internally designated appeal process.[27] Although the fundamental principles of the judiciary's independent power are outlined in Article 156 of the constitution, these court systems fall outside the scope of the authority of the judiciary.

Family Courts

These courts in Iran have weathered several changes, although a detailed analysis of these changes falls beyond the scope of this chapter. Pursuant to the amended Family Protection Act (amended and approved by parliament on 21 August 2011), family courts were established to fulfil the constitutional requirements of Article 21, ordering the government to establish competent courts to protect and preserve families and aiming at ensuring women's rights in 'all respects, in conformity with Islamic criteria', and accomplishing goals 'establishing competent courts to protect and preserve the family' (the Iranian Constitution, Article 21, note/annex 3). These courts have exclusive authority to examine cases pertaining to family matters such as marriage (permanent and temporary), the annulment of a marriage and divorce.[28]

Prosecutor's Office (Dadsara)

This office is responsible for discovering crimes, filing lawsuits and protecting the rights of the public, and the enforcement of rulings and dealing with probate matters (the New Islamic Penal Procedure Code, Articles 22–7). The Office of the Prosecutor will issue an indictment after the preliminary investigation and the prosecution of the accused have been completed (the New Islamic Penal Procedure Code, Articles 64–122). In its capacity as an important judicial institution, this office has responsibility for criminal proceedings, but it has been subject to closures and resurrections within the judicial system. The closure of the prosecutor's office, for instance, resulted in consequences such as 'lack of specialization of the courts, wasting the court's time, lack of clarity concerning who has the duty to prosecute on behalf of the public and the overlapping of the duties of the prosecution and crime investigators' ('Third Periodic Report of Iran', paragraphs 44–5, 2010).[29] Following its closure for eight years, the general and revolutionary prosecutor's office was re-established, albeit this time possessing greater jurisdiction in relation to general and revolutionary offences ('Third Periodic Report of Iran', paragraph 46, 2010).

Reconciliation/Dispute Settlement Councils

The Law on Mandatory Arbitration was passed with the multiple aims of: (1) increasing and promoting people's participation in the settlement of disputes, (2) reducing referrals to the courts, (3) settling disputes locally and (4) settling minor disputes lacking judicial character (Article 189 of the Law on the Third Development Plan).[30] Councils have authority to settle disputes and examine cases relating mainly to disputes over the beneficiaries of a will or intestacy, residential tenant eviction, disputes ranging from a maximum of 20 million Rials in rural areas to 50 million Rials in urban areas (the latter amount has recently been increased from 50 to 200 million Rials) and also supervising and exercising the guardianship of properties belonging to minors, the insane, the absent and those suffering from incapacity and intestacy without any known beneficiaries (the Law on Dispute Settlement Councils, Articles 8–17). Any appeals are heard by the public courts (the Law on Dispute Settlement Councils, Article 31). The scope of authority and power of these councils, together with their compositions and the appointment of their members, are in accordance with implementing regulations that are approved by the head of the judiciary, proposed by the minister of justice and also approved by the Council of Ministers ('Fourth Development Plan of the Islamic Republic of Iran', Article 134). The councils are divided into two public and two specialized divisions. The head of the judiciary is authorized to establish a special branch of councils in each province, in order to deal with matters concerning specialized cases (the Law on Dispute Settlement Councils, Article 2). The civil and criminal branches are two examples of such special branches. However, their jurisdiction and competence are still limited to hearing disputes in line with the previously stated cap, and any dispute beyond these parameters must be heard by the courts.

Within the judicial system, councils have played an important role in the reconciliation and settlement of disputes as well as being effective and productive in achieving the primary objectives of enhancing people's participation in dispute settlement, reconciliation and reducing referrals to the courts. A recent statement by the director of the councils affirms how they have functioned productively and improved their performance; in 2013, for instance, approximately 3.4 million cases were referred to the councils, of which approximately 35 per cent were settled through reconciliation and the remaining cases resulted in rulings. In addition, it is important to note that 50 per cent of all cases were referred to these councils.[31] The exponential growth of these branches could be another indication of their successful operation, as over 8,000 branches (4,700 in urban areas and 3,300 in rural areas) across the state have been established so far. Nonetheless, the councils' performance has been subject to criticism on various grounds, including criticism of 'Article 189 of the third program Act of economic, social and cultural development of the Islamic Republic of Iran', which established the councils in the first place. Examples of these denigrations revolve around: (1) how the councils' jurisdiction has been expanded to include disputes of a judicial nature; (2) the fact that the Law of Dispute Settlement Councils contradicts itself, because its Article 1 states that the objective of the councils is to settle disputes through reconciliation, whilst Article 26 authorizes them to deliver rulings if disputes through reconciliation have not been settled; (3) the fact that the councils' members are at times deemed unqualified to work as judges, which is also considered to be in violation of Shari'a; and (4) the fact that Article 189 is seen to be inconsistent with both the constitution and established legal principles.

The aforementioned criticisms should not be interpreted as if these councils completely and collectively operate with judges who lack legal qualifications. In essence, under the Law on Dispute Settlement Councils, each council comprises three main and two substitute members,[32] and in each jurisdiction one or several qualified judges (known as judges of the council) are appointed to assess, act upon and carry out their duties in accordance with the legal procedures that follow the Civil and Penal Code of Procedures, and additionally the councils operate under direct supervision of the judiciary.[33] Therefore, irrespective of these inconsistencies, the councils in general have taken progressive steps towards settling disputes, which, as this book asserts, is an important issue.

Sources of law

This section shall consider the sources of law and their hierarchically ordered relationship, before then proceeding to examine how these sources, their underlying principles and the codified law are interpreted and applied. Taking these sets of approaches and functions into consideration, it can be seen how Shari'a law is the dominant legal principle and source for laying down the constitutional and legal foundations of the State's legal system.

The Law

In general, 'law' is understood by ordinary Iranian people to include all governmental rules and regulations set out by authoritative institutions with legislative and/or executive powers (Katouzian 2013). However, using more specialist terminology, law is regarded as legislation created by legislative powers and institutions. Within the Iranian legal system, law encompasses the required process (as set out within the constitution) that falls under the authority of parliament through legislation or, via direct recourse to the popular vote, through referenda (the Iranian Constitution, Articles 58 and 59), which means that the term 'law' possesses a unique meaning. Hierarchically, laws are divided into three groups, namely: (1) constitutional laws; (2) ordinary laws; and (3) government regulations/decrees (Katouzian, 2013), all of which must be structured and passed in line with a set framework and parameters, as laid out within the constitution.

Reviewing the law-making process in more detail, once a proposed bill promulgated by parliament has been approved by the Guardian Council, without recourse to the Expediency Council, it is a constitutional requirement for that bill to go through three additional stages before it is recognized in law. First, after parliament has passed a bill, it must be forwarded to the president for his signature (Article 58); second, following the presidential signature, the proposed bill is then forwarded to the judicial authorities for implementation (Article 123); and third, the texts of the law must be published within 72 hours of the notification in an official gazette used for notification purposes (the Iranian Constitution, Articles 58 and 123; and the Civil Code, Articles 1–3). The president's signature on the bill indicates his full agreement, and thus the proposed bill is formally declared a law. An example of this process was seen earlier when discussing the New Islamic Penal Procedure Code. In cases where the president might refuse to sign the proposed bill, alternatively the chairman of parliament can order the publication in the official gazette within the required 72 hours' legal timeframe (the Civil Code, Articles 1–3), and hence the bill will become law without the president's signature.

As seen previously in this chapter, parliament, under the constitution, is empowered to pass laws as long as these laws are compatible with the *'ahkam* [or the judgements] of the official religion of the country or to the Constitution' (the Iranian Constitution, Article 72), whereby the official religion represents Islam and Shari'a (Article 12). As such, 'All civil, penal [...] and other laws and regulations must be based on Islamic criteria. This principle applies absolutely and generally to all articles of the constitution as well as to all other laws and regulations, and the *fuqaha'* of the Guardian Council are judges in this matter', as stipulated in Article 4 of the constitution. This strong emphasis on Islamic criteria highlights how Shari'a dominates the Iranian legal system. Shari'a, with its religious foundations and disciplines, is based upon primary and secondary sources, whereby the primary sources encompass the Qur'an and *sunna*, and the secondary sources contain consensus, or *ijma*, and reason, or *aql* (Hashemi 2013).[34]

Urf

In Chapter Nine, we explained that *urf* (or *orfi*) courts have a long history in Iran, going back to the beginning of the sixteenth century. We also mentioned that the limits of *urf* were (re)defined in terms of *maslahat-e nezam* (the expediency of the regime) after the Islamic Revolution of 1979 (see Mohammadi 2008: 127). In this section, we provide a view of *urf* that explains how it is employed within the legal system itself. We reiterate that *urf* consists of customary rules embedded in cultural practices, which provide continuity in exchanges between ordinary people while exerting a normative force on their relationships. In other words, *urf* concerns customary practices that have a binding effect on the way in which people normally organize their everyday lives. This binding element imposes a legal obligation upon those who commonly adhere to these rules, which can be invoked as part of the court's judgement (Katouzian 2011, 2013). These customary rules are often unwritten or unspoken, and they are formed habitually, emanating from general consciousness and public norms but without the intervention or inclusion of any legislative authority or fulfilling any formalities (Katouzian 2011). In other words, the difference between laws and customary rules lies in their formulation processes – whereby laws are enacted by legislators following a formal procedure, whereas customary rules are the product of the evolution of a society and are driven by practices intended to regulate, normalize and shape the behaviours, beliefs and attitudes of the general public. Therefore, the question is how do laws and *urf* interact with one another within the Iranian legal system?

The interplay between laws and *urf* takes place differently within different areas of the Iranian legal system, signifying that the laws at times refer directly to *urf*. For example, under civil law, 'the wording of a contract shall be read according to the meaning understood by customary law', while 'if certain points that are customarily understood in a contract by customary law or practice are not specified [...] they are nevertheless to be considered as mentioned in the contract'.[35] Specifically, civil law defines laws and customary rules within a contractual context, thereby highlighting how a 'contract not only binds the parties to execute what it explicitly mentions, but both parties are also bound by all consequences which follow from the contract in accordance with customary law and practice, or by virtue of a law'.[36]

Therefore, *urf* plays a significant role in various aspects of Iranian custom and culture whilst at the same time providing a secondary source of law. This is not to say that enacted laws and *urf* have the same legal weight in the Iranian legal system. *Urf* plays a significant role in relation to family law, wherein legally a man is able to marry more than one wife (four permanent wives and as many temporary ones as he wishes). Despite this legal right, however, not many men practice polygamy in the country, since *urf* directs otherwise. According to Daniel and Mahdi (2006: 167), polygamy is not 'widely practiced in Iran, and the Iranian society does not generally approve of it'. Looking at this issue from another angle, legitimacy is a dominant power and at times takes priority over legality. *Urf* plays a role in dispensing punishments, whereby a judge can enjoy a certain degree of discretion. One such example can be seen in how *ta'zir*, or corporal punishment, is meted out for crimes against the person and property. In these cases, judges may exercise discretion and take mitigating factors into consideration when deciding on the type of punishment. This level of flexibility in *ta'zir* is in contrast to *hadd* (plural *hudud*) punishments, which refer to crimes against God and which have fixed retributions provided in the Qur'an.

As previously mentioned in this chapter, Article 167 of the constitution does not refer specifically to *urf* in its guidance to judges in their rulings; alternatively, it directs judges to apply 'authoritative Islamic sources and authentic fatwa' when facing 'the silence of or deficiency of law in the matter'. This constitutional requirement is reflective of the objective of the legislative authority to find a legal solution within Shari'a and its sources, instead of *urf*, when applying laws.

Judicial Precedent and Legal Scholarly Thoughts/Writings

The Iranian Constitution requires the country's supreme court to ensure the uniformity of judicial procedure (Article 161). Such uniformity provides precedence as a source of reference and a legal standard for all similar, future cases by all courts (the New Islamic Penal Procedure Code, Articles 471–3).

Judicial decisions, and the writings and thoughts of legal scholars, play a vital role and have a significant influence on the legal system in Iran. This is also important in the further development and scrutiny of sources of law and the constitution, in order to ensure that the legal system provides a set of coherent and consistent approaches in legal matters. The two constitutive elements of the sources of law can be considered one of the more pertinent values of the legal system. Judicial precedents and legal scholarly thoughts and writings present practical application towards the appropriate and uniform interpretation of laws. That is to say, judicial decisions provide the best application of the rules for legal systems by assessing legal rules and setting out the valid application. Precedents set in previous rulings can help judges to apply and to interpret law consistently and uniformly, which could be a significant step in maintaining and preserving justice. Even though legal systems (besides common-law systems) provide set parameters in order to follow rules and principles, there is a level of flexibility within the interpretation thereof, and consequently judges' previous rulings can provide alignments in legal interpretation.

Dr Naser Katouzian emphasized the importance of judicial decisions and legal thought in legal systems similar to that of Iran, by classifying this importance into three groups. First, when a law is passed, long before a dispute is heard in a court, legal scholars engage in analysing and interpreting the law and will share the advantages and disadvantages of the potential new law as well as examine the intended objective of the legislator. Dr Katouzian maintained that these scholarly writings neither anticipate all possible shortcomings and difficulties nor provide all necessary solutions relating to the implementation and enforcement of laws; however, they do provide the basis for research and reflection by judges. Second, legal scholarly thought can indirectly or directly influence judges in the validity of their rulings. A judgement that is accepted and supported within the legal scholarly community is likely to gain stature and higher credibility, which will then make it more likely to be used as an established precedent for future cases. Third, there is a one-to-one relationship between any ruling and any special circum-stances leading to the related dispute. Even though the ruling is unique to the conditions of the case, the scholarly community can collectively analyse all such cases and consider a common and uniform solution, applicable in similar cases, thus paving the way for the formulation of precedents as well as playing a role in legal development and the decision-making process (Katouzian 2011, 2013).

Concluding Reflections on the Autonomy of the Iranian Courts

The Iranian legal system is unique in so far as it combines political ideas based on Shi'i doctrine, according to which Imams are the true and rightful successors of the Prophet, with modern legal institutions, which are then ultimately supervised by Islamic jurists who, in turn, constitute the country's political elite. Its court system consists not only of public courts, but also of special security tribunals such as Islamic revolutionary courts and special courts for the clergy. While routine cases concerning crimes against the person and property, as well as family and private law disputes (pertaining to property, contract, compensation, etc.) are referred to the public courts, cases involving national security, smuggling and blasphemy are channelled to the special tribunals. As we mentioned in Chapter Nine, Islamic revolutionary courts have been criticized internationally for operating in contravention of international human rights law (Moschtaghi 2010: 6). Similarly, the Special Court for the Clergy, which amongst other things prosecutes dissident clergy, operates outside the framework of the legal system and is not accountable to any legal authority besides the Leader (see Künkler 2009: 20).

The creation of two parallel court systems – one 'public' and the other 'special' – has a number of implications for the way in which justice is delivered in Iran. It limits the jurisdiction of public courts in relation to non-political cases, thus curtailing the authority of the ordinary courts and the judiciary over political matters, and, at the same time, by moving cases involving political dissidents out the ordinary courts it subjects them to other procedures and substantive rules. In theory, the revolutionary courts are expected to follow the codes of criminal procedure, but in practice they violate these without having to account to any higher legal authority for their breach of due process.[37] Thus, we are confronted with autonomous political tribunals, which, although operating in the name of the law, are not subjected to the scrutiny of the judicial order. The extent to which public courts act autonomously and in accordance with the principle of legality is a complicated matter, which was demonstrated by the importance of the sources of law and the implications of Article 167 of the constitution.

Our interviews with the lawyers revealed the tension between the independent section of the legal profession – attorneys who are members of the Iranian Bar Association – on the one hand, and the judiciary and the regime, on the other. It was suggested by several lawyers that they were being misrepresented and their professional standing was being systematically questioned by the state-run media. One of the lawyers stated that attorneys were penalized for defending the right of their clients to a fair trial (see interview 2:9:21, page 94), whilst others said that the judiciary would humiliate them in court and place obstacles in their way, in order to stop them representing their clients.

> 2:5:28: 'All government agencies disrespect lawyers. In my legal work, I am up against a daily set of problems which have nothing to do with the law; yet, they prevent me from doing my job as a lawyer within the court system.'

Thus, not only is the court system fragmented by the separation of 'public' from 'special' courts, but the legal profession is also divided between a politicized judiciary and independent lawyers. This brings us back to the question that we posed at the outset: what holds the fragmented legal institutions of the Islamic Republic, with its conflicting authorities and legal powers, together as one unified system?

In theory, Shari'a, as defined, interpreted and enforced by the Guardian Council and the Expediency Council, determines the legislative process and sets the contours within which laws are formed and the Iranian legal system operates. However, the Guardian Council and the Expediency Council, as well as parliament and the executive and the judiciary, are directly or indirectly under the overarching authoritative powers of the Leader. Similarly, the special courts, which operate in the name of law, are also ultimately under the control of the Leader. As Rezaei (2002) points out, according to Article 4 of the constitution, part of which is quoted at the beginning of this chapter, 'it is the Islamic rulings as determined by Islamic jurists [who, due to Article 110, are appointed by the Leader] that in fact constitute the supreme law in Iran'. The central role that the Leader plays in this regard impacts, directly and indirectly, on the autonomy of the judicial order, for, in his person, religious, legal and political authority is conflated. Constitutionally speaking, the Leader may be regarded as the most foundational *political* source of law, or *Grundnorm*, to borrow from Kelsen (1967), while an ideologized interpretation of Shari'a can be seen as the primary framework of the legal system. Thus, the dominant role of the Leader, combined with the regime's interpretation of Shari'a, holds this fragmented body together.

This point becomes significant against the backdrop of our empirical study, where the overwhelming majority of those we interviewed regarded parliament as the primary source of law. Admittedly, we could argue that ordinary people have not read the constitution and are unfamiliar with the way in which laws are enacted and the courts operate, which is why they erroneously believe that parliament is the primary source of law and legal authority in their country. It could even be argued that their belief in parliament is a form of 'false consciousness', and is reflective of the fact that they vote to elect members of parliament. However, even those lawyers that we interviewed named parliament as the primary source of law, which suggests that the Islamic ideology underpinning the Iranian Constitution does not enjoy widespread legitimacy amongst ordinary Iranians. Therefore, 'Does the Iranian Constitution have a socio-historical basis in Iranian legal culture?' remains a question in need of further empirical research. Nevertheless, our study shows that after 35 years of living under the Islamic Constitution, the overwhelming majority of Iranians that we interviewed regarded parliament, and not the Leader or Shari'a, as their primary source of law.

APPENDIX

Interviews with Male Taxi Drivers in Tehran

Date:
Number of the interview:
Age of the interviewee:

The Interview Questions:

Part One: Attitudes to Driving and to the Automobile

1) Could you tell us about yourself? When did you start driving?
2) Besides being a necessity in your line of work, could you tell us what driving a car means to you?
3) What do you regard as a serious car accident?
   - *Have you been involved in any accidents?*
4) What is your general view of the traffic situation in Tehran?
   - *How does the traffic situation in the city affect your work as a taxi driver?*
5) Why do you think Iran has improved in most respects over the last decades (compared to 30 years ago people are generally healthier, wealthier and better educated), but the reckless and dangerous driving of Iranians has not changed?

Part Two: Attitudes to Traffic Rules and Conventions

6) The traffic rules were changed last year and more severe penalties were introduced in order to improve the traffic

behaviour. In your opinion, what impacts have the new traffic rules had on Iranians driving habits? *(if the reply is none – ask why?)*

7) Why do many drivers disregard the traffic rules?

8) In your opinion, who are the worst and the best drivers?

9) How do you see pedestrians, when you are behind the wheel and driving? Would you stop so that someone can cross the road?

   - *What rights and duties do pedestrians have in the traffic?*

10) Are there any informal or unspoken rules of driving which affect drivers' and pedestrians' actions and behaviour?

11) What is your view of the way traffic rules are enforced?

Part Three: Causes of Accidents

12) What do you think is the main cause of traffic accidents (1) inside the city and in ordinary streets, (2) in the motorways and bypasses and (3) in roads between the cities?

Part Four: Attitudes to Car and Road Safety

13) What are your views on car and road safety?

   - *Do you wear a seat belt when driving? Do your passengers wear seatbelts?*

Part Five: Attitudes to Law

14) What comes to your mind when you hear the word law (*ghanon*)?

15) Who or what do you regard as the primary source of *ghanon*?

16) Who do you consider as the main source of legal authority?

17) To whom would you turn for help if you had a dispute say with your neighbour (a disputes about a shared wall) or in regard to a business transaction (for example someone owes you money but refuses to pay back)? And what would be your expectation?

   - *At what stage would you turn to the legal system?*

18) What experience have you had with the law and the legal system?

   - *Have you used the courts?*

    - Have you ever appeared before a court?

    - Have you used the services of a lawyer?

19) Do you think the majority of people follow and obey the law?

20) How effectively do think these laws are enforced?

21) In your opinion, how is justice (*edalat*) connected with law (*ghanon*)?

    - If they are not connected where and how would you find justice?

22) To end our discussion, it would be useful if you could tell us how in your opinion one can improve the driving behaviour and the traffic situation?

NOTES

Chapter 1 Introduction: What have Driving Habits Got to do with Law, Gender and Class Conflicts?

1. Interview number 3:2:1.
2. The World Health Organization's 2013 document 'Global Status Report on Road Safety' ranks Iran in third place, after Thailand and Venezuela, in respect of the number of deaths caused by road accidents. Also, see *BBC News*, 10 June 2012, wherein it is claimed that Iran has the highest rate of road fatalities in the world.
3. This study argues that there are many forms of modernity, and that the Iranian brand of modernity must be conceptualized in its own socio-historical terms and not as a distorted reflection or an extension of the European Enlightenment (for a discussion on Iranian modernity, see Jahanbegloo 2004 and Kamrava 2008). We shall argue that Iranian traditionalists are in favour of promoting the sciences, modern technology and a market economy, albeit within the ethical framework of Islam. Iranian modernists, on the other hand, are not necessarily anti-Islamists, although they might insist on the separation of state and religion and advocate a largely liberal interpretation of the central doctrines of Shari'a.
4. Part of the Iranian middle classes never supported the revolution and did not aspire to establish an Islamic state. The section of the middle classes that actively participated in the revolution came from religious, traditionalist and secular liberal groups, many of whom did not favour the establishment of a theocracy in Iran. However, the Iranian middle classes have grown in size and today include a large number of people with more diverse traditional and religious backgrounds.
5. Before and after the 1979 revolution, the Islamists employed the dual idea of the 'oppressors' (*mostakberin*) and the 'oppressed' (*mostazafin*) to mobilize the disadvantaged masses and the traditionalists to wage war on the secular sections

of society, including parts of the middle classes as well as the opponents of the regime (Abrahamian 1993: 47). Domestically, this class antagonism also served as a means of supressing women's rights and introducing draconian policies aimed at controlling sexuality, while internationally it helped to create an ideological platform to launch Iran's foreign policy. For a more detailed discussion, see Chapter Nine.

6. The rate of literacy among women rose from 28 per cent in 1976 to 80 per cent in 1996 (Olivier 2004: 14).

7. See Kamrava (2008: 22) and Gheytanchi (2006: 286).

8. Ghajarieh et al. state that 'the only major cause of death other than chronic diseases is road traffic accidents (RTAs), which is mainly in younger individuals' (Ghajarieh 2010: 342). RTAs are also one of the main causes of mortality among children aged 5–14 and the age group 20–29 (Abbasi-Shavazi 2004: 11).

9. According to the *Daily Mail*, 22 April 2008, 'Dangerous drivers in Iran face being flogged under a tough new law'.

10. The primary cause of mortality in 2007 was coronary heart disease, which claimed 25 per cent of all those who died in Iran that year. It was followed by RTAs, which claimed 12.5 per cent during the same period. See Amani and Kazemnejad (2010) and Abbasi-Shavazi (2004).

11. For examples of studies conducted by medical doctors, see Zamani-Alavijeh et al. (2010), Vafaee-Najar et al. (2010), Vafaee et al. (2009), Ardalan et al. (2009), Naghavi et al. (2009), Karkhaneh et al. (2008), Karbakhsh and Zargar (2006), Muntazeri (2004), Ayati (2004) and Roudsari (2004). It should be mentioned in passing that although car ownership has increased rapidly in Iran over recent decades, this increase in itself cannot account for the very high level of RTAs, as a similar increase in the number of automobiles in European countries has been accompanied by a decrease in the rate of road traffic fatalities (Mohammadi 2013: 184–5).

12. There are other, similar tendencies in Iran to use the secular language of medicine to transform sociopolitical issues. For example, homosexuality is considered a cardinal sin and prohibited in law, and yet the authorities allow transsexuals to be 'treated' medically, i.e. to undergo sex-change operations. Through the secular methodology of medicine, transsexuality is defined as a 'gender identity disorder' (Javaheri 2010: 369), allegedly brought under control by restricting it to the individual's body and treating it through medical intervention.

13. See, for example, Zamani-Alavijeh et al. (2010).

14. To give an example, Naghavi et al. conclude their study by arguing that in order to bring RTAs under control the country needs to 'keep reinforcing traffic safety regulations, build more public health infrastructure, and increase people's access to health services and control the growth of motorized vehicles' (Naghavi et al. 2009: 293). Most importantly, Iran should build fewer and safer cars and motorcycles.

15. For studies of the relationship between the automobile and sociocultural dimensions of behaviour, see Urry et al. (2005), Urry (2007), Miller (2001), Evans (1991), Neal (1985), Lewis (1980) and Dettelbach (1976).

16. For detailed discussions of the concept of legal culture, see also Nelken (2007) and Banakar (2008).

17. For various approaches to defining and analysing the notion of culture, see Geertz (1973), Rosen (2006), Cotterrell (2006), Alexander (2003) and Swidler (1986).

18. Sociolegal scholars often distinguish between the written law, or 'law in books', and the practice of the law, or 'law in action' (see Pound 1910). The former refers to legislation and other rules of law and ordinances, while the latter refers to how the rules of law are interpreted and enforced by various authorities and institutions, and then used by various individuals and groups for public good or out of self-interest. This book treats all the manifestations of the law as representations of how society has been organized and how its constitutive institutions operate (Durkheim 1933).

19. Both ancient and modern Iranian states (including the current Islamic Republic) have been internally fragmented (see Kamrava 2008; Axworthy 2007) and consisted of rival factions representing competing centres of political power and normativity – a fact that has added to the overall arbitrary character of the way successive Iranian regimes have exercised power, but that has also provided social space for dissent. The 'polycentric' make-up of the Iranian Government will be discussed in Chapter Eight.

20. The concept of 'state' refers often to the nation state, which is a modern idea and cannot be used meaningfully to discuss the forms of government that existed during the Achaemenid Empire (550–330 BC) or the Sasanian Empire (AD 224–651) in Iran. Thus, references to the 'state' herein refer to the rulers of Iran and their form of government, which, as a rule, was based on the exercising of arbitrary power, or *estebdād*.

21. These four chapters are organized and presented according to the order in which the interviews were carried out. This order has a methodological significance in so far as we learnt about the limits of our methodology and the leading questions we were using as we carried out the interviews. Early on, we learnt, for example, that at least one of the questions that had been formulated to examine informal rules of driving did not work, and caused confusion in the mind of the interviewee. This question was subsequently removed from the list. As the interviews progressed, we noted that some questions regarding the causes of RTAs and car safety were quickly exhausted (almost all interviewees answered in a similar fashion) and did not generate any new insights. Subsequently, we did not emphasize these questions in the remaining interviews, and instead devoted more time to exploring the questions that concerned culture and law. To give another example, as our interviewees repeatedly referred to the 'culture of driving' and *farhang-sazi* (culture building), we asked them to define these and sought to reflect more on them. Thus, the sequence of chapters in Part Two reflects the way in which this study has developed.

Chapter 2   Conducting Research in Iran

1. According to Amirpur (2011: 341), 'the High Council of Cultural Revolution was responsible, among other things, for purging universities of counter-revolutionaries'. Certain members of the council, it is claimed, 'intended to close down universities for the next 20 years' (Amirpur 2011).
2. Shiraz was Iran's sixth largest city, with a population of 1,500,000, in 2014.
3. For example, Manavipour (2012) uses a population of 380 schoolchildren in Tehran as a basis for a quantitative study of the structure of moral development in Iranian culture. No consideration is given in his study to the fact that the culture of pupils in the capital might not be representative of all schoolchildren in Iran. This understanding of Iranian culture as a homogeneous entity is typical of many studies conducted by mainly Farsi-speaking Iranian researchers. These studies are most often conducted by using quantitative methods.
4. According to Holliday (2011: 24), *Iraniyat*, or the idea of being Iranian, is a pre-Islamic notion related to *melliyat-i Irani* (Iranian nationhood). At times, it has been employed as a nationalistic concept that, by implication, defies *Islamiyat* (being Islamic or Muslim) and the Islamic notion of *Ummeh*. While the *Iraniyat* refers to Iranians only and to Iran as a geopolitical construct, the *Ummeh* refers to all Muslims across geographical boundaries. However, *Iraniyat* and *Islamiyat* mean different things to different groups – whereas some political groups have employed them as opposing ideas in political discourse, others have tried to integrate them within Iranian culture.
5. For in-depth discussions of Shi'ism, see Dabashi (2011) and Halm (2007).

Chapter 3   *Estebdād*: Pilot Study in Shiraz and Tehran

1. Cambyses II, son of Sirus the Great, who ruled Persia between 530 and 522 BC.
2. In a recent study, Manoukian (2012: 4) describes Shiraz as a 'city of knowledge', i.e. a city renowned historically as a centre of learning, and goes on to 'consider the making of Shiraz as the emblem for the culture of Iran'.
3. References to the poor driving of Shirazis appear in the interviews we conducted in Tehran. See, for example, interview 2:11:6 in Chapter Five.
4. The questions used in the second part of the interviews draw on a comparative study of legal cultures conducted by Kurkchiyan (2011).
5. 'Positive laws' are transient rules of law promulgated, passed or *posited* by people, in contrast to 'natural laws', which originate from divine sources such as the Qur'an and are thus treated as eternal. 'Positive law', as it is used here, refers in the first place to legislation made by Parliament.
6. This policy was reversed in August 2014, when the use of contraception and the advertising of birth-control measures were banned in Iran. According to the *Washington Post* (12 August 2014), Iran's Supreme Leader publicly encouraged young Iranians to have more babies as a method of counteracting 'undesirable aspects of [the] Western lifestyle'. It is suggested that this radical change of

policy reflected the concerns of conservative clerics about the rising number of women in the universities and workplaces. By encouraging them to have more children, they hoped to restore women's traditional roles as mothers and confine them to the private sphere.

7. Krämer (2007: 25) points out that in Shari'a, justice could refer to a wide range of ideas, 'from straightness and evenness, to fairness, equity and impartiality [...]. Justice could also be inextricably linked to God's will, but it is not necessarily or exclusively so'. In other words, the fact that the interviewees did not refer to the 'will of God' or Islamic values when asked to define justice, does not mean that they necessarily have a secular conception of it.

8. Lawrence Friedman distinguishes between internal and external legal cultures – the former referring to the legally oriented values, attitudes and practices of the judiciary and other functionaries of the law, and the latter to how the citizenry views and experiences the law and the pressures that various social groups exert on the legal system in order to promote their interests (see Friedman 1994).

9. As we explained in the Introduction, reference to the 'state' here is not to the modern nation state but to forms of government that have existed in Iran over the centuries. The word 'ruler' might therefore be more appropriate in one sense, although it does not capture the fact that a system of government was in place in the Achaemenid Empire (550–330 BC) and the Sasanian Empire (AD 224–651) in Iran.

10. Others also have noted that regarding Iran as a totalitarian state is misleading. Contemporary Iran 'is not a totalitarian state like those of the Soviet bloc during the Cold War', writes Axworthy (2007: 291); instead, it 'is a complex polity, with different power centres and shades of opinion among those in power'.

Chapter 4   *Farhang-Sazi*: Interviews with Male Taxi Drivers

1. According to the UK *Telegraph* (01 July 2012), 'Unemployment in Iran's industrial heartland has soared to an unofficially estimated 35% because factories unable to import vital goods and equipment due to sanctions are forced in turn to sack their workers'.

2. The list of interview questions is presented in the Appendix. All the interviewees were men between the ages of 21 and 65. When presenting the interviews, we shall not refer to the age of the interviewee as the scope of our data is too small to establish any correlation between age and interviewees' responses. Only one of them suggested that he had a university education, though many of them had work experience from other walks of life and had been drawn to taxi driving in order to make a living.

3. Most Iranian cities and towns are divided up into similar, separate zones. We find an identical spatial socio-economic division between the south and the north of Shiraz.

4. We were, however, told that youths from the south drove 'uptown' to have fun, speed driving and meeting girls (see Khosravi 2008). Moreover, the fact that north Tehran is a space associated with secular lifestyles, does not mean that people in the south do not, for example, drink. Finally, the general attitude in Tehran is that driving behaviour is much worse in the south than in the north of the city.

5. In a study conducted by a group of medical doctors (see Peymani et al. 2012: 279), the causes of high fatal-accident rates amongst pedestrians are described in the following terms: 'Evaluation of the injury site and the cause of death found that they were significantly associated with age [and the] interval between injury and death. The type of roads played an important role in mortality'. There are, thus, no references to the culture of driving or the drivers' attitude to the traffic rules – or to pedestrians.

6. *Shakhsiyat* can be translated as 'character' and 'personality', but also 'self-respect' or 'dignity', and a person with *shakhsiyat* is polite and well mannered (he or she is said to be *ba-shakhsiyat*). By contrast, a person whose behaviour is offensive and who lacks etiquette is *bi-shakhsiyat*, or without respect. See Koutlaki (2002: 1742).

7. *Taarof* has many manifestations and can involve various forms of offers and compliments. One of its manifestations, which one encounters in everyday life, 'involves both parties insisting they are not worthy of the other', as 'when people refuse to walk through a door first, cab drivers refuse to accept payment as passengers beg them to...' (Bahrampour 2007: 1).

Chapter 5 Trust: Interviews with Lawyers

1. The Holy Qur'an contains the words of God as they were communicated through the Prophet, and therefore they cannot be treated as a source of positive (man-made) law.

2. *Zerang* is an adjective referring to a smart or sly person, while *zerangi* is an adverb referring to acting craftily.

3. *Mehrieh* is a single payment specified in the marriage contract, payable by the husband to the wife on her request – albeit a request that is normally made in the event of divorce. *Mehrieh* may be regarded as a form of marriage insurance for women in a legal system that grants men special privileges in marriage (such as the right to demand divorce or the right to polygyny while denying women equal rights. As Parvin Paidar points out, although all women are entitled to *mehrieh*, most of them do not benefit from it for a host of reasons (Paidar 1995: 299).

4. The Council of Guardians consists of 12 jurists, six of whom are appointed by the Supreme Leader. The head of the judiciary recommends the remaining six, who are officially appointed by Parliament. The Council of Guardians is authorized to interpret the Constitution and determines if the laws passed by Parliament are in line with Shari'a (Islamic law). If a law passed by Parliament is deemed incompatible with the Constitution or Shari'a, it is referred back to Parliament for revision.

5. The Expediency Council mediates between Parliament and the Council of Guardians. Serving as an advisory body to the Supreme Leader, it is one of the most powerful governing bodies in the country. It also examines presidential and parliamentary candidates to determine their fitness to run for a seat. This competency is conferred upon the Expediency Council by Articles 99 and 118 of the Constitution.

6. *Diyah* (*dyya* and *dyyat* in Arabic) is a legal doctrine in Shari'a with roots in the pre-Islamic tribal customs of the clans in Arabia, according to which the culprit must pay monetary compensation in lieu of criminal damages. According to Article 17, Chapter Four in the Iranian Criminal Code of 2014, *diyah*, 'whether fixed or unfixed, is a monetary amount under Holy Shari'a which is determined by law and shall be paid for unintentional bodily crimes against life, limbs and abilities or for intentional crimes when for whatever reason *qisas* [retaliation in kind" or revenge} is not applicable' (Iran Human Rights Documentation Centre 2014). Thus, *diyah* may be paid for both intentional and unintentional crimes, including murder. In Iran, the payment does not completely absolve the offender in cases of intentional crime, such as murder, although it does have a mitigating effect on the sentence, for, in cases of serious intentional crime, the State remains obliged to punish the offender. Moreover, the minimum rate of *diyah* prescribed for the wrongful killing of a woman is half the amount set for a man.

Chapter 6   Social Class: Interviews with other Professionals

1. Admittedly, the disadvantaged groups live in the south – but not all of them are religious.

Chapter 7   Gender and Domination: Interviews with Female Taxi Drivers

1. The above exchanges are borrowed from an internet blog in Farsi, which describes a foreign journalist's interview with a group of female cabbies in Tehran. For a more complete account of the interview, see Alavi (2005: 206).

2. An excellent Australian documentary entitled *Iran: Women Taxi Company* is available on YouTube at http://www.sbs.com.au/news/dateline/story/iran-wom ens-taxi-company.

3. The complete text of this quote is provided in Chapter Ten under interview 4:4:79.

4. *Siygheh* is temporary marriage, which allows men and women to have short- or long-term relationships. According to Haeri (1989: x), Iranians have had an ambivalent attitude to *siygheh*. We are often told that 'before the revolution of 1979, the secular Iranian middle classes dismissed temporary marriage as a form of prostitution' (Haeri, 1989). On the other hand, the section of the clergy, who

had become wary of the growing autonomy of women, presented *siygheh* as 'God's mercy on humanity, necessary for an individual's health as well as for maintaining social order' (Haeri 1989). However, Haeri goes on to explain, these viewpoints simplify 'a complex and dynamic social institution', adding that 'The ambiguities inherent in this form of marriage have sustained it through its long history and allowed it to be intimately interconnected with other aspects of social life in Iran. Sometimes the institution has been dismissed by the state as archaic, a remnant of backwardness [...]. At other times it has been advanced by the religious establishment as one of the "brilliant laws of Islam" [...]. Sometimes it is used by women as a means of asserting autonomy and exerting some degree of control over their lives; at other times they are abused by the same set of laws. Often men abuse the law, but other times they are manipulated by women into submission and obedience of their wants and desires. Sometimes, temporary marriage is used to reinforce the structure of sex segregation, at other times as a means of subverting it' (Haeri 1989).

5. She uses the word *havoo*, which refers to a polygamist man's second wife: 'It is as if we are their *havoos*'.

6. It has been argued that the Iranian Government agreed to the introduction of a women-only taxi agency in November 2006 'in response to increasing instances of rape and sexual assault in Tehran. Police estimated that 30% of sexual offenses were committed by male taxi drivers, and women were advised not to travel alone in cabs'. See Jezebel (10 August 2008).

7. As these lines are written, Maryam Mirzakhani, who was born and raised in Iran, became the first woman to be awarded the most prestigious mathematics award. See *Guardian* (13 August 2014).

Chapter 8   Culture: Reflections on Individualism and Community

1. This section borrows text from Chapter Eight on comparative law in Banakar (2014: 145).

2. The analysis and discussions presented here will be limited by the scope and the concerns of our interviews, and will not endeavour to provide a comprehensive overview of Iranian culture in its totality as such a task falls outside the remit of this chapter. See Chapter Two for a discussion of the methodological limitations of this study.

3. Supreme Leader's Speech on 14 October 2012 to the Youth of North Khorasan. At: http://english.khamenei.ir.

4. For discussions on the role of *mahalleh* in contemporary Iranian cities, see Amirshekari et al. (2013); Sharifi and Murayama (2013); and Ehlers and Floor (1993).

5. According to Amjad (1984: 36), 'following Mohammad's death in AD 632 Muslims were divided in two groups. The majority argued that Mohammad's successor should be selected by the Islamic community (*Ummah*). This group is

called *Sunni*, or follower of the tradition (*Sonnat*) of the Prophet. A minority, called *Shi'a*, argued that Mohammad had already chosen his cousin and son-in-law, Ali, to take the leadership of the *Ummah* following his death. Shi'as also believed that Imamate (i.e. political and religious leadership) is the right of the male descendants of Ali. Imamate, however, ends with the twelfth Imam (Mahdy) who lives in occultation (*Ghaybat*). According to *Shi'a* doctrine, the only legitimate ruler after Mohammad was Ali, who was the caliph for a short period of time. After Ali's assassination in AD 661 his first son, Hassan, replaced him as the new caliph. The governor of Sham (Syria), Moavia, rebelled against Hassan and defeated him in a series of battles. After these victories, Moavia founded the Omayyid dynasty. Ali's descendants were never able to regain [. . .] state power.

Martyrdom (*Shahadat*) is a very important aspect of Shi'ism. None of the Imams died of a natural cause. Ali was assassinated in a mosque by political opponents. Imam Hossein (the Third Imam and Mohammad's grandson) was killed in a battle against the army of the Omayyid Caliph Yazid in Karbala (Iraq). The rest of the Imams were poisoned by their respective caliphs. The martyrdom of Imam Hossein, however, provides the most emotional and heart-rendering aspect of Shi'ism. Imam Hossein and 72 of his followers rebelled against the injustice and tyranny (*Zolm*) of the Omayyid Caliph Yazid, but fell in the battle in AD 683 Hossein's martyrdom is commemorated throughout the year especially during the holy month of Moharram'.

6. Ashura is a holy day, on which the martyrdom of Imam Hossein is celebrated by the Shi'as. A minority of Shi'i Muslims commemorate the day with a self-flagellation ritual.

7. The *Basij* was created in 1980 to police the populace and punish deviations from the countless moral laws of the Islamic Republic.

8. *Mujtahid* means an Islamic scholar who has achieved the stage of *ijtihâd*, i.e. he can 'strive for a correct legal conclusion through individual reasoning when all other sources of law are silent on the issue' (Burns 2014: 31).

9. For a historical overview of sexual politics in Iran, see Afary (2011).

10. 'Living law' is contrasted with 'positive law', which refers to the compulsive norms of the State that require official enforcement. Conversely, 'living law' consists of the rules of conduct that people in fact obey spontaneously as they interact with each other to form social associations. See Ehrlich (1936) and Banakar (2008).

11. The Iranian semi-official news agency reported in October 2014 that attackers riding on motorbikes had thrown acid in the faces of at least eight women who were driving with their windows down. These incidents sparked protests by horrified Iranians in Isfahan and Tehran. The protesters believed that the female victims had been targeted because of the way they dressed. However, the Iranian authorities denied this accusation. According to the *Guardian* (28 October 2014), 'Iranian officials are particularly angry with any suggestion that attackers were driven by religious extremism, or that victims were targeted because they

wore clothing that could be deemed inappropriate in the eyes of hardliners. But despite the state's condemnation of the Isfahan incidents, many in Iran believe that a long-standing strict policy on women's clothing has encouraged such attacks'. The Iranian authorities reacted by criticizing the coverage of the attacks and the subsequent protests, and by arresting several reporters.

12. In Farsi, *amoozesh* means 'education', but it can also mean 'learning', 'training' and 'instruction'.

13. Although *taarof* can have non-verbal dimensions, it is fundamentally a linguistic game.

14. As one of the interviewees pointed out, 'The car changes the *shakhsiyat* of a person who drives it, in the sense that they disrespect the rights of others, including pedestrians and drivers, while driving, but their behaviour changes as soon as they get out of the car'.

15. See Chapter Seven, interviewee 4:7:16, page 133: 'I always respect pedestrians. I put myself in their shoes; they might be my mother or sister'.

Chapter 9   Iranian Legal Culture: Law, Gender and Class Divisions

1. Libson's account (1997) is based on Hanafi tradition, which is one of the four Sunni schools of jurisprudence (or *fiqh*), which grants custom a more prominent place in its jurisprudence than other traditions.

2. In October 2003, Ayatollah Ali Khamenei issued a *fatwa* forbidding the production, stockpiling and use of nuclear weapons. See Eisenstadt and Khalaji (2011: iv).

3. 'A prominent hard-line Iranian cleric has denounced high-speed mobile Internet and 3G services as "immoral and unlawful"'. See *Washington Post* (30 August 2014).

4. Ayatollah Khomaini had elaborated on the permissibility of sex change in his 'Arabic master a treatise' in 1964 (Najmabadi 2014: 6). 'Twenty years later', writes Najmabadi (2014), 'in 1984, this time in Persian as the supreme political authority of the state, he reissued this earlier opinion in response to a transwoman's plea'.

5. System is born out of, and for its existence continues to be dependent on, *lifeworld*. It coordinates and organizes large and complex action systems, such as the market and the political system, so that they run smoothly and efficiently. Thus, it has a macro existence of its own that, in accordance with its instrumental/strategic form of rationality, maximizes efficiency and system stability (thus integrating complex forms of macro social action) through the media of power and money. According to Habermas (1984), both *lifeworld* and system are needed for a satisfactory operation and the coordination of a modern society, yet there is fundamental tension defining their relationship, caused by their essentially opposing forms of operational rationality. *Lifeworld* operates in accordance with communicative rationality, which is geared to mutual

understanding and brings about *social integration*. In contrast, system operates on the basis of strategic rationality, which is designed to satisfy the impersonal demands of the capitalist economy and produces *system integration*. Problems arise when steering media of the economy and administrative systems, due to dysfunctions and crises of various types, expand their instrumental, rational steering capacity at the expense of the communicative rationality of the *lifeworld*.

6. The regime's legitimacy crisis led to the 2003 student riots and the widespread 2009 protests, both of which were suppressed using force against civilians. In 2012, under the pressure of embargoes, the economy of the country almost collapsed. The 2012 crisis of legitimacy and the collapse of the system were avoided through new elections in 2013, which brought the moderate government of Hassan Rouhani to power.

7. Our interviews demonstrate that female taxi drivers are subjected to prejudicial treatment and are viewed negatively in Iranian society. In other countries, such as the USA, where women have started working as cab drivers, they regularly encounter prejudiced attitudes and even insults from their male passengers (see Her website 2012) In New York City, for example, only 117 out of 46,000 taxi cabs are driven by women, which shows the male-dominated nature of the taxi industry (see International Women's Day website 2014).

8. Let us not forget that the government could not have implemented the decision to grant women taxi licences had the conditions not been created by women who had already normalized their presence in the public sphere and established their position in the labour market. In *Revolutionary Iran*, Axworthy (2013: XX) maintains that during the Iran–Iraq war, women could 'quietly and without any kind of concerted plans' take 'advantage of the war and the absence of men to aggrandize their position in society (as has happened in wartime in other countries)'.

9. These theological discourses involve multiple, and at times conflicting, interpretations of the Qur'an, reflecting the cognitive and political interests of the jurists (for a study of the diversities of opinions and conflicting exegesis of the Qur'an, see Amirpur 2011).

10. According to Petersen and Zahle (1995: 8), '"legal polycentricity" indicates an understanding of "law" as being engendered in many centres – not only within a hierarchical structure – and consequently also as having many forms. In this way it resembles the term "legal pluralism". [...] Whereas legal anthropologists and legal sociologists may mostly tend to understand and describe the legal landscape from outside, legal polycentricity approaches legal science from within and tries to reach another understanding. Legal polycentricity attempts to reform the understanding of law from inside, it may even influence the approaches taken by legal doctrine'.

11. The *Basij* militia is a volunteer paramilitary force consisting of Islamic government loyalists, created in the 1980s during the Iran–Iraq war.

12. According to Memarian and Nesvaderani (2010: 49–50), 'Unemployment among youth has almost doubled since 1990. Young people between 15 and 29

make up 35 percent of the population but account for 70 percent of the unemployed. Among males, roughly one in four is unable to find a job. Among women with higher education, unemployment is estimated at around 50 percent'.

13. According to Torabi et al. (2013: 271), the 'recent rise in the age at marriage of Iranian women happened while pro-marriage policies were being implemented'.

14. As we explained above, traditionalists in Iran are 'modernists' in a narrow sense of the word and as far as modern ideas are compatible with their Islamic beliefs and practices. Similarly, modernists are not necessarily anti-Islamic although they insist on the separation of religion and politics (see endnote 3, Chapter One).

15. One example we gave above concerned the introduction of women's taxi services. A more pertinent example concerns sex-change surgery. The Islamic government has legalized transsexual surgery and introduced a legal process that leads to medical interventions in transsexual cases. This policy was initially based on a legal opinion (a *fatwa*) issued by Ayatollah Khomeini, declaring the permissibility of sex-change operations (Najmabadi 2014: 174). A recent empirical study conducted by Saeidzadeh (2014) shows a disparity between the cultural values existing in Iranian society (which are, in part, formed by religious beliefs) and policies propagated by the Islamic regime in respect to transsexuality. While the government is supportive of sex-change operations as long as transsexuality is defined as a pathological disorder in need of medical intervention (and thus 'misrecognized'), Iranian society and its culture remain largely hostile to the idea of transsexuality, irrespective of how it is defined.

16. To support their objections, the traditionalists might even resort to using the critique of Westernization, which has been advanced by a range of Iranian reformist thinkers such as Jalal Al-e Ahmad and Ali Shariati (for a discussion on Iranian modernity, see Jahanbegloo 2004).

17. For a general exposition of Gurvitch's sociology of law, see Banakar (2001).

18. Various ideologies, however, were represented, among which the Islamic trend was the most dominant in comparison with Marxist–Leninism or liberal conservatism (see Katouzian 2010: 46). Needless to say, the Iranian revolution received ideological impetus from a number of sources, but these were at the level of the ideologues rather than at the level of the 'street'.

19. The Persian title of this book is: *Resaleh Mosumeh be Yek Kaleme*. Yusef Khan Mustashar od-Dawlah (d. 1898) was an Azerbaijani scholar, a political reformist and Iran's *chargé d'affaires* in Paris (see Seyed-Gohrab and McGlinn 2007; Kia 1994; Atabaki 1993: 20).

Chapter 10   The Reproduction of Meaning and Women's Autonomy

1. 'Optional' within the regulated choices.
2. Not the strictest form.
3. See Schwartz et al. (2008) and also Schwartz and Boehnke (2004).

4. The interviewee 'buys a taxi' instead of 'driving passengers with a private automobile', which is common in Tehran and other cities, and she thinks that *driving with a taxi* gives her a better status than *driving with a private car*. Here, *'people looking down'* on her refers to the perceptions towards a woman who works as a driver with a private automobile.
5. Patriarchy-related meanings.
6. Terminology is borrowed from Hydén (2008).
7. See also interview 4:6:5, page 129, in Chapter Seven.

Chapter 11   The Iranian Legal System

1. The legal principle requiring that no person is punished for conduct that is not prohibited by law.
2. The Constitution of the Islamic Republic of Iran, which replaced the 1906 constitution, was adopted on 24 October 1979, came into force on 3 December 1979 and was subsequently amended in 1989. The amendment was made after the death of Ayatollah Khomeini, and encompassed changes to Article 5 (Office of Religious Leader), Article 107 (the task of appointing the Leader), Article 109 (Leadership qualification), Article 110 (Leadership duties and powers), Article 111 (Leadership Council) and Article 176 (Supreme Council for National Security). As a result of the changes, the new constitution holds and refers to the 'Leader' (*rahbar*), because it is not required for the Leader to be a supreme theological authority (*Marja' taqlid*). As a sign of respect, however, the title 'Supreme' Leader is commonly used.
3. See Articles 5, 110 and 107.
4. According to Article 72, the 'Islamic Consultative Assembly cannot enact laws contrary to the official religion of the country or to the Constitution. It is the duty of the Guardian Council to determine whether a violation has occurred, in accordance with Article 96'.
5. According to Article 93, the 'Islamic Consultative Assembly does not hold any legal status if there is no Guardian Council in existence, except for the purpose of approving the credentials of its members and the election of the six jurists on the Guardian Council'.
6. According to Article 112: '[u]pon the order of the Leader, the *Majma-e-Tashkhis-e-Maslahat-e Nezam* (Expediency Discernment Council of the System) shall convene at the order of the Leader to determine such expedience in cases where the Council of Guardians finds an approval of the *Majlis* against the principles of Sharia or the Constitution, and the *Majlis* in view of the expedience of the System is unable to satisfy the Council of Guardians, as well as for consultation in matters referred to it by the Leader, and for discharging other functions laid down in this law'.
7. See Articles 91(1) and 110, Article 4 and Article 91(2).
8. See Articles 110 and 157, and Article 99.
9. See Articles 99 and 118, Articles 114 and 117, Article 110.

10. See Article 113 and Article 114.
11. See the discussion on the sources of law relating to the roles of law and *urf* later in this chapter.
12. The constitution, Article 73, states that it does not intend to prevent 'the interpretations that judges may make in the courts of cassation'.
13. The Civil Code of Procedure for public and revolutionary courts, which was approved in 2000, is a collection of laws and rules governing the procedure, methods and practices that must be followed by courts in a civil litigation process. These include the following requirements to be met: (1) the requirements for the commencement of the legal proceedings; (2) the pre-trial and trial procedure; 3) the requirements on the hearing and the judgement. The civil procedure code requires the public, revolutionary, appeal and supreme courts to comply with its rules in civil proceedings.
14. The New Islamic Penal Procedure Code, Article 477. This penal procedure code was passed by parliament on 23 February 2014, approved by the Guardian Council on 17 March 2014 and published in the *Official Gazette* on 23 April 2014.
15. The Civil Code of Procedure, Articles 367 and 368.
16. The Civil Code of Procedure, Article 368.
17. The Civil Code of Procedure, Articles 331 and 332.
18. Other specialized courts include medical courts, computer-crime courts and driving and traffic courts. There are also specialized courts that hear commercial disputes, disputes related to the intellectual property law and international disputes. Labour disputes and employment-related matters will be heard and settled by designated special councils.
19. See Articles 294–6, 298, 304, 315, 402 and 408–17 of the New Islamic Penal Procedure Code. Children and juveniles courts have jurisdiction to prosecute crimes concerning minors, i.e. children and adolescents under the age of 18; see Articles 298, 304, 315, 402, and 408–17 of the New Islamic Penal Procedure Code for detailed information on these courts' jurisdiction and composition. For information on recent amendments relating to the appellate authority to appeal the judgements delivered by children and juveniles courts, see the New Islamic Penal Procedure Code, Articles 444–7.
20. See Articles 302 and 305, in accordance with Article 352 and Article 168, of the New Islamic Penal Procedure Code.
21. The New Islamic Penal Procedure Code, Articles 305 and 352.
22. Armed Forces Procedure Code, Articles 2 and 3.
23. The Administrative Procedure Code, Articles 2–5.
24. The Procedural Code for the Special Courts for the Clergy, Article 1, 3–8 and 10.
25. The Procedural Code for the Special Courts for the Clergy, Article 13.
26. The Procedural Code for the Special Courts for the Clergy, Article 14.
27. The Procedural Code for the Special Courts for the Clergy, Articles 48–51.
28. The amended Family Protection Act, Article 4.

29. This report is provided in accordance with Article 40 of the International Covenant on Civil and Political Rights, 31 May 2010.
30. The Law on the Third Development Plan of the Islamic Republic of Iran, Article 189, adopted and amended on 5 April 2000. The Law on Dispute Settlement Councils (which contains 51 articles and ten notes/annexes) was passed by parliament on 8 July 2008 and approved by the Guardian Council on 6 August 2008.
31. See interviews with the Director of the Council (Deputy Head of the Judiciary), conducted by the Iranian Students' News Agency (ISNA), on 16 February 2014.
32. The Law on Dispute Settlement Councils, Article 3.
33. See the Law on Dispute Settlement Councils, Article 4, 20 and 1 respectively.
34. The primary source, the Qur'an, as the direct word of God, is the principal religious book of Islam and was revealed to the Prophet Muhammad, while *sunna* in the Shi'i tradition means the words, deeds and acknowledgements of the Prophet Muhammad, the 12 Imams and the Prophet's daughter. The secondary source – consensus, or *ijma* – comprises those agreements which are passed by *fuqaha'* – Shi'i jurists – unanimously on a case or problem; and reason, or *aql*, constitutes cases in which *fuqaha'* reach a legitimate decision on a matter with reference to the primary sources through logic and reasoning in cases when a solution has not been found in the primary sources).
35. See Iranian Civil Law, Articles 224 and 225.
36. Iranian Civil Law, Article 220.
37. The trial of Mohsen Air Aslani, which ended with an execution verdict, is a case in point. See Iran Human Rights Documentation Centre (2015).

BIBLIOGRAPHY

Abbasi-Shavazi, Mohammad Jalal, 'Preliminary notes on trends and emerging issues of mortality in Iran', *Economic and Social Commission for Asia and the Pacific* (Bangkok: UNESCAP, 2004). Available at http://www.unescap.org/esid/psis/meetings/health_mortality_sep_2004/H_M_Iran.pdf (accessed 12 August 2012).

Abrahamian, Ervand, *Khomeinism: Essays on the Islamic Republic* (Berkeley: University of California Press, 1993).

——— *A History of Modern Iran* (Cambridge: Cambridge University Press, 2008).

Afary, Janet, 'The Sexual Economy of the Islamic Republic', *Iranian Studies* 42/1 (2009), pp. 5–26.

——— *Sexual Politics in Modern Iran* (Cambridge: Cambridge University Press, 2011).

Afrachteh, Kambiz, 'Iran', in M. Ayoob (ed), *The Politics of Reassertion* (London: Taylor and Francis, 2014), pp. 90–119.

Afshar, Haleh, *Islam and Feminisms: An Iranian Case-study* (London: Macmillan Press Ltd, 1998).

Aghajanian, Akbar and Vaida Thompson, 'Recent divorce trend in Iran', *Journal of Divorce & Remarriage* 54/2 (2013), pp. 112–25.

Alavi, Nasrin, *We are Iran: The Persian Blogs* (London: Portobello Books, 2005).

Alexander, Jeffrey C., *The Meanings of Social Life: A Cultural Sociology* (Oxford: Oxford University Press, 2003).

Amani, Firouz and Kazemnejad, Anoushiravan, 'Changing pattern of mortality trends in Iran, South, South-West Asia and World, 1970–2010', *Iranian Journal of Public Health* 39/3 (2010), pp. 20–6.

Amirpur, Katayun, 'The changing approach to the text: Iranian scholars and the Quran', *Middle Eastern Studies* 41/3 (2011), pp. 337–50.

Amirshekari, Salma et al., 'Recognition of the concept of community, neighborhood unit and Mahalleh as a clear explanation of urban space divisions', *Journal of Social Issues & Humanities* 7/1 (2013), pp. 206–11.

Amjad, Mohammad, 'Shi'ism and revolution in Iran', *Journal of Church and State* 31/1 (1984), pp. 35–53.

Arasteh, Reza A. and Joséphine Arsateh, *Man and Society in Iran* (Leiden: E.J. Brill, 1964).

Ardalan, Ali et al., 'Road traffic injuries: a challenge for Iran's health system', *Iranian Journal of Public Health* 38/1 (2009), pp. 98–101.

Arjomand, Saïd Amir, 'Islam and constitutionalism since nineteenth century: the significance and peculiarities of Iran', in S.A. Arjomand (ed.), *Constitutional Politics in the Middle East* (Oxford: Hart, 2008), pp. 33–62.

——— 'Shi'ite jurists and the Iranian law and constitutional order in the twentieth century', in S.A. Arjomand and N.J. Brown (eds), *The Rule of Law, Islam, and Constitutional Politics in Egypt and Iran*. Pangaea II: Global/Local Studies Series (Albany: State University of New York Press, 2013), pp. 15–56.

Atabaki, Touraj, *Azerbaijan: Ethnicity and the Struggle for Power in Iran* (London: I.B.Tauris, 1993).

Axworthy, Michael, *Iran: Empire of the Mind* (London: Penguin, 2007).

——— *Revolutionary Iran: A History of the Islamic Republic* (London: Penguin, 2013).

Ayati, Esmaeel, 'Drowsiness and fatigue, the most frequent causes of severe accidents among heavy vehicle drivers in Iran', paper submitted to the 3rd International Conference on Traffic and Transport Psychology (ICTTP 2004), Nottingham, UK, 2004. Available at www.psychology.nottingham.ac.uk/IAAPdiv13/ICTTP 2004papers2/Impairment/Ayati.pdf (accessed 1 April 2105).

Bahadori Monfard, Ayad, et al. 'Reduction of fatal road traffic crashes in Iran using the Box-Jenkins time series model', *Journal of Asian Scientific Research* 3/4 (2013), pp. 425–30.

Bahramitash, Roksana, 'Women's employment in Iran', in R. Jahanbegloo (ed.), *Iran: Between Tradition and Modernity* (Lanham, MD: Lexicon Books, 2004), pp. 161–8.

Bahrampour, Tara, 'Courtesy around the camp fire', *Washington Post*, 7 July 2007. Available at http://www.washingtonpost.com/wp-dyn/content/article/2007/07/06/AR2007070601974.html (accessed 26 April 2015).

Banakar, Reza, 'Integrating reciprocal perspectives: on Georges Gurvitch's theory of immediate jural experience', *Canadian Journal of Law and Society* 16 (2001), 67–91.

——— 'The politics of legal cultures', *Retfærd: The Nordic Journal of Law and Justice* 4/123 (2008), pp. 37–60.

——— 'The sociology of law: from industrialisation to globalisation', *Sociopedia.isa.*, 2011. Available at Social Science Research Network: ssrn.com/abstract=1761466 (accessed 1 April 2015).

——— *Normativity in Legal Sociology* (Stuttgart: Springer, 2015).

Banakar, Reza and Shahrad Nasrolahi Fard, 'Driving dangerously: law, culture and driving habits in Iran', *British Journal of Middle Eastern Studies* 39/2 (2012), pp. 241–57.

Bausani, Alessandro, *The Persians: From Earliest Days to the Twentieth Century* (London: Elek Books, 1971).

Bayat, Asef, 'Tehran: paradox city', *New Left Review* 66/November–December (2010), pp. 99–122.

——— *Life as Politics: How Ordinary People Change the Middle East* (Stanford, CA: Stanford University Press, 2013).

Bayatrizi, Zohreh, 'Knowledge is not power: state-funded sociological research in Iran', *Current Sociology* 58/6 (2010), pp. 811–32.

Burns, Jonathan G., *Introduction to Islamic Law: Principles of Civil, Criminal, and International Law under the Shari'a* (TellerBooks: JuraLaw, 2014).

Chehabi, Houshang E., 'A political history of football in Iran', *Iranian Studies* 35/4 (2002), pp. 371–402.

Cotterrell, Roger, *Law, Culture and Sociology: Legal Ideas in the Mirror of Social Theory* (Aldershot: Ashgate, 2006).

———— *Iran, the Green Movement and the US: The Fox and the Paradox* (London: Zed Books, 2010).

———— *Shi'ism: A Religion of Protest* (Cambridge, MA: Harvard University Press, 2011).

Daniel, Elton L. and Ali Akbar Mahdi, *Culture and Customs of Iran* (Westport, CT: Greenwood Press, 2006).

Dettelbach, Cynthia C., *In the Driver's Seat. The Automobile in American Literature and Popular Culture* (Westport, CT and London: Greenwood Press, 1976).

Dumas, Firoozeh, 'The real supermarkets of Orange County', 2010. Available at www.nytimes.com/2010/11/21/magazine/21lives-t.html?_r=0 (accessed 1 April 2015).

Durkheim, Emile, *The Division of Labor in Society* (New York: Free Press, 1933, orig. publ. 1893).

Durkin, Kevin and Andrew Tolmie, 'The development of children's and young people's attitudes to driving: a critical review of the literature'. Road Safety Web Publication No. 18 (London: Department for Transport, 2010).

Edalati, Ali and Ma'rof Redzuan, 'Perception of women towards family values and their marital satisfaction', *Journal of American Science* 6/4 (2010), pp. 132–7.

Ehlers, Eckart and Wilhelm Floor, 'Urban change in Iran, 1920–1941', *Iranian Studies* 26 (1993), pp. 251–75.

Ehrlich, Eugen, *Fundamental Principles of the Sociology of Law* (Cambridge, MA: Harvard University Press, 1936, orig. publ. 1913).

Eisenstadt, Michael and Mehdi Khalaji, 'Nuclear Fatwa', Policy Issue No. 115 (Washington, DC: Washington Institute, 2011). Available at https://www.washingtoninstitute.org/uploads/Documents/pubs/PolicyFocus115.pdf (accessed September 2014).

Elek, Elvira et al. 'Influences of personal, injunctive, and descriptive norms on early adolescent substance use', *Journal of Drug Issues* 36 (2006), pp. 147–72.

Enayat, Hadi, *Law, State, and Society in Modern Iran* (London: Palgrave Macmillan, 2013).

Evans, Leonard, *Traffic Safety and the Driver* (New York: Van Nostrand Reinhold, 1991).

Fayyaz, Sam and Roozbeh Shirazi, 'Good Iranian, bad Iranian: representations of Iran and Iranians in time and newsweek (1998–2009)', *Iranian Studies* 46/1 (2013), pp. 53–72.

Fischer, Michael J., *Iran: From Religious Dispute to Revolution* (Cambridge, MA: Harvard University Press, 1980).

Friedman, M. Lawrence, 'Is there a modern legal culture?', *Ratio Juris* 7/2 (1994), pp. 117–31.

Geertz, Cliford, *The Interpretation of Cultures: Selected Essays* (New York: Basic Books, 1973).

Ghajarieh Sepanlou, Sadaf et al. 'Reducing the burden of chronic diseases: a neglected agenda in Iranian health care system, requiring a plan for action', *Archives of Iranian Medicine* 13/4 (2010), pp. 340–50.

Gheytanchi, Elham, 'Women in the Islamic Iranian Republic', in N. Gole and L. Ammann (eds), *Islam in Republic* (Istanbul: Bilgi University Press, 2006).

Golkar, Saeid, 'Politics of piety: The Basij and moral control of Iranian society', *Journal of Middle East and Africa* 2/2 (2011), pp. 207–19.

Griffiths, John, 'The social working of legal rules', *Journal of Legal Pluralism and Unofficial Law* 48 (2003), pp. 1–85.

Gurvitch, Georges, *Sociology of Law* (London: Routledge & Kegan, 1947).

Habermas, Jürgen, *Legitimation Crisis* (Boston, MA: Heinemann Education, 1975).

―――― *The Theory of Communicative Action*. Vol. I. (Boston, MA: Beacon Press, 1984).

Habibi, Ehsanollah et al., 'Investigating the predictive of risk-taking attitudes and behaviors among Iranian drivers', *Journal of Education and Health Promotion* 3/19 (2014). Available at www.ncbi.nlm.nih.gov/pmc/articles/PMC3977409 (accessed 1 April 2015).

Hadizadeh Moghadam, Akram and Parisa Assar, 'The relationship between national culture and e-adoption: a case study of Iran', *American Journal of Applied Sciences* 5/4 (2008), pp. 369–77.

Haeri, Shahla, *Law of Desire: Temporary Marriage in Shi'i Iran* (Syracuse, NY: Syracuse University Press, 1989).

Halm, Heinz, *The Shiites: A Short History* (Princeton, NJ: Markus Wiener, 2007).

Hashemi, S.M., *The Islamic Republic of Iran's Basic Rights*, Vols. I and II (Tehran: Mizan Legal Foundation, 2013).

Hegland, Mary E., 'Educating young women: culture, conflict, and new identities in an Iranian village', *Iranian Studies* 42/1 (2009), pp. 45–79.

Herodotus, *The Persian Wars*, Book III (Cambridge, MA: Harvard University Press, 1922).

Hobbes, Thomas, *Leviathan*, Vol. 3, edited by Noel Malcolm (Oxford: Clarendon Press, 2012).

Hofstede, Geert, *Culture's Consequences: International Differences in Work-related Values*, 2nd edition (Beverly Hills, CA: Sage, 1984).

―――― *Cultures and Organizations: Software of the Mind* (Maidenhead: McGraw-Hill Professional, 1991).

Holliday, Shabnam, *Defining Iran: Politics of Resistance* (Farnham: Ashgate, 2011).

Hunter, Shireen T., *Iran Divided* (Lanham, MD: Rowman & Littlefield, 2014).

Hydén, Håkan, 'Putting law in context: some remarks on implementation of law in China', in H. Hydén and P. Wickenberg (eds), *Contributions in Sociology of Law* (Lund: Media-Tryck, 2008), pp. 147–76.

Jahanbegloo, Ramin (ed.), *Iran: Between Tradition and Modernity* (Lanham, MD: Lexington Books, 2004).

Javaheri, Fatemeh, 'A study of transsexuality in Iran', *Iranian Studies* 43/3 (2010), pp. 365–77.

Kallgren, Carl A et al., 'A focus theory of normative conduct: when norms do and do not matter', *Personality and Social Psychology Bulletin* 26/8 (2000), pp. 2002–12.

Kamali, Masoud, 'Multiple modernities and Islamism in Iran', *Social Compass* 54/3 (2007), pp. 373–87.

Kamali, Mohammad H., *Shari'a Law* (Oxford: Oneworld, 2012).

Kamrava, Mehran, *Iran's Intellectual Revolution* (Cambridge: Cambridge University Press, 2008).

Kar, Mehrangiz and Homa Hoodfar, 'Personal status law as defined by the Islamic Republic of Iran: an appraisal', *Women Living under Muslim Laws Special Dossier* 1 (1996), pp. 7–35.

Karbakhsh, Mojgan and Zargar Mousa, 'Road traffic accidents in Iran: results of National Trauma Project in Sina Trauma Research Center', 2006. Available at http://www.researchgate.net/publication/260387023_Road_Traffic_Accidents _in_Iran_Results_of_National_Trauma_Project_in_Sina_Trauma_Research_ Center.

Karkhaneh, Mohammad et al. 'Epidemiology of bicycle injuries in 13 health divisions, Islamic Republic of Iran 2003', *Accident Analysis & Prevention* 40/1 (2008), pp. 192–9.

Katouzian, Homa, 'Arbitrary rule: a comparative theory of state, politics and society in Iran', *British Journal of Middle Eastern Studies* 24/1 (1997), pp. 49–73.

————— *The Persians: Ancient, Mediaeval and Modern Iran* (New Haven, CT: Yale University Press, 2009).

————— 'The Iranian Revolution at 30: the dialectic of state and society', *Middle East Critique* 19 (2010), pp. 35–53.

————— 'The revolution for law: a chronographic analysis of the constitutional revolution of Iran', *Middle Eastern Studies* 47 (2011), pp. 757–77.

Katouzian, Naser, *Philosophy of Law*, Vol. II (Tehran: Enteshar, 2011).

————— *Introduction to the Study of Law in Iranian Legal System* (Tehran: Enteshar, 2013).

Kazemi, Asghar, 'Roots of the post elections crisis', *Iranian Journal of Law and Politics* (2010). Available at http://aakazemi.blogspot.se/2009/10/iran-roots-of-post-elections-crisis.html (accessed 15 December 2010).

Kelsen, Hans, *Pure Theory of Law* (Berkeley: University of California Press, 1967).

Keshavarzian, Arang, *Bazaar and State in Iran: The Politics of the Tehran Marketplace* (Cambridge: Cambridge University Press, 2007).

Kia, Mehrdad, 'Constitutionalism, economic modernization and Islam in the writings of Mirza Yusef Khan Mostashar od-Dowle', *Middle Eastern Studies* 30/4 (1994), pp. 751–77.

Khorasani-Zavreh, D., 'The requirements and challenges in preventing of road traffic injury in Iran: a qualitative study', *MBC Public Health* 9/486 (2009), pp. 1–9.

Khosravi, Shahram, *Young and Defiant in Tehran* (Philadelphia: University Pennsylvania Press, 2008).

Koutlaki, Sofia, 'Offers and expressions of thanks as face enhancing acts: *Tæ'arof* in Persian', *Journal of Pragmatics* 32/1 (2002), pp. 733–56.

Krämer, Gudrun, 'Justice in modern Islamic thought', in A. Amanat and F. Griffel (eds), *Shari'a Islamic Law in Contemporary Context* (Stanford, CA: Stanford University Press, 2007), pp. 20–38.

Künkler, Mirjam, 'The special court of the clergy and the repression of dissident clergy in Iran', 2009. Available at papers.ssrn.com/sol3/papers.cfm?abstract_ id=1505542 (accessed 1 April 2015).

Kurkchiyan Marina, 'Perceptions of law and national order: a cross-national comparison of collective legal consciousness', *Wisconsin International Law Journal* 29/2 (2011), pp. 366–92.

Lambak, Salman and I. Mohad Tahir, 'Juristic analysis of common law in Malaysia Takaful Act 1984 based on Doctrine al-'Urf', *Asian Social Science* 9/9 (2013), pp. 262–9.

Lewis, David (ed.), *The Automobile in American Culture* (Ann Arbor: University of Michigan Press, 1980).

Libson, Gideon, 'On the development of custom as a source of law in Islamic law', *Islamic Law and Society* 4/2 (1997), pp. 31–55.

Locke, John, *Questions Concerning the Law of Nature* (Ithaca, NY: Cornell University Press, 1990).

Luhmann, Niklas, *Trust and Power* (London: John Wiley and Sons, 1979).

Lupton Deborah, 'Road rage: drivers' understandings and experience', *Journal of Sociology* 38/3 (2002), pp. 275–90.

Madanipour, Ali, *Tehran: The Making of a Metropolis* (Chichester: Wiley, 1998).

Mahdi, Ali Akbar, 'Sociology in post-erevolutionary Iran', *Journal of Iranian Research and Analysis* 19/2 (2003), pp. 32–48.

——— 'Sociology in Iran: between politics, religion and western influence', in S. Patel (ed.), *The ISA Handbook of Diverse Sociological Tradition* (London: Sage, 2010), pp. 268–79.

Manavipour, Davood, 'Moral developmental scale in Iranian culture', *Journal of Psychology in Africa* 22/2 (2012), pp. 289–93.

Manoukian, Strag, *City of Knowledge in Twentieth Century Iran: Shiraz, History and Poetry* (London: Routledge, 2012).

Mashaw Jerry L. and David L. Harfst, *The Struggle for Auto Safety* (Cambridge, MA: Harvard University Press, 1990).

McAndrews, Carolyn A., *Road Safety in the Context of Urban Development in Sweden and California*, doctoral thesis submitted at University of California, Berkeley, 2010.

McCartt, Anne T and Lori L. Geary, 'Longer term effects of New York state's law on handheld cell phone use', *Injury Prevention* 10/1 (2004), pp. 11–15.

Mehran, Golnar 'The creation of the new Muslim woman: female education in the Islamic Republic of Iran', *Convergence* 24/4 (1991), pp. 42–52.

Memarian, Omid and Tara Nesvaderani, 'The youth', in R.B. Wright (ed.), *The Iran Primer: Power, Politics, and U.S. Policy* (Washington, DC: USIP, 2010).

Miller, Daniel (ed.) *Car Cultures* (London: Bloomsbury, 2001).

Mirgholami, Morteza and Sidha Sintusigha, 'From Traditional Mahallehs to Modern Neighbourhoods: The Case of Narmak, Tehran', *Comparative Studies of South Asia, Africa and the Middle East* 32/1 (2012), pp. 214–39.

Mir-Hosseini, Ziba, 'Sharia and national law in Iran', in J.M. Otto (ed), *Sharia Incorporated: A Comparative Overview of the Legal Systems of Twelve Muslim Countries in Past and Present* (Leiden: Leiden University Press, 2010a), pp. 318–71.

——— 'Iran', in Z.M.-Hosseini and V. Hamcic (eds), *Control and Sexuality: the Revival of Zina Laws in Muslim Countries* (London: WLUML, 2010b), pp. 83–115.

Mirsepassi, Ali, 'The crisis of secularism and rise of political Islam', in A. Mirsepassi (ed.), *Intellectual Discourse and the Politics of Modernization: Negotiating Modernity in Iran* (New York: Cambridge University Press, 2000), pp. 65–95.

Moghadam, Afsaneh, *Death to the Dictator!: Witnessing Iran's Election and the Crippling of the Islamic Republic* (London: Bodley Head, 2010).

Moghissi, Haideh, 'Islamic cultural nationalism and gender politics in Iran', *Third World Quarterly* 29/3 (2008), pp. 541–54.

Mohammadi, Ghorbanali, 'Road traffic injuries and fatalities in the city of Kerman, Iran', *International Journal of Injury Control and Safety Promotion* 20/2 (2013), pp. 184–91.

Mohammadi, Majd, *Judicial Reform and Reorganization in the 20th Century Iran: State Building, Modernisation and Islamization* (London: Routledge, 2008).

Moschtaghi, Ramin, 'Rule of law in Iran', in M. Koetter and G.F. Schuppert (eds), *Understanding of the Rule of Law in Various Legal Orders of the World*, Working Paper Series No. 11 of SFB 700 Governance in Limited Areas of Statehood (Berlin: Free University Berlin, 2010).

Muntazeri, Ali, 'Road-traffic-related mortality in Iran: a descriptive study', *Public Health* 118/2 (2004), pp. 110–13.

Mustashar od-Dawleh, Y.K., *One Word – Yak Kalame* (Leiden: Leiden University Press, Iranian Series, 2007, orig. publ. 1870).

Naficy, Hamid, 'Veiled voice and vision in Iranian cinema: the evolution of Rakhshan Banietemad's Films', *Social Research* 67/2 (2000), pp. 559–76.

Nafisi, Nadreh, *Persepolis: The Pearl of Persia* (Tehran: Goya Art House, 2005).

Naghavi, Mohsen et al., 'Adverse health outcomes of road traffic accidents in Iran after rapid motorization', *Archives of Iranian Medicine* 12/3 (2009), pp. 284–94.

Najmabadi, Afsaneh, *Professing Selves: Transsexuality and Same-sex Desire in Contemporary Iran* (Durham, NC: Duke University Press, 2014).

Namazie, Pari, 'Factors affecting the transferability of HRM practices in joint ventures based in Iran', *Career Development International* 8/7 (2003), pp. 357–66.

Nazarian, Ali, et al., 'The relationship between national culture and organisational culture: the case of Iranian private sector organisations', *Journal of Economics, Business and Management* 1/1 (2013), pp. 11–16.

Neal, Arthur G., 'Animism and totemism in popular culture', *The Journal of Popular Culture* 19/2 (1985), pp. 15–24.

Nelken, David, 'Using the concept of legal culture', *Australian Journal of Legal Philosophy* 29 (2004), pp. 1–28.

————— 'Defining and using the concept of legal culture', in E. Örücü and D. Nelken (eds), *Comparative Law* (Oxford: Hart, 2007), pp. 109–32.

Nevadeh Khodadadi, Sodabeh et al., 'Driving environment in Iran increases blood pressure even in healthy taxi drivers', *Journal of Research in Medical Sciences* 13/6 (2008), pp. 287–93.

Olivier, Roy, *Globalized Islam: The Search for a New Ummah* (New York: Columbia University Press, 2004).

Paidar, Parvin, *Women and the Political Process in Twentieth-century Iran* (Cambridge: Cambridge University Press, 1995).

Peden, M. et al., *The Injury Chart Book: A Graphical Overview of the Global Burden of Injuries* (Geneva: World Health Organization, 2002). Available at whqlibdoc. who.int/publications/924156220x.pdf (accessed 1 April 2015).

Petersen, Hanne and Henrik Zahle, 'Preface', in H. Petersen and H. Zahle (eds), *Legal Polycentricity: Consequences of Pluralism in Law* (Aldershot: Dartmouth, 1995), pp. 7–11.

Peymani, Payman et al., 'Epidemiological characteristics of fatal pedestrian accidents in Fars Province of Iran: A community-based survey', *Chinese Journal of Traumatology* 15/5 (2012), pp. 279–83.

Pound, Roscoe, 'Law in books and law in action', *American Law Review* 44 (1910), pp. 12–36.

Redshaw, Sarah, *In the Company of Cars: Driving as a Social and Cultural Practice* (Aldershot: Ashgate, 2008).

Rezaei, Hassan, 'The Iranian criminal justice under the Islamization project', *European Journal of Crime, Criminal Law and Criminal Justice* 10/1 (2002), pp. 54–69.

Rezaei, Satar et al., 'Extent, consequences and economic burden of road traffic crashes in Iran', *Journal of Injury and Violence* 6/2 (2014), pp. 57–63.

Rosen, Lawrence, *Law as Culture: An Invitation* (Princeton, NJ: Princeton University Press, 2006).

Roudsari, Bahman Sayyar, 'Sex and age distribution in transport-related injuries in Teheran', *Accident Analysis & Prevention* 36/3 (2004), 391–8.

Rousseau, Jean-Jacques, 'On the social contract', in Jean-Jacques Rousseau, *The Basic Political Writings* (Indianapolis, IN: Hackett Publishing, 1987), pp. 141–203.

Sadri, Ahmad, 'The varieties of religious reform: public intelligentsia in Iran', in R. Jahanbegloo (ed), *Iran: Between Tradition and Modernity* (Lanham, MD: Lexington Books, 2004), pp. 117–28.

Saeidzadeh, Zara, *The legality of Sex Change and Reconstruction of Transsexuality in Contemporary Iran*, Master's thesis, Lund University, 2014.

——— 'Redefinition of Law and Re-conceptualization of Transsexuality/Gender in Iran', MA dissertation, Lund University, 2015.

Salamati, Payman et al., 'Health status in Iran', *Maghreb Review* 34/1 (2009), pp. 5–17.

Salehi-Esfahani Haideh, 'Rule of law: a comparison between ancient Persia and ancient Greece', *Iranian Studies* 41/5 (2008), pp. 629–44.

Salisu, Taiwo M., '*Urf/Adah* (custom): an ancillary mechanism in Shari'ah', *Ilorin Journal of Religious Studies* 3/2 (2013), pp. 133–48.

Schwartz, Shalom H. and Boehnke Klaus, 'Evaluating the structure of human values with confirmatory factor analysis', *Journal of Research in Personality* 38 (2004), pp. 230–55.

Schwartz, Shalom H., Johnny R.J. Fontaine, Ype H. Poortinga and Luc Delbeke, 'Structural equivalence of the values domain across cultures: distinguishing sampling fluctuations from meaningful variation', *Journal of Cross-Cultural Psychology* 39/4 (2008), pp. 345–65.

Seyed-Gohrab, Ali Asghar and Sen McGlinn, *The Essence of Modernity: Mirza Yusof Khan Mustashar ad-Dowla Tabrizi's Treatise on Codified Law (Yak Kaleme)* (Amsterdam, Utrecht: Rozenberg, 2007).

Shadi-Talab, Jaleh, 'The Iranian women: their requirements and expectations' [publ. in Farsi], *Journal of Social Sciences* 18 (2001), pp. 31–62.

——— *Tose-'e va čāléshā-ye zanān-e Īrān* (Development and the Iranian Women's Challenges) (Tehran: Qatreh Publications, 2002).

Shahidian, Hammed, *Women in Iran: Gender Politics in the Islamic Republic* (Westport, CT: Greenwood Press, 2000).

Shahshahani, Soheila, 'Chapter seven pedestrians in Tehran Mega City', *Global Bioethics* 19/1 (2006), 85–95.

Sharifi, Ayyob and Akito Murayama, 'Changes in the traditional urban form and the social sustainability of contemporary cities: a case study of Iranian cities', *Habitat International* 38 (2013), pp. 126–34.

Simmel, Georg, 'The metropolis and mental life', in D.N. Levine (ed.), *Georg Simmel on Individuality and Social Forms* (Chicago, IL: University of Chicago Press, 1971a, orig. publ. 1903), pp. 324–39.

——— 'The stranger', in D.N. Levine (ed.), *Georg Simmel on Individuality and Social Forms* (Chicago, IL: University of Chicago Press, 1971b, orig. publ. 1903), pp. 143–9.

Swidler, Ann, 'Culture in action: symbols and strategies', *American Sociological Review* 51 (1986), pp. 273–86.

Taleghani-Nikazm, Carmen, 'Politeness in Persian interaction', *Crossroads of Language, Interaction, and Culture* 3 (1998), pp. 4–11.

Taremi, Kamran, 'Iranian strategic culture: the impact of Ayatollah Khomeini's interpretation of Shi'ite Islam', *Contemporary Security Policy* 35/1 (2014), pp. 3–25.

Tavakol, M. and M. Rahimi. Sajasi, 'Sociological theorization in Iran: a study from the perspective of sociology of sociology', *International Journal of Humanities and Social Science* 2/8 (2012), pp. 200–11.

Tayeb, Monir, 'Cultural Determinants of Organizational Response to Environmental Demands', M Litt. Thesis, Oxford University, 1979.

Tellenbach, Silvia, 'Aspects of the Iranian Code of Islamic Punishment: the principle of legality and the temporal, spatial and personal applicability of the law', *International Criminal Law Review* 9 (2009), pp. 689–705.

Thrift, Nigel, *Spatial Formations* (Thousand Oaks, CA: Sage, 1996).

Tizro, Zahra, *Domestic Violence in Iran: Women, Marriage and Islam* (London: Routledge, 2012).

Tönnies, Ferdinand, *Community and Association (Gemeinschaft und Gesellschaft)* (London: Routledge and Kegan Paul, 1955).

Torabi, Fatemeh et al., 'Marriage postponement in Iran', *Population, Space Place* 19 (2013), pp. 258–74.

Tutan, Mehmet U., 'Bazaaris' interest on the Iranian economy', *Ege Academic Review* 8/1 (2008), pp. 256–66.

Urry, John, 'The "system" of Automobility', *Theory, Culture and Society* 21/4/5 (2004), pp. 25–39.

——— *Mobilities* (Cambridge: Polity Press, 2007).

Urry, John et al. (eds), *Automobilities* (London: Sage, 2005).

Vafaee-Najar A. et al., 'Epidemiologic study of motor vehicle accidents resulting in injury and death in Mashhad, Iran (2006–2007)', *Journal of Applied Science* 9/13 (2009), 2445–50.

Vafaee-Najar A. et al., 'Motorcycle fatal accidents in Khorasan Razavi Province, Iran', *Iranian Journal of Public Health* 39/2 (2010), pp. 95–101.

Venkatesan M., 'Experimental study of consumer behavior, conformity and independence', *Journal of Marketing Research* 3/November (1966), pp. 384–7.

Windfuhr, Gernot (ed.), *The Iranian Languages* (London/New York: Routledge, 2009).

Wuthnow, Robert, *Meaning and Moral Order: Explorations in Cultural Analysis* (Berkeley: University of California Press, 1987).

Zamani-Alavijeh, Fereshteh et al., 'Risk-taking behaviors among motorcyclists in middle east countries: a case of Islamic Republic of Iran', *Traffic Injury Prevention* 11/1 (2010), pp. 25–34.

News Items

All internet addresses were correct at time of research

BBC News (25 November 2008) 'Taxi revolution in the streets of Tehran'. Available at http://news.bbc.co.uk/2/hi/middle_east/7747677.stm (accessed 26 April 2015).

——— (18 June 2009) 'Profile: Basij militia force'. Available at http://news.bbc.co.uk/2/hi/middle_east/8106699.stm (accessed 26 April 2015).

——— (10 May 2012). 'Iran comes top in the number of global road accident deaths'. Available at http://www.bbc.com/news/world-middle-east-18023809 (accessed 26 April 2015).

———— (22 September 2012) 'Iranian Universities ban on women causes consternation'. Available at http://www.bbc.com/news/world-middle-east-19665615 (accessed 26 April 2015).

Daily Mail (22 April 2008) 'Dangerous drivers in Iran face being flogged under a tough new law'. Available at http://www.dailymail.co.uk/news/article-1016408/Irans-answer-dangerous-drivers-flog-them.html (accessed 26 April 2015).

The Economist (29 July 2010) 'The bazaar strikes back'. Available at http://www.economist.com/node/16705481 (accessed 26 April 2015).

Guardian (13 August 2014) 'Fields medal mathematics prize won by a woman for first time in its history'. Available at http://www.theguardian.com/science/2014/aug/13/fields-medal-mathematics-prize-woman-maryam-mirzakhani (accessed 14 August 2014).

———— (28 October 2014) 'Iranian journalists detained after reporting on acid attacks', Available at http://www.theguardian.com/world/iran-blog/2014/oct/28/iranian-journalists-detained-reporting-acid-attacks (accessed 26 April 2015).

New York Times (6 December 2010) 'Iran's divorce rate stirs fears of society in crisis'. Available at http://www.nytimes.com/2010/12/07/world/middleeast/07divorce.html?_r=0 (accessed 26 April 2015).

Payvand Iran News (1 September 2014) 'Iran Police Chief stirs controversy over women working in coffee shops'. Available at www.payvand.com/news/14/sep/1000.html (accessed 1 April 2015).

Telegraph (1 July 2012) 'Iran's food costs soar and unemployment spirals as nuclear sanctions begin to bite'. Available at http://www.telegraph.co.uk/news/worldnews/middleeast/iran/9368117/Irans-food-costs-soar-and-unemployment-spirals-as-nuclear-sanctions-begin-to-bite.html (accessed 26 April 2015).

Washington Post (17 December 2013) 'Iran's hard-liners resist nuclear deal'. Available at http://www.washingtonpost.com/opinions/david-ignatius-irans-hard-liners-resist-nuclear-deal/2013/12/17/b7927d04−6742−11e3−8b5b-a77187b716a3_story.html (accessed 20 October 2014).

———— (12 August 2014) 'Iran bans vasectomies, wants more babies'. Available at http://www.washingtonpost.com/blogs/worldviews/wp/2014/08/12/iran-bans-vasectomies-wants-more-babies/ (accessed 20 December 2014).

———— (30 August 2014) 'Iranian cleric issues fatwa against the internet'. Available at http://www.washingtonpost.com/news/morning-mix/wp/2014/09/02/iranian-cleric-issues-fatwa-against-the-internet/ (accessed 19 September 2014).

Websites

All internet addresses were correct at time of research

Al Monitor (6 November 2013) 'Iran's crisis on the road'. Available at http://www.al-monitor.com/pulse/ar/originals/2013/11/iran-traffic-deaths-crisis-roads.html (accessed 26 April 2015).

Center for Preserving and Publishing the Works of Grand Ayatollah Sayyid Ali Khamenei. 'Supreme leader's speech on 14 October 2012 to the youth of North Khorasan'. Available at http://english.khamenei.ir//index.php?option=com_content&task=view&id=1714&Itemid=4 (accessed 26 April 2015).

———— 'Supreme leader's speech on 6 June 2014 on the 25th anniversary of Imam Khomeini's death (r.a.)'. Available at http://english.khamenei.ir/index.

php?option=com_content&task=view&id=1921&Itemid=4 (accessed 26 April 2015).

——— 'Supreme leader's speech on 2 July 2014 at the meeting with university professors'. Available at http://www.leader.ir/langs/en/index.php?p=content Show&id=12052 (accessed 26 April 2015).

Civil Code of the Islamic Republic of Iran [Islamic Republic of Iran], 23 May 1928. Available at www.unhcr.org/refworld/docid/49997adb27.html (accessed 1 April 2015).

Constitution of the Islamic Republic of Iran [Islamic Republic of Iran], 24 October 1979. Available at www.unhcr.org/refworld/docid/3ae6b56710.html (accessed 1 April 2015).

Court of Administrative Justice (2013), 'The administrative procedure code'. (Farsi Website), Available at http://www.divan-edalat.ir/show.php?page=law (accessed 10 April 2015).

Dispute Settlement Councils (2008), 'The law on dispute settlement councils'. (Farsi Website) Available at http://www.shoradad.ir/Default.aspx?tabid=1366 and http://www.shoradad.ir/Default.aspx?tabid=1367 (accessed 10 April 2015).

Encyclopaedia of the Institutions of Islamic Revolution (1982 and 1983), 'The supreme judicial council'. (Farsi Website), Available at http://daneshnameh. irdc.ir/?p=1842 (accessed 10 April 2015).

Expediency Council of the system: approved policies (Farsi Website), Available at http://maslahat.ir/DocLib2/Approved%20Policies/Noncompatabilities.aspx (accessed 10 April 2015).

Global Burden of Road Injuries (2011) 'Incidents of Road Injuries in Iran'. Available at roadinjuries.globalburdenofinjuries.org/iran (accessed 19 September 2014).

Her (2012) 'Girls with drive'. Available at herkansascity.com/feature-story/girls-drive-taxi-drivers-talk-about-their-uniqueness-and-share-their-cab-confessions (accessed 1 April 2015).

Hofstede Centre (2014) 'Iran'. Available at geert-hofstede.com/iran.html (accessed 1 April 2015).

International Women's Day (2014) '170 out of 46,000 New York City taxi drivers are women'. Available at www.internationalwomensday.com/article.asp?m=6&e=21 (accessed 1 April 2015).

Iran Car Accidents (2010). Available at www.car-accidents.com/country-car-accidents/iran-car-accidents.html (accessed 1 April 2015).

Iran Human Rights Documentation Centre (2011) 'The third and fourth periodic reports of States parties, Iran, The International Covenant on Civil and Political Rights, Human Rights Committee, Consideration of reports'. Available at http://tbinternet.ohchr.org/_layouts/treatybodyexternal/TBSearch.aspx?Lang=en&Treaty ID=8&DocTypeID=45&DocTypeID=29 (accessed 17 April 2015).

——— (2013) 'Iranian lawyers call on Iranian authorities to cease infringements on independence of legal profession in Iran'. Available at http://www.iranhrdc.org/english/news/press-statements/1000000252-iranian-lawyers-call-on-iranian-authorities-to-cease-infringements-on-independence-of-legal-profession-in-iran.html (accessed 21 June 2014).

——— (2014) 'English translation of books I & II of the new Islamic penal code'. Available at http://www.iranhrdc.org/english/human-rights-documents/iranian-codes/1000000455-english-translation-of-books-1-and-2-of-the-new-islamic-penal-code.html (accessed 26 April 2015).

—— (2015) 'The chronicle of an execution'. Available at www.iranhrdc.org/english/publications/legal-commentary/1000000565-chronicle-of-an-execution-the-case-of-mohsen-amir-aslani.html (accessed 1 April 2015).

Iranian Students' News Agency (16 February 2014) '50 per cent of the cases are referred to Dispute Settlement Councils' (Farsi Website). Available at http://isna.ir/fa/news/92112718348/ (accessed 17 April 2015).

Islamic Parliament Research Center (1985) 'The armed forces code of procedure of the Islamic Republic of Iran' (Farsi Website). Available at http://rc.majlis.ir/fa/law/show/91072 (accessed 21 December 2014).

—— (2000) 'The Islamic Republic of Iran's civil code of procedure for public and revolutionary courts' (Farsi Website). Available at http://rc.majlis.ir/fa/content/law_cd (accessed 21 December 2014).

—— (2005), 'The amended procedural code for the special courts for the clergy' (Farsi Websites) Available at http://www.dadkhahi.net/modules.php?name=News&file=print&sid=150 and http://www.tebyan.net/newindex.aspx?pid=33453 (accessed 10 April 2015).

—— (2011) 'The Amended Family Protection Act' (Farsi Website). Available at http://rc.majlis.ir/fa/content/law_cd and http://haghgostar.ir/ShowPost.aspx?id=241 (accessed 21 December 2014).

Islamic Penal Code of The Islamic Republic of Iran (2013) (Farsi Website). Available at http://www.refworld.org/cgi-bin/texis/vtx/rwmain/opendocpdf.pdf?reldoc=y&docid=5447c9274 (accessed 10 April 2015).

Islamic Republic of Iran, Management and Planning Organization (2005–9) 'English translation of the fourth development plan of the Islamic Republic of Iran'. Available at http://unpan1.un.org/intradoc/groups/public/documents/APCITY/UNPAN021522.pdf (accessed 1 April 2015).

Jezebel (10 August 2008) 'For Iranian women, cars represent both limitations and freedoms'. Available at jezebel.com/5060696/for-iranian-women-cars-represent-both-limitations-and-freedoms (accessed 1 April 2015).

Judiciary of the Islamic Republic of Iran, 'High Council for Human Rights'. Available at en.humanrights-iran.ir (accessed 1 April 2015).

Laws and Regulations Portal of Islamic Republic of Iran. (Farsi Website), Available at http://law.dotic.ir/AIPLaw/index-ghanoon-home.jsp (accessed 10 April 2015).

Life (23 November 2013) 'Go with the flow in Tehran'. Available at http://www.theaustralian.com.au/life/travel/go-with-the-flow-in-tehran/story-e6frg8rf-1226765478891(accessed 5 April 2015).

Official Gazette No. 20,135 (23 April 2014) 'The new Islamic penal code' (Farsi Website). Available at http://www.dadiran.ir/LinkClick.aspx?fileticket=2GaAXV4uecI%3D&tabid=40 (accessed 21 December 2014).

—— (1985), No. 11728 'The armed forces code of procedure of the Islamic Republic of Iran' (Farsi Website). Available at http://www.dastour.ir/brows/?lid=%20%20%20%20122672 (accessed 10 April 2015).

United Nations Children's Fund (2007) 'Iran Representative: early safety training for children best way to reduce high rate of injuries and accidents'. Available at www.unicef.org/iran/media_3810.html (accessed 1 April 2015).

—— (2014) 'Road traffic injuries in Iran and their prevention, a worrying picture'. Available at www.unicef.org/iran/media_4783.html (accessed 1 April 2015).

United Nations Office of the High Commissioner for Human Rights (1976) 'International covenant on civil and political rights'. Available at http://

www.ohchr.org/en/professionalinterest/pages/ccpr.aspx (accessed 1 September 2014).

———— (1976) 'International covenant on economic, social and cultural rights'. Available at http://www.ohchr.org/EN/ProfessionalInterest/Pages/CESCR.aspx (accessed 1 September 2014).

United Nations Treaty Collection. Available at treaties.un.org (accessed 1 September 2014).

World Bank (2014) 'Literacy rate, youth female (% of females ages 15–24)'. Available at data.worldbank.org/indicator/SE.ADT.1524.LT.FE.ZS (accessed 15 November 2014).

World Health Organization (2013) 'Global status report on road safety'. Available at www.who.int/violence_injury_prevention/road_safety_status/2013/en (accessed 1 April 2015).

INDEX

Printed and bound by CPI Group (UK) Ltd, Croydon, CR0 4YY